The Fine Green Line

· JOHN PAUL NEWPORT ·

The Fine Green Line

✤

My Year of Adventure on
the Pro-Golf Mini-Tours

Broadway Books

New York

BROADWAY

A hardcover edition of this book was published in 2000 by
Broadway Books.

THE FINE GREEN LINE. Copyright © 2000 by John Paul Newport. All
rights reserved. Printed in the United States of America. No part of this
book may be reproduced or transmitted in any form or by any means,
electronic or mechanical, including photocopying, recording, or by any
information storage and retrieval system, without written permission
from the publisher. For information, address Broadway Books, a
division of Random House, Inc., 1540 Broadway, New York, NY 10036.

Broadway Books titles may be purchased for business or
promotional use or for special sales. For information, please write to:
Special Markets Department, Random House, Inc.,
1540 Broadway, New York, NY 10036.

BROADWAY BOOKS and its logo, a letter B bisected on the diagonal, are
trademarks of Broadway Books, a division of Random House, Inc.

Visit our website at www.broadwaybooks.com

The Library of Congress has cataloged the hardcover edition as follows:
Newport, John Paul, 1954–
The fine green line : my year of adventure on the pro-golf mini-tours /
by John Paul Newport.
p.   cm.
1. Golf—Tournaments—United States.
2. Newport, John Paul, 1954–   I. Title.
GV970.N49   2000
796.352′66—dc21   99-089271

Designed by Fritz Metsch

ISBN 0-7679-0117-7

For Polly

Contents

A certain man of La Mancha filled himself with
books on knight errancy, so then in fact he began
to feel it proper that he become errant himself
and go out in the world.

—MIGUEL DE CERVANTES SAAVEDRA

Don Quixote

Preface:
A Fine Green Line
Runs Through It

FORT WORTH, TEXAS, where I grew up, is a semifamous golf town. Ben Hogan and Byron Nelson both grew up there, rival caddies and players from the east side. The Colonial National tournament in Fort Worth is the oldest PGA Tour event held continuously at the same site. Dan Jenkins, the funniest golf writer of all time, hails from Fort Worth and went to the same high school I did, R. L. Paschal (although much before my time). Back in the sixties, Jenkins wrote a funny, much-anthologized article in *Sports Illustrated* called "Glory Days at Goat Hills" about gambling at the bone-dry Worth Hills municipal course, which was a block from my house and where I hit my first golf ball.

Even so, growing up, I hardly gave golf a second thought. I was of the opinion, like most of my peers in Texas at the time, that only two sports mattered: football and spring football. All my athletic dreams as a boy, which is to say all my dreams period, revolved around playing quarterback at Baylor University and then leading the Dallas Cowboys to an NFL championship. I devoted myself to football. For a period of two or three years in my early teens, I disciplined myself to throw a hundred passes a day—rain or shine, cold or heat—mostly through tires and hoops set up in my backyard. As a result, I actually did get pretty good at throwing the old pigskin and was quarterback of my high school team. But I couldn't get an athletic scholarship to

Baylor and so ended up at Harvard. I played football there for a year but hurt my knee and lost interest, in no small part because football players ranked absolutely lowest in the status sweepstakes among early-seventies Radcliffe girls. I might as well have been a Nixon Republican. And so all my years of athletic toil came to nothing.

But then, in my early thirties, I discovered golf. And to my delight and surprise, I had a knack for the game.

It wasn't as if I'd never played golf before. Back when I was ten or eleven, I had spent many desultory afternoons whacking shag balls on the aforementioned Worth Hills golf course, which the city of Fort Worth had recently sold to Texas Christian University for an eventual expansion of its campus. It was the perfect way to learn how to hit a golf ball: no pressure, an open field, and the opportunity to do the one thing you really care about doing at age ten: hit the snot out of the ball. For a couple of summers during junior high school, some buddies and I played a couple of times a week at the old Benbrook muni on the edge of town, though I never recall any of us breaking 90 without serious cheating.

And that was it, with maybe a half dozen isolated golf experiences in the interim, until one splendid autumn afternoon in Vail, Colorado, in 1985.

At the time I was a writer for *Fortune* magazine and had somehow been picked to help represent the editorial side at an ad sales conference at the Snowmass resort. One of the main qualifications for being an ad salesperson for *Fortune* back then was a low golf handicap; a lavish golf outing with customers was the primary sales technique, and the publisher himself was a single-digit member of Pine Valley. Naturally one of the primary orders of business at the conference was daily golf. In the first afternoon's round I played in a fivesome with the publisher, and on the fifth hole—I will never forget it—I accidentally caught a drive dead on the screws. It was an exhilarating feeling I had never had before. All my various limbs and body parts happened to fire in precisely the right sequence, the clubface hit the ball smack in the middle, and the thing took off like a rocket.

"Holy shit!" the publisher said. Those glorious words are seared in my mind.

He was so excited by my drive that he paced it off: 340 yards. Granted, at over a mile of altitude golf balls travel at least 10 percent farther than they do at sea level, plus the wind was with us, and the drive had cleared a crest and landed on the downhill fairway. But still—it was certainly the best shot I had ever hit in my life. For the rest of the round the publisher kept looking at me funny, as if waiting for another miracle. It never came, though I did pull off a handful of other decent shots with my long irons. After we putted out on the final hole, he took me aside, clamped both hands on my shoulders, looked me full in the face, and said, "You simply *must* take up golf."

I must admit, I was flattered. And obviously, I took his advice. Within a week of returning to Manhattan, I purchased my first set of clubs. Unfortunately, the publisher was fired before I could get good enough at golf to rate an invitation to play Pine Valley.

OVER THE NEXT few years I became a card-carrying golf addict. This wasn't easy, living in Manhattan. In the summers I rented a beach house with friends in the Hamptons and spent many miserable predawn hours waiting in line to get onto the only decent public course in the area, Montauk Downs. Whenever I traveled for business I took along my sticks, if only to hit balls at a decent driving range somewhere.

My infatuation with the sport was baffling, even to me. Almost none of my friends in New York played golf. Most, in fact, viewed the game as a shameful, bourgeoisie absurdity (this was before the "golf boom" certified the game as acceptable to yuppies). But I was forever dreaming about the next fix.

Part of golf's appeal must have had to do with the divorce I was going through. It was a refuge. In my personal life I hardly knew which end was up, but on the golf course the rules were clear and order prevailed. Plus, you had the tweeting birds and the gentle breezes and the bright green grass—the same elements that make sanitariums such pleasant places to spend time.

And I was continually getting better, which was good for my battered ego. In only my second summer of adult golf I broke 80 by holing out a wedge shot on the eighteenth hole. "Seventy-nine! Seventy-nine! Seventy-nine!" I shouted like an idiot from the fairway. In the rush to high-five my playing buddy, I forgot about the club in my hand and almost fractured his nose.

Then, shockingly, the following year I shot a 69. I say shockingly because until that fateful midsummer afternoon I still hadn't broken 80 more than a few times. My best score ever was 76, and on off-days I easily ballooned into the upper eighties and low nineties. How was a 69 possible?

Even now I can't totally explain it. The weather was splendid— upper seventies, nearly windless—and I was playing at a comfortable, familiar course, Island's End, on the North Fork of Long Island where I now spent my summers. I was, perhaps, a wee-bit hung-over, which produced a pleasant fatigue which was augmented by some basketball that morning, I looked forward to the round primarily as an opportunity to spend time with a friend I was just getting to know, Ed Tivnan. My scoring expectations were minimal.

We had the course almost to ourselves, and from the first tee to the final green I felt absolutely relaxed and totally in control. My pre-shot routine, which usually involved a lot of neurotic pacing and throwing of grass and practice swinging and second thoughts, was minimal: I simply waggled the club a few times, looked down the fairway at where I wanted the ball to go, and then, most of the time, hit it there. On the greens, I saw the line of each putt as if a highway crew had painted a yellow stripe to the hole—all I had to do was set the ball in motion and watch it tumble into the jar. Between shots Ed and I chatted and strolled. I was not *un*aware of my accumulating score, but for some reason—and this may be the strangest aspect of the round—I didn't focus on it. If I had, I surely would have chunked shot after shot and finished with a string of double-bogeys. Instead, I birdied the par-five seventeenth hole with a wedge to five feet and a firm putt into the back of the cup, and parred the long, par-four eighteenth with a good drive, a six-iron to the green and two routine putts.

Presto! Sixty-nine. Nothing ever seemed easier.

Only after I said good-bye to Tivnan, returned to the house my friends and I were renting for the summer, and took my seat on the terrace did I begin to think about the round. I was pleased, of course, but nowhere near as idiotically exhilarated as I had been after my first 79. In this case the score seemed oddly secondary. I was mainly struck by my mental state: throughout the round I had felt calm, focused, preternaturally at peace with the world. As a sometime athlete, I had experienced being "in the zone" before, but those episodes were usually brief and were dependent on adrenaline rushes and an intensity of will. This state, which lasted for more than four hours, seemed altogether more mature and under my control. I had slipped back and forth between hitting fine shots and chatting with Ed without losing a beat. I felt powerful yet serene, totally in charge. Even now, sitting on the terrace with a cocktail in hand, I was luxuriating in the afterglow of this mood or dimension or whatever you want to call it, and I wanted to experience it again and again.

I passed around the scorecard for my housemates to see: three birdies, one eagle, and two bogeys. "You ought to turn pro," Jane Clark said offhandedly.

"Right," I responded.

It was an ignorant suggestion. Jane knew as much about golf as I knew about quantum physics. Still, the remark got me to thinking (strictly from an intellectual point of view, you understand): Why couldn't I turn pro? If I could shoot 69 once, why couldn't I learn to shoot 69 frequently? For that matter, why couldn't I learn to shoot 69 all the time? I assumed there were many sound reasons why I couldn't, I was simply curious to know what those reasons were, exactly. Shooting 69 the first time had seemed so very, very easy.

And this, I blush to admit, was the big bang origin of the book you hold in your hand.

NOT LONG AFTERWARD I quit my job at *Fortune* to go freelance. I never intended to become a "golf writer" per se, but right off the bat I pursued a couple of assignments about golf to indulge my new curiosity, and before long I was nearly as obsessed with writing and learning about the sport as I was with playing. I justified this by coming up with a nifty, self-serving definition of my duty to society as a freelancer: to go places, do things, and ask questions that people stuck in more responsible, traditional jobs would want to do if they only had the time.

One of the first assignments I snared, for *Details* magazine, was a piece about Q School—the annual nightmare where more than a thousand of the world's best professional golfers try to earn one of forty available "cards" to play on the PGA Tour the following year. Some guys I met there had clearly gone over the edge. They slept with subliminal suggestion tapes running beneath their pillows, sang Christmas carols in the shower as part of strange pre-round rituals, and talked incoherently of things like "true gravity" and "cosmic consciousness." They had been driven batty by an advanced version of the same question I had posed: Why, when they were demonstrably capable of shooting rounds in the mid-sixties or better on a regular basis, did they invariably regress for a hole or two per tournament and finish out of the big money?

The next golf story I took on was about the Space Coast Tour, a so-called mini-tour in central Florida. Here were guys—some former Tour players but mostly aspiring cadets in their twenties—who could knock the cover off the ball, but who obviously lacked some intangible something that their betters on the Big Tour possessed. What was it? Mental discipline? The perfect temperament? An extra iota of hand-eye coordination? They had no idea and I didn't either.

I was also lucky enough during this period to write a few stories about big-name Tour players like Greg Norman and Tom Lehman. But frankly their struggles didn't intrigue me as much as those of the guys on the fringe. One day, while idly thumbing through the PGA Tour media guide for 1993, I came across two statistics which crystallized the questions that had been bouncing around in my head.

The first statistic was Nick Price's scoring average. Price was Player of the Year. He won six tournaments and $1.4 million and his average score was 69.63. The second statistic was Ed Fiori's scoring average. Fiori, a journeyman pro, won $107,000 and finished 127th on the money list, which was not high enough for him to retain his playing privileges the following year. His average score was 70.95—*a difference compared to Price of only 1.32 strokes per round.* How could this be? Was all that stood between Nick Price, the best player in the world in 1994, and an obscure pro I'd never heard of really just one-stroke-and-a-third per round—one drive that just misses the fairway and perhaps a lipped-out putt?

Over the next few months I began to think of the difference between Price and Fiori as the Fine Green Line, and became convinced that all of golf's secrets would be revealed if I could just understand the phenomenon. Not just secrets that pertain to golf at the high-end professional level, but the secrets of golf at every level. The primary cause of golf's maddening addiction, it seemed to me, was the certainty every golfer feels that they are actually a whole lot better than their scores would indicate. Golfers are sure of this because they've proved it to themselves over and over. Every golfer in every round hits a few sensational shots of the kind that only golfers with significantly lower handicaps ought to be able to hit. Every so often everything comes together and the golfer posts an extraordinary score. Forever after, in the golfer's mind, this score becomes the norm, the standard by which subsequently, every higher score is judged inadequate. Ed Fiori must have experienced this frustration every time he missed a cut in 1994, or made the cut but went home with a paltry, last-place paycheck of $2,666. It's enough to drive a sane person crazy.

. . .

CERTAINLY IT WAS enough to drive me crazy. Two summers after shooting the 69, I still had not repeated the miracle, though I had reduced my handicap to around three and shot par or better a half dozen times. By hack amateur standards I was fairly accomplished, but I was also stuck. No matter how hard I worked at my game, I couldn't push my handicap any lower and I couldn't narrow the gap between my good rounds and bad rounds; I might shoot 75 one day and 85 the next. I had bumped into the Fine Green Line for myself, up close and personal. And I was miserable.

The low point came on a New York City subway. Unable to afford a summer rental that year, I spent more time than I would like to admit commuting via public transportation from my Manhattan apartment to the nearest driving range, a bare-dirt affair at the city-run Mosholu course in the Bronx. There I would squander entire afternoons whacking balls, usually getting worse and angrier by the hour, until daylight expired and I hiked to the subway for the seventy-minute trip home.

On one such return trip I noticed two teenage girls giggling at me from across the aisle. When I saw my reflection in the window, I couldn't blame them. What a pathetic spectacle. There I was, thirty-seven, fully grown and formally educated, attired in a brown moth-eaten sweater and a backward golf hat, slumping dejectedly over my golf bag in the corner of a graffiti-covered subway car, cursing savagely, and making odd sledgehammer motions with an inter-locking grip.

At that moment I decided the time had come either to give up golf entirely or pursue my obsession to the logical extreme.

I chose the latter.

IT WASN'T EASY arranging the Year of Golf that followed. For one thing, I had no money. For another, just as I was about to set forth, I met a woman too fabulous not to marry. Since neither of us were exactly spring chickens (Polly was already in her forties), we had a baby right away. But this only delayed the adventure. I explained to

Polly that getting to the bottom of golf's dark hold was essential to my happiness and she, perhaps unduly distracted by the glorious bouncing baby girl on her knee, agreed. Meanwhile, I had secured a contract to write a book about my experiences. This gave us the confidence to push ahead despite the money problem.

I organized the Year around two objectives. The first was to see how much better I could get at golf in twelve months' time. I would enlist the aid of a top golf instructor and various golf psychologists and mental game gurus, scam as much top quality equipment as I could from manufacturers, and compete in tournaments around the country. Other than a three-month stint on the mini-tours in Florida at the start of the year—Florida seemed like a fine place to spend the winter, especially since Polly and our daughter could be there with me—I didn't know where I would compete. That was part of the adventure. At some point, I knew, I would have to turn pro.

The second objective was to test myself at the end of the Year by entering the PGA Tour's Q School. Only in my wildest fantasies did I entertain the hope of actually making it onto the Tour, but I did feel it might just be possible, if I made spectacular progress, to advance from the first stage of Q School into the second stage (out of three stages total). That became my specific, ultimate goal. Making it to the second stage was something worthy to shoot for, and had the added benefit of making my goal for the Year the same as that of virtually every other aspiring pro in the country. In golf's bush leagues, the Tour's Q School each October is the glittering prize that counts.

And so, my heart surging, the Year began.

· SECTION ONE ·

Teeing It Up

If it hadn't been golf, it would have been something else. I might have become a drunk or a drug addict.

—JOHN UPDIKE

1 . *The Broken Stick*

My YEAR OF GOLF BEGAN OFFICIALLY—NOT
that there were any officials keeping track—in
October 1995, with a lesson from Michael
Hebron. It was my first golf lesson ever, and in
addition to the predictable paranoia anyone
would feel handing over something valuable to
a stranger (one's soul to a priest, one's mind to
a shrink, one's swing to a golf coach), I was
intimidated by Hebron's reputation. One of
the country's most respected teachers, just a
notch of renown below the celebrity instructors like David Leadbetter and Butch Harmon
who hang out on the PGA Tour practice tee,
he is the author of (among other titles) *The Art
and Zen of Learning Golf*, a title which

intrigued me. Among his former students were Tour stars like Vigay Singh, Steve Pate, and Ian Woosnam.

Given my tight budget, I hoped to talk Hebron into giving me lessons for free, or at least at a steep discount, and most of my thoughts during the drive to the lesson concerned how to make my case. "I am no ordinary student," I rehearsed out loud in the car. "I am on a quest. I am embarking on an everyman adventure sure to be of interest to all living Americans. My goal is to penetrate the very heart of golf. I will practice like crazy. My hands will bleed. I will purify my thoughts and become the ball. And all I need to succeed is your instruction—and your support." In practicing these remarks I made dramatic gesticulations with my nonsteering hand. By the time I arrived at the Smithtown Landing Country Club on Long Island, where Hebron teaches, I felt reasonably confident.

At the pro shop, however, the clerk insisted that I pay $150 in advance—so much for the free lesson—and when I walked down the hill to the covered teaching tee and spotted Hebron working with a strong young Japanese player, my self-assurance melted. The student, so far as I could tell, possessed an absolutely flawless swing. Which particular, minute detail of the swing he and Hebron might have been working on was impossible to determine. After each swipe at the ball the Japanese guy held his finish like someone posing for the PGA Tour logo. Nevertheless, Hebron always stepped in to suggest some adjustment: a one-centimeter forward shift of the upper torso, perhaps, or a half-degree left swivel of the hips. I had to assume the Japanese guy couldn't putt; otherwise it seemed certain that I would have recognized him from the Tour.

When the lesson ended they shook hands, then bowed to each other in the Oriental fashion, and Hebron walked over to where I stood trying to look nonchalant and introduced himself. He was a decent-looking man in his early fifties, fit and of average height, with sandy, gray-speckled hair and a boyish face that was just beginning to show the effects of years in the sun. But his eyes are what caught my attention. They were striking, vivid blue and penetrating, yet strangely nonrevealing, like a reptile's.

"What can I help you with?" he asked.

The words of my carefully composed little speech deserted me. Whatever confidence I had had in the car was now completely gone, replaced by need—raw, unadulterated, heartfelt need. I stood before Hebron's reptile gaze stripped of all pretense, suddenly as awestruck as a child who finally gets to the front of the Santa Claus line at the department store. I could only sputter nonsense. What I really, desperately wanted, I realized, was the same thing all golfers want.

"I wanna get better," I said. "I wanna get better at golf."

Hebron nodded understandingly and said, "Let's see you hit a few balls." He told me later that new students often break down in this kind of confessional way ("It can get emotional out here," he said), so in hurrying me to the practice mat he was probably trying to keep things from getting messy.

I chose my pitching wedge to hit with because the wedge is generally one of the hardest clubs to screw up with. I took my time, stretching a little while trying to regain my emotional equilibrium, and slapped a half dozen balls towards the 125-yard sign. The results were better than I could have expected. I hit every ball on the noggin, and one actually hit the 125-yard sign. My confidence came back.

When I turned around to face Hebron, however, he was nodding ominously—like a doctor who has seen the lab report but is not yet ready to divulge the disheartening results. "Yes, I see a few things," he said noncommittally.

Then he asked me to hit a few more balls with a video camera rolling, and after he ejected the tape we walked up a cart path (my cleats clattering on the pavement) to a small, cinder block shed a pitch shot away. He asked me what my handicap was.

"Five," I told him. "No wait. Actually, three." In fact at that moment it was 2.7, but the Japanese guy and Hebron's enigmatic nods had left me feeling insecure.

I decided to broach the subject of my grand plans for the Year of Golf. "My intention, you see, is to work really hard on golf for an entire year." I tried to sound positive, but couldn't bring myself to mention anything about Q School or turning pro. "I'm going to practice really, really hard and my object is to see how good I can get in that time."

"I know the answer to that one," Hebron said brightly. "Not very."

"Not very?"

"That's right."

"But . . . don't you think if I absolutely commit myself to golf for an entire year, I can get better?"

"Not much," he said.

"Not much?"

"That's right."

I didn't quite know how to respond. Wasn't a teacher supposed to be encouraging? We walked on, my cleats echoing in the uncomfortable silence. Finally I said, "Why is it you think that?"

"Because the golf swing is complicated. You've got seventy bones and two hundred muscles and they all have to work together. That isn't easy to make happen."

Hebron could tell that I wasn't satisfied with this response. "Let me put it another way," he continued. "College golfers usually start out with a handicap about like yours, three or four. They play 250 days a year, three or four hours a day, for four or five years, and usually by the time they graduate they're scratch players. The ones who go on to do well after that are the ones who happen to be very good in the short game, but that's another issue. And grown-ups like yourself don't have nearly that much time to devote to the game, so it takes even longer."

"But I *do* have that much time," I said excitedly. I told him about my plans to write a book about the Year ahead and how I had always been a good student in school and how I was intensely motivated. He didn't seem very impressed.

"Generally we tell low single-digit handicappers it takes three or four years to drop a single stroke."

Three or four years! Had he been paying attention? I was dismayed. A year from now I would be going to Q School. By then I needed to be at least scratch!

"That's impossible," I blustered.

"Some students are better than others," he shrugged. "Maybe in your case we could take a stroke off in just one year."

By this time we had entered the cinder block shed, which was lined on three walls with mirrors. A red circle was painted in the middle of the floor, intersected by various other multicolored lines and multicolored footprints like you might see at a dance studio. The Sheetrock near the video installation was plastered with photos of famous golfers in mid-swing.

We sat down at the video table and watched my swing, which I had never seen on tape before. I was pleasantly surprised. My timing seemed smooth—not too fast, not too slow—and I finished on balance.

"Is that similar to what you thought it would look like?" Hebron asked.

"Actually it looks better than I expected," I said. "Because when I'm standing over the ball I don't feel nearly as comfortable as I look like I am here."

"Hmmmm," he responded, and took out a black grease pencil. He froze the tape at the instant of impact—the view was head-on, with me facing the camera—and drew a straight vertical line on the screen through the ball. "How much of your body is behind the ball?"

"About half, I guess," I said, thinking this was probably the right answer.

"And how much of the body of Davis Love over there is behind the ball?" He pointed to a picture on the wall of Davis Love III at a similar instant of impact.

I studied the photo and saw that *all* of Davis Love III was behind the ball.

"So that would be my first observation about your style," Hebron said. "The second would have to do with your spine. See how the upper part of your spine is leaning slightly toward the target at the top of your backswing?" He played the tape back and forth sadistically. "In the swings we like, the spine leans away from the target. Look at Davis again."

Sure enough, there was geeky Davis Love tilting his spine perfectly. I was embarrassed. I was guilty of reverse pivot, a flaw I was well acquainted with from reading instructional books. In fact, when friends asked me to look at their swings, reverse pivot was often one of the first things I pointed out. I myself had stopped reverse pivoting years ago—or so I thought.

Hebron led me out on the floor and we worked on attaining the correct spine-tilt. I stood in the middle of the painted circle and checked my posture in the mirrors as I swung. When I had done this enough to feel thoroughly awkward, Hebron introduced another correction. He had noticed on the range that the ball was too close to my feet at address, and so we established a new setup that felt like I was leaning over the edge of a cliff. In passing he also mentioned that I would eventually need to change my grip.

Then he talked about my broken stick.

"If your left arm is 30 inches long and your club is another 30 inches long, what we want at impact is a straight 60-inch stick, but a 60-inch stick that is *leaning*, with your hands *ahead* of the ball."

He took me back over to the video machine and froze my swing. "Would you say that we're looking at a straight, leaning stick in this picture?"

"No."

"The best players in the world play golf with straight sticks." He pointed to Davis Love III again.

"You're playing with a broken stick. Look at this—your hands are actually *behind* the ball at impact. That means your system can't be producing enough power."

He sat back in his chair and sighed. "When you paint, is the paintbrush in front of your hand or are you pulling the brush behind your hand?"

"I'm pulling the brush behind my hand."

"Is the brush straight or is it leaning?"

"Leaning."

"Is a hockey stick straight up and down when it hits the puck or is it leaning?"

"Leaning."

"Is the baseball bat out ahead of the hitter's hands at impact, or is he pulling the bat through the strike zone with his hands ahead of it?"

"His hands are ahead of it."

"The straight, leaning shaft compresses the ball and that's what makes the ball jump off the clubhead. This is a fundamental. I'm only going over very fundamental concepts with you today. There are three reasons people don't get better. Lack of a plan, misinformation, and trying to learn the big things before the small things. We're going to start with the small things."

I nodded obediently as Hebron continued talking about broken sticks and proper alignment, but I stopped paying close attention, counting on my whirring tape recorder to preserve the wisdom for later. My mind wandered back to how good my wedge shots had been, the ones that were the basis for all this withering dissection. I'd made solid contact each time. The trajectories were uniform. The balls all landed within a few yards of each other.

"The thing I don't understand," I interrupted when Hebron paused for a moment, "is why, if my swing has all these deficiencies, my shots on the range went so straight. They were all pretty good shots, weren't they?"

"*Pretty* good?" Hebron burst out. "Well, that was a *pretty* good paper you wrote back in college, John Paul, but it wasn't an 'A' paper, was it? That was a *pretty* good round you shot at the U.S. Open last year, Mr. Norman, but you still came in second. What's *pretty* good? If pretty good is all you're after, you're already *pretty* good. Why did you come to me for help?"

Hebron's reptile eyes were merry. He arched his eyebrows quizzically and craned his head forward in a stagy manner and said in a sappy voice, "*Why bother getting better at all?*" Then he laughed out loud—a friendly, ironic, welcome-to-the-nuthouse sort of laugh—and gave me a big wink.

This sudden transformation of Hebron from dour instructor to fellow traveler filled my heart with joy. It made me think we shared a fundamental conviction, namely that the game of golf is absurd. Admitting to yourself that whacking a dimpled ball around some pasture with hard-to-manipulate clubs is a boneheaded pursuit seems to me the first necessary step in any serious golfer's journey. Once you can accept this, you are freed from ever having to think about it again, and thus can get on with the business at hand.

"Why bother getting better at all," I repeated. "That's the million-dollar question, all right."

2 . *P l a i d   P a n t s*

TWENTY-ONE MONTHS BEFORE MY FIRST LES-
son with Hebron, Polly and I had moved to the
village of Orient on the far eastern tip of Long
Island's North Fork, 110 miles from Manhattan. Orient had only six hundred residents and
looked like a Disney movie set: shady streets,
white Victorian-style homes, a general store,
and a historic one-room schoolhouse, with
views all around of the rocky beaches and
sparkling waters of Peconic Bay. It was the
community where I had rented summer houses
with friends and passed many idyllic hours
swimming, playing golf and tennis, reading
books, and grilling fresh fish for dinner.

With our daughter Anna on the way, we
figured that moving out of the city made

sense. Polly was an artist who could use a room of our house as her studio. And I worked at home, too, communicating with the magazines I wrote for via telephone and modem. Plus, of course, the golf was far better on Long Island than in midtown Manhattan. In my mind's eye, our neighborhood consisted of Island's End golf course in East Marion, just seven minutes from our house; the sprawling grass practice range there; the Orient schoolyard, where I could hit sand wedge through six-iron at a splendid array of targets (soccer goals, softball backstops, an old wooden scoreboard); and the usually vacant fairgrounds in nearby Greenport, where I could hit as much as a three-wood if I was careful. Island's End, a semiprivate course, had a friendly staff, was easy to get on except weekend mornings, and had several nice holes, especially the par-three sixteenth on the cliffs overlooking Long Island Sound. I played most of my rounds there with a handful of friends who came out from the city on weekends, and local characters I picked up with on, say, Tuesday mornings at eleven when I grew weary of banging my forehead against my computer keyboard.

Just fifteen miles across the bay in Southampton (though an hour away by car) lay Shinnecock, the legendary links course where Corey Pavin won the 1995 U.S. Open, and its historic neighbor, the National Golf Links of America, designed by Charles Blair Macdonald. Over the years I had wangled invitations to both of these courses, and these experiences made the entire East End, to my golf-addled mind, seem like hallowed ground.

In the days immediately after my lesson with Hebron, I spent a lot of time in our backyard working on spine-tilt. The goal was to keep my spine tilted slightly away from the target at the same angle from start to finish of the swing. It wasn't easy. Never have I paid so much attention for so many hours to any nonsexual part of my body.

The more I struggled with this problem, the more fascinating it became. Spine-related insights popped into my head at all hours. For instance, while trimming the bushes one day it struck me that the backward-tilting spine and a firmly planted right leg, converging into the waist from opposite angles, form the letter "K." This was an exciting discovery. I dubbed it my "O.K. Theory of Power Generation" and worked hard at trying to "carry the K" into my finish. I was proud of the concept. Unfortunately, the first time I took my O.K. Theory of Power Generation to the range at Island's End, I could barely hit the ball. Shanks and drubs. I was frankly surprised at the degree of my awfulness. Everything felt awkward. Positioning the ball further from my feet, as Hebron had instructed, made matters worse. And when I tried to add in both the "leaning stick" and the "body behind the ball" phenomena, I became totally disoriented. Wasn't it physically impossible to keep your wrists *ahead* of the ball while simultaneously keeping all of your body *behind* the ball? Couldn't you get hurt trying something like that?

But then (every golfer has had this experience) just as I was about to skulk off the range in despair, I connected with three swings in a row. The ball practically *leaped* off the clubface.

"Whoa! Where did that come from?" I said out loud. The sensation of those swings was new and sleek—more than enough to keep me soldiering on.

ONE AFTERNOON, TOWARD the end of a lengthy spine-tilting session behind the house, I happened to glance up at the second-floor window of Polly's studio. She was staring down at me with a look of mild horror on her face. I was not using a club at this point, but simply twisting from side to side, somewhat sassily, with arms akimbo. To anyone observing, I must have looked like a calisthenics instructor aboard a Celebrity Cruise ship.

"I'm working on spine-tilt," I called up to Polly defensively.

She nodded slowly, clearly unable to extract meaning from this explanation. After a while she asked, "Is it helping?"

"I think so. I can feel the power of the K."

She nodded again, ran what I had said through the data bank of everything she had ever known or heard, came up with nothing, and finally said, "Well, good."

Then silently she lowered the blind.

Polly and I have many things in common—values, temperament, a paranoid fear of being mistaken for yuppies—but golf is not one of them. If anyone was ill-equipped to appreciate the implications of Hebron's question, "Why bother getting better at golf at all?" that person would be Polly. From her point of view, being pretty good at golf was plenty good enough for anyone. Though she was supportive of my interest in the game, she was also basically clueless.

At the time we met, the only thing Polly knew for sure about golf was that golfers wore plaid pants. That this happened not to be true made no difference. I have learned over the years that whenever someone deploys the phrase "plaid pants" in connection with golf, you can be sure that, a) they have never actually played a round of golf, and b) they know all they ever need to know to ridicule golf for the rest of their lives.

Polly had some exposure to golf growing up in Ohio. Her doctor father played. But from the time she was fifteen, when her parents shipped her off to boarding school, until the day she met me, her only encounter with golf was a viewing of the movie *Caddyshack*. During most of those years she lived in tenement lofts on the Bowery in Lower Manhattan and produced abstract paintings.

But Polly's skepticism about golf did not bother me, because I brought my own prejudices to the game. Growing up in Fort Worth, I never much cared for the kids who hung out at the country clubs—most of them seemed like spoiled brats. In junior high the parents of one of my best friends were blackballed from Colonial Country Club because they were Jewish. Such was my naïveté at the time that this actually shocked me, and left a distaste in my mouth for the social aspects of golf clubs that persists to this day.

Nevertheless, I considered it a central mission of my marriage to convince Polly that golf was actually hip. It was a kind of running game we played. In an attempt to diffuse her negative plaid pants image of the sport, for instance, I argued that back in the fifties and sixties, when some golfers actually did wear plaid pants, doing so was a form of subversion. "Dean Martin didn't wear plaid pants because he was a fashion retard," I said. "He wore plaid pants because he was a drinker. Everybody drank back then. You had three martinis at lunch because the work world was so repressive, and you wore plaid pants at the golf course because they were silly. It was like putting a lampshade on your head at a party."

Polly was unconvinced: "I don't care what you say, there's no excuse for plaid pants ever, under any circumstance."

Another ploy I used was dropping the names of celebrities Polly admired who also golfed. "It's not just Republicans, you know. Sean Connery—Mr. James Bond—is an *avid* golfer. So is Willie Nelson. And Kris Kristofferson. And Clint Eastwood. Hootie and the Blowfish. Michael Jordan. Dennis Quaid. Harvey Keitel. . . ."

"Harvey Keitel?" she interrupted. "I find that hard to believe."

She had caught me. I meant to say Joe Pesci, but didn't want to admit it. "Yes, Harvey Keitel. Harvey's a *big* golfer. Plays out of Winged Foot."

She knew I was lying. "Okay, maybe not Harvey Keitel, but the point remains: the stereotypes of golf are crumbling!"

One of the best bits of hip golf propaganda I came across—or so I thought—was about a well-known New York artist who, according to a friend of mine, had recently become enthralled by golf. Supposedly the artist had set up a net in his downtown studio and spent hours a day hitting balls. But when I eagerly called Polly from a pay phone to spring this news, she said she'd already heard it. "It's sad, isn't it?" she replied. "He's lost. He no longer paints. A total pothead."

Sometimes when I watched golf on TV, Polly joined me on the couch and offered commentary. "How come nobody looks like they're having fun?" was the sort of thing she said. "From the expression on their faces, you'd think it was the Cuban missile crisis." The physiques of some of the Tour's more portly athletes (like Craig Stadler and John Daly) came in for special ridicule, as did the clothes. "I can see wearing a shirt like that if you're climbing a mountain and might need to be rescued, but on a golf course? Please."

I think Polly secretly enjoyed this little game as much as I did. At parties she comically rolled her eyes whenever I launched into the subject of golf and kept me, I think, from becoming too much of a bore. But for all her personal lack of fascination with the game, she was an artist and respected that golf meant a lot to me at some (to her) unfathomable level. Her grandfather, Maxwell Perkins, had been F. Scott Fitzgerald and Ernest Hemingway's editor. Perkins always encouraged his writers to follow their instincts wherever they led, and the last thing Polly wanted to do was discourage me from writing a book about what I loved. Even if it was golf.

Polly's support, however, did not mean that I was without my own doubts about the wisdom of the Year. As a carefree bachelor it had been all fine and good to squander my summers playing golf and travel for weeks at a time researching stories. But now I was a family man and, as for most family men, money was a major issue. My best estimate for the golf-related costs of the Year was $25,000. That included the cost of all my travel and accommodation, entry fees into tournaments (which would escalate into the $400 to $500 range once I turned pro), range balls, equipment, and a final $3,000 hit for my entry fee into Q School. Even given the advance I had secured from my publisher, we would end the Year in debt—and I would still have to write the book.

Guilt, you should know, was a major component of my upbringing. My father is an ordained Southern Baptist minister, and my mother comes from a long line of Southern Baptist teachers and missionaries herself. Southern Baptism is not usually the stern, humorless, right-wing religion people up North tend to think it is, but it does subscribe to the notion of Original Sin—basically, that we're all born as sinners and only get worse after that—and to other bleak tenets on the Calvinist model. For Baptists and Calvinists, virtue is largely a matter of how much pleasure one can forswear.

Playing golf for a year while my wife and baby went hungry (if only metaphorically) did not comfortably fit into this worldview. Emotionally, if not theologically, I had to make peace with my guilt. I never seriously considered *not* going through with the Year—you can't plan for something as long as I had, sell a publisher on the idea and then back out—but I wanted to feel right about the project. What if I had too much fun? What if I got so swept up in the glory of golf, travel, and competition that I thoroughly enjoyed myself? That might be hard to take.

But then I thought about Colin Montgomerie and the other golfing Scotsmen I knew: wretched, guilt-racked souls, every one. And I realized this was *golf* I was pursuing, not yachting, and golf originated in Scotland, which is also where Calvinism achieved its gloomiest expression. Too much carefree fun would be the least of my problems.

Moreover, I rationalized further, the Year would be a period of self-discovery, which tied directly into the soul-searching religious nature of my youth.

During the vulnerable years after my first marriage ended, golf, along with psychotherapy and confessional dating, had been how I learned useful things about myself. But dating was now out of the question and psychotherapy was way too expensive. That left golf. I was delighted being married to Polly and ecstatic as a new father, but that didn't mean I'd figured everything out. In little more than a year my life had been turned topsy-turvy: we'd moved, gotten married, then had a baby. Golf was one of the few links I had to my past self. If I were to abandon the Year, the "me" I had invested so much time and energy developing, in part through golf, might be obliterated. I wasn't precisely sure what golf had to teach me, but all my instincts told me the Year was important to my life, not just my golf game.

"Continue what ya' started," I advised myself—oddly, in a Scottish accent. "Find oowt who ya' are."

And so, after months of this possibly pointless self-rationalization,

I dropped the Hamlet act altogether. And it wasn't like I was abandoning the family. In fact, after two months of practice, the plan called for all three of us—Polly, Anna, and myself, plus our two cats—to move for the winter to Florida, where my playing career would begin.

3 · The White Polar Bear Club

THE SESSION WITH MICHAEL HEBRON HAD
indeed been my first golf lesson—unless you
count the ten minutes my brother Frank spent
showing me how to grip a golf club back when
I was nine. His hope was that by introducing
me to a time-consuming activity like golf, I
would leave him alone. He was fifteen already
and liked to have friends over, but we shared a
room. I was "the Brat" or "the Babe." And so
one summer day he demonstrated the basics
of the interlocking grip (the grip Hebron now
said needed to be changed), loaded me down
with a cheap vinyl flight bag of old shag balls (I
still remember their rubbery smell) and the
set of Lawson Little–label clubs my dad had
used when he played golf before I was born,

and directed me to Worth Hills with the parting encouragement, "Don't forget to play in the traffic on your way home."

The Worth Hills municipal course, universally known as Worthless Hills even before it was abandoned, had been one of those legendary golf betting parlors back in the fifties and early sixties, like Tennison Park in Dallas where Lee Trevino cut his teeth or Airco Park in St. Petersburg, Florida. The famous hustler Titanic Thompson often dropped by Worth Hills. He could always count on rounding up a big money match with the likes of Moron Tom, Cecil the Parachute, and Magoo—whom Dan Jenkins later immortalized in his *Sports Illustrated* article—the highlight of which was a multiply-wagered six-man cross-country scramble from the first tee at Worth Hills, down Alton Road and Simondale, over a couple of chain link fences to the third green at Colonial Country Club.

I knew about none of this nonsense at the time, of course. But I was glad to have the vacant, seldom-mowed course as a place to hit balls. I loved the sheer animal violence of walloping something as hard as you could without getting into trouble, and I would recommend a similar approach to anyone taking up golf. It reduces a new golfer's frustration level immensely, and once you learn what it takes to make the ball go a long way, you never forget. It's like riding a bicycle. The knowledge burns deep into your muscles.

The drawback to learning golf in the wild is that later in life you have no conceptual understanding of what happens in a golf swing. You just do it, which can work beautifully so long as you stay relaxed and don't ask questions, but the moment you start to think about the swing, as inevitably you will once you begin to take the game seriously and hit several bad shots in a row, you're toast. You have no resources to fall back on.

My three handicap at the time of my first lesson with Hebron owed primarily to my length off the tee. When I was "on" I could more or less overpower a course from the white tees, leaving myself simple pitch shots onto the greens and reaching most par fives in two. Also, I was deft at chipping and pitching because I loved to practice those skills (it seemed like pure play) and that saved me many a stroke.

But I knew in my heart that the three drastically overstated my competence. In the first place, the Island's End course where I played most of my rounds ideally suited my erratic, power-golf game. Except for two or three holes with out-of-bounds, it was almost impossible to get into trouble off the tee, which meant I could swing from the heels on almost every shot and not pay the price for malfeasance.

Second, the formula the United States Golf Association uses to determine handicaps takes into account only the ten best scores of one's most recent twenty. I seldom went twenty rounds without posting a low number or two, but I was streaky and easily discouraged, and my bad scores were pretty awful. If such a thing as a "reverse" handicap existed, figured on the basis of those dog scores the computer normally throws out, mine would have been eleven. This was significantly higher than the reverse handicaps of other low handicappers. I know because I covertly inspected their posted scores on the computer printouts in the locker room at Island's End and their reverse handicaps came out mostly in the five to eight range.

Consistency, therefore, was what I most hoped to gain from my lessons with Hebron. I wanted to "eliminate the downside," in business parlance.

The obvious danger, however, was that in doing so I would lose the upside—that too much self-consciousness about mechanics would annihilate my fearless old Worth Hills rhythm. Because in every aspect of my life *except sports*, I was anal-retentive. I tended to overanalyze, overthink, overintellectualize. When planning a trip, for instance, I would send away for dozens of travel brochures and peruse every one, just to make sure we weren't missing some must-see wax museum or amazing cavern or something. It drove Polly nuts, and frankly it drove me nuts, too, which was why sports were such a great release—in sports I could let loose and fly.

In this context, taking lessons was like opening Pandora's box. It brought to mind one of my college roommates, John Kiernan. Kiernan (no one ever called him John) was an English major like me and our dorm life consisted primarily of rambling, late-night bullshit conversations about books, movies, politics, whatever. It was fun. We winged it. Then Kiernan went to law school. The summer after his first year I happened to ask him how he liked such-and-such a movie and he began, "I liked it for the following three reasons: a) The narrative subplot as epitomized by . . . , b) The director succinctly set forth . . ." and so on. His mind had irretrievably become that of a lawyer. I was afraid of something similar happening with my golf swing.

Given my Q School deadline, eleven short months away, I was also concerned about my timetable for improvement. Like most golf fans, I'd read the inspiring tale of Nick Faldo completely rebuilding his swing under the tutelage of instructor David Leadbetter. But it took Faldo three years, during which time he slumped badly. Tour locker rooms are filled with other sad accounts of pros like Bobby Clampett and Ian Baker-Finch (like Faldo, a student of Leadbetter) never recovering from attempts to retool their swings. Hebron's comment that it normally takes low handicappers three to four years to drop a single stroke hung over me ominously.

Despite these reservations, there was never really much chance that I would choose to forgo lessons and trust the Year entirely to my instincts. The fact was, I had ceased to make progress as a golfer, and not making progress is not only un-American, it is un-golferly. Belief in the possibility of progress is what sustains golfers—for proof, just ask any old codger out at the course what part of his game he is working on. There's always something. If Nick Faldo could remake his swing and go on to win three Masters and two British Opens, then surely lessons represent hope for the rest of us.

AT MY SECOND lesson with Hebron, two weeks after the first, somehow we got started talking about the difficulties of teaching golf. "Even with all the video cameras and training aids and the increased number of instructors, handicaps are going up, not down," he said. "I'd say only a few out of every hundred people who come to me actually get better in any sustained way."

The problem is not that instructors don't know what they're talking about or don't understand the golf swing, he said, but that most don't work hard enough trying to convey information in ways that strike a chord, that relate to motions and activities students already know. That explained why Hebron's teaching tee was littered with items like mops, tennis rackets, and hockey sticks.

"There are pockets of enlightenment in golf instruction, but that knowledge usually doesn't become general for a long time. Most people who are teaching now were taught themselves by someone who is, like, eighty. I suspect that in the next century people will look back on what we're doing today as pretty rudimentary. Because the fact is people just aren't learning."

Golf magazine tips came in for particular scorn. "They're like pearls without a string," he said. "They aren't wrong or misinformed necessarily, they just aren't geared to people's particular learning styles or athletic backgrounds, to their individual sizes or natural swing shapes or frequency of play or their ambitions. They get people confused. They're really more for entertainment than they are useful."

He watched me hit a few balls and complimented my spine-tilt. "That's a *little* better, I guess," he said.

"Yeah, but my shots are pretty lame. I'm getting worse," I said.

"You can't worry about results at this stage. You're doing fine."

I nodded without resistance.

Hebron's concept-of-the-day was swing plane. Ben Hogan in *Five Lessons: The Modern Fundamentals of Golf* popularized the image of a golfer standing with his head poking through a tilted sheet of glass. The glass, visualized as resting on the golfer's shoulders and extending down to the ball, paralleled the ideal plane the club should stay on during the entire swing. Hebron actually had such a sheet of glass—Plexiglas, actually—sitting at one end of his tee. He invited me to poke my head through the hole in the middle and, after he adjusted the contraption for my height, to swing.

Bam! I hit the glass on my backswing with each attempt. My swing plane was too flat, which caused me to do all kinds of wicked things to compensate, like "come over the top," which was another elementary swing flaw (like reverse pivoting) I had thought I was immune to.

Swing plane was the *only* subject we dealt with in my forty-five minutes. Even so, I was mentally exhausted.

Before I left, Hebron loaded me down with copies of several books he had written, including a large-format, 420-page monster called *Building and Improving Your Golf Mind, Golf Body, Golf Swing*. It was basically an encyclopedia, containing a history of golf instruction, illustrated sections on the human skeleton, golf-related discussions of the laws of physics, photographs of athletes from others sports getting their bodies behind throws and hits, informed monographs on nutrition and the mental barriers to change, sections on stretching and the Alexander technique, and other material. Clearly Hebron had done his homework.

This book appealed mightily to my scholarly instincts. It had the totemic quality of a sprawling ancient text on alchemy, as if all the wisdom of the universe were contained therein. Every night for weeks, after tucking Anna into bed and maybe drinking a glass of wine with Polly, I would sneak off to my room, throw up the footrest on my recliner, and dive in. Through my reading I was finally beginning to get a sense of where the magical power of a golf swing originates—from coiled tension, the whip effect, the perfectly sequenced tripping of a series of powerful levers—and the knowledge excited me.

I accompanied these readings and my daily practice sessions with extensive scribbling in a journal. Some of my entries were purely description. For instance, on October 21, I proclaimed (to myself) that I had finally solved "the vexing problem of my right hip." Two pages of detailed analysis followed, the sum and substance of which was that I'd learned to bend my right knee.

Other entries strove for a more elevated tone, such as this rhapsodic description on November 1 of the moment of impact. "It is an invisible instant, a wrinkle in time, a blackout. You set the swing carefully in motion with the backswing and then POOF—the next thing you know you're in a perfect high finish, watching the ball fly high, straight, and true!"

I got such a kick of out this passage that I called up my best golfing buddy, John, to read it to him.

"Uh-oh," he responded.

"What do you mean, uh-oh?"

"I mean uh-oh, you think too much." He assured me that I would bomb on the mini-tours. "Those other guys out there, you know how much they have going on upstairs? Absolutely nothing. That's what makes them so good."

I wondered whether this was true. The mini-tour players I'd met so far had not struck me as stupid—golf-addled, obsessive, addicted, yes, but not stupid. They all seemed reasonably verbal, read newspapers, kept up with the culture as much as most twenty-something-year-olds. But maybe it was true that my intellectual fascination with golf was counterproductive. Certainly, standing over the ball, you didn't want to be thinking about how the laws of physics might affect the hook spin on your ball. You wanted total quiet upstairs. You wanted to be in the moment, as I had been shooting the 69. "When you seek it you cannot find it," Hebron had quoted some guru in *The Art and Zen of Learning Golf*. "Zen is practice, experience—not explaining, interpreting, investigating." It was a concept I had underlined in red ink and marked with an exclamation point, though in making an intellectual issue of it I was already violating the injunction.

Which brought to mind another paradox, a story I once heard in some literature class about Leo Tolstoy. It seems that when Leo was a boy he formed a club, the White Polar Bear Club, of which he was the only member. No one else could pass the initiation ritual, in which for a designated thirty-minute period the candidate had to sit in the corner of a room, facing the wall, and *not* think about a white polar bear. Obviously this test required the honor system, but Tolstoy claimed to have passed. I could pass, too, if they told me *afterward* that the thing I was not supposed to have thought about was a white polar bear. But if they told me immediately *before* the test began that I couldn't think about white polar bears, I wouldn't last a second, a second being about how long—as I begin my take-away on an approach shot into a green with a water hazard on the left—I usually manage not to think about the water hazard on the left. Which, of course, usually causes the ball to plop directly into the water hazard on the left.

It's extremely confusing to think about trying not to think, but I will say this: if Tolstoy really did pass the entrance exam for the White Polar Bear Club, he was in the wrong profession writing novels. He should have been a golfer.

As OCTOBER SLID into November the weather turned nasty: highs were typically in the forties, often accompanied by high wind and rain, sometimes by snow. The leaves were gone from the trees.

Whenever the sun broke through the clouds, however, or the wind died a bit, I grabbed my clubs and dashed for the Orient schoolyard or the Greenport fairgrounds to hit balls. The practice wasn't always satisfying—to keep warm I had to wear restricting long underwear and a pair of cold-weather golf gloves I had ordered from a catalog— but I had so many different things to work on I usually felt that I accomplished something. By design I never played actual rounds, though Island's End remained open; I wanted to work on the elements of my reformed swing without the distraction of score.

One dark, blustery afternoon at the Greenport fairgrounds—a vast, semi-grassy expanse near the high school where each summer the carnival sets up shop—I was struggling to eliminate an annoying little fade that had recently cropped up when a man appeared next to me out of nowhere. I had thought I was the only one crazy enough to be out in the weather, but nonetheless, there he was. He was small and wiry, in his fifties or sixties, with a white mustache and dark skin, and was wearing a green military jacket with a cap from a U.S. Navy destroyer. Next to him was a bicycle.

"Hey," I said.

"Hey what?" he replied brusquely.

"Hey hello," I said.

He had his arms crossed and was staring at me, and it occurred to me that he might be bent on foul play. I was vulnerable, a lone golfer in the middle of a field, and Greenport has its rough section.

"What kind of clubs you got there?" he asked.

"Dunlops," I said. They were the original set I had bought after my Eureka experience in Colorado.

"Good clubs," he nodded. "Let's see you hit." This was when I noticed a half dozen clubs strapped to his bicycle and a paper bag of what appeared to be golf balls bungee-corded beneath the seat.

I hit a few unintentional fades.

"Break the right wrist more," he said. "That'll make 'em go straight."

"I hardly think that's the problem," I replied, irritated at his presumption to give *me* advice, I who was planning to turn professional in just a few months. Even so, on the next few shots I couldn't not think about breaking my right wrist more, and sure enough it worked. The shots went straight, even drew slightly left-to-right.

"See?" he said.

"Yeah, well . . . I adjusted my stance a little, too."

"My name is Indian Joe. I'm from India," he said. We shook hands, he got his clubs, and we proceeded to hit balls in opposite directions, standing back to back.

Over the next few weeks I ran into Indian Joe almost every time I visited the fairgrounds. I think he could see the field from his apartment and hopped on his bike when he saw me arrive. He said he was a retired Con Edison electrician who lived on a pension and didn't much like people and had played only one round of golf on a real course in his entire life, that being the year before when a Greenport cop took him as his guest to Island's End.

"I don't have much use for playing at country clubs," he said when I asked what he shot. "I just like hitting balls."

I had mixed feelings regarding Indian Joe. His persistence in showing up every time I did, often stealthily, was annoying. His presence made it difficult to concentrate. On the other hand, on the days he didn't show up I kind of missed him. He was, after all, a fellow golfer, and there were not many of us out and about in the gloomy cold of November.

As I got to know Indian Joe better, I discovered he knew a lot about golf—not necessarily the types of things I needed to know, since he never played "real" golf, but an amazing array of odd facts and opinions nonetheless, picked up mostly from his two golf magazine subscriptions and from watching pretty much every golf tournament on TV from start to finish.

In trying to help me with my game, Indian Joe invoked tips from Lee Trevino (his favorite player), Ray Floyd, Paul Azinger, and Fuzzy Zoeller. I tried out most of them. Even when they didn't work, which was most of the time, they were fun to goof around with. Each failure gave me more information, I told myself. I was learning how different approaches to the ball, different grips and pronations, different stances and ball positions affected the flight and distances of my shots.

Ben Hogan, in a phrase I always liked, talked about how he "dug his game out of the dirt." Maybe that's what I was doing now, digging it out by trial and error. In any case, Indian Joe and I spent countless hours at the fairgrounds, whacking golf balls. It took me back to my innocent golf days at Worth Hills. Despite the chill and drizzle, we were both happy as larks.

4 . *The Throw-Up Zone*

ONE GUY WHO WAS DEFINITELY *NOT* HAPPY AS
a lark—even though he was getting ready to
play golf on a real course in a much better cli-
mate—was the guy I spotted standing off to
the side of the first tee at the Bear Lakes
Country Club in West Palm Beach, Florida.
Precisely three minutes remained until his tee
time, but he was not idly loosening up like the
other players in his group. He was bent over,
feet wide apart, hands on his knees, about to
throw up.

I had flown to Florida on the last day of
November to educate myself at the final stage
of Q School, and this was the first tableau that
presented itself as I hiked in from the parking
lot. The vomiter had bleached blond hair, a

deep tan, a fashionable black-and-gold Aureaus golf shirt hanging from a set of powerful shoulders and appeared to be in his mid-twenties. He was heaving but nothing came out.

After a minute or so (I was riveted by the drama) he stood up, walked to the tee box, shook the hands of his fellow competitors, and hit—first. The drive drilled on a low arc about 280 yards down the center of the fairway. Despite his jangled emotional state, he had made it look as effortless and graceful as a kid tossing pebbles down a well.

"Atta boy, Steve," called out a middle-aged man next to me.

The player acknowledged the remark without eye contact, simply nodding, and retreated to the back of the tee box where he closed his eyes and engaged in a series of deep, deliberate breaths. When the other players finished hitting, he handed the driver to his caddie without a word and walked down the fairway. It was the first of 108 holes he would play over the next six days (assuming he made the cut after four rounds) to determine whether he would have a spot on the PGA Tour for the following year.

"He hit a good drive," I remarked to the man who had said, "Atta boy, Steve."

"I'm amazed," he replied. "That's my nephew. He's staying with us during Q School. The poor guy didn't get two hours' sleep last night."

"At least he didn't actually vomit," I said optimistically.

"There was nothing left. He threw up twice this morning already."

THE PGA TOUR Qualifying Tournament has been known as Q School since its makeshift origins back in the early 1960s. Back then the only way to earn a regular, guaranteed spot on Tour was to work your way into the top fifty on the money list by "Monday qualifying" one tournament at a time. That meant you had to travel each week to the tournament site and compete on Monday against a varying number of other pros for one of usually about sixty open spots in the field. The pros who did this regularly were called "rabbits" after the way they hopped from city to city, but as Palmer, Nicklaus, et al. increased the popularity of professional golf, the rabbit population got out of hand, as rabbit populations will. So the Qualifying Tournament was introduced—originally twice a year but now just once, in the fall—to create a more orderly system. At the same time, the number of spots available each week through Monday qualifying was drastically reduced, usually to no more than four.

No one seems to know who first called the qualifying tournament Q School, but everyone understands why: at Q School you learn lessons you never forget. Such as how easy it is to play like a superstar on the mini-tours for eleven months and then play like a duffer when Q School rolls around. Or how strangely your body behaves down the stretch when your whole career is on the line. Or how easy it is to four-putt from ten feet on the final hole to miss earning your "card" by a single stroke.

The annals of Q School are filled with such tales, not all regarding obscure personalities. Paul Azinger and Mark Calcavecchia each washed out of five Q Schools before making it to the Tour. Mac O'Grady failed a record *seventeen times* before finally earning a card in 1982. Future two-time U.S. Open winner Curtis Strange, the top-rated amateur in the country before turning pro for the 1976 Q School, bogeyed the last three holes to miss by one.

"It was the most pressure I'd ever felt, and I just flat choked," Strange said later. "I couldn't handle it. You know you are choking when you are helpless, and I felt helpless. I had no control over my swing, and most of all, I had no control over my thoughts. When I finished I felt I was a failure."

The pressure on Q School competitors has gotten worse, because the big money and exposure the Tour offers these days is luring many more superb golfers into the pipeline. Each year upward of twelve hundred pros somehow come up with the three thousand dollars it costs to enter. (And last year the Tour raised the entry fee to four thousand!) Except for some players coming off the Tour who are exempted into the final stage, the competition begins at a dozen or so sites around the country—the so-called first stage, which is what I was planning to enter next October. The survivors face another round of elimination in the second stage, at five sites around the country.

Only 190 players or so survive to the final stage, and those who make it arrive feeling extremely lucky and extremely nervous. Just to get to the final stage, beating seven-to-one or eight-to-one odds, is an accomplishment—one the players know they may never repeat no matter how many times they reenter Q School. But getting to the final stage means next to nothing if they can't beat the odds once more by nailing down a Tour card. The precious cards go to only the top forty finishers, plus ties. Forty winners out of twelve hundred entrants! That thought alone is enough to make most people's stomach twitch. It is true that most of those who reach the final stage but fail to get their card will be offered some kind of status for the following year on the PGA Tour's developmental circuit, the Nike Tour (now the Buy.com Tour). But the Nike Tour is no bargain. The purses are skimpy and the expense of traveling from event to event can easily chew up $30,000 or $40,000 a year—money most players don't have. Except for the top few money-winners, the Nike Tour is even more grueling than the old rabbit days on the PGA Tour. There's a lot less hanging-out-with-the-guys type of fun and a lot more pressure.

Only, the Big Tour itself is worth being on. It is the Land of Milk and Honey, the Be All and End All of a bush-league golfer's world.

AFTER WATCHING STEVE the Vomiter hit his tee shot, I found the media center in the clubhouse and got permission to leaf through the biographical information sheets the players had been asked to fill out. I was curious to see who was there and what they'd been doing to get so good.

Some of those in the tournament were well-known, former PGA Tour winners: Andy Bean, Tim Simpson, Bob Gilder, Gary Hallberg, and Billy Ray Brown. They had lost their cards by failing to finish higher than 125th on that year's Tour money list. You could tell instantly from the bio sheets which contestants had once been at or near the top of golf—they were the ones who didn't deign to do more than scrawl their names across the top. Simply *being* at Q School was ignominy enough, Tim Simpson must have figured, without having to fill in the blanks about his hobbies, achievements and marital status for who knows who to read.

The up-and-comers were more fastidious, as if they somehow hoped good penmanship and complete responses would help get them on the Tour. Thus you got, in the case of Joseph Cioe of Cranston, Rhode Island, not just a comprehensive list of the Q Schools he had entered ('87, '89, '92, '93, '94, '95) but also the stage at which he had washed out of each. Steve Hart itemized all fourteen Q Schools he had attended—every year since 1981. Six times he had played well enough at Q School to earn a card (those years he indicated by asterisks), but he had never played well enough on Tour to keep his spot.

Virtually every player listed at least some experience on the mini-tours, which I expected. But I was shocked at the multitude of mini-tours I had never heard of: the Prairie Tour, the Desert Tour, the Moonlight Tour, the Power-Bilt Tour, the 40-Plus Tour, the Lone Star Tour, the Hurricane Tour, and the VX Sweet Caroline Titanium Woods Tour, just to name a few.

Mini-tours are a necessary evil for pros excluded from the Big Time. Pros desperately need someplace to play between Q Schools, and for most mini-tours are the only solution. The tours have no official status or connection with the PGA Tour or even with one another. Most were begun by entrepreneurs who simply put out the word of a tournament schedule and waited to see if anyone showed up. If enough pros did, they had a mini-tour. Most mini-tours operate within a finite geographical region—the Space Coast Tour I had written about was in Orlando—and the prize money usually consists of nothing more than the pooled entry fees of the players—less course costs and a cut for the entrepreneur. The mini-tours are a long, long way from the Land of Milk and Honey.

As I jotted down the names of various mini-tours in Florida that I might investigate as a place to play come January, I asked a local golf reporter sitting next to me what he had heard about the Gold Coast Tour. Several of the players had mentioned winning tournaments on this tour, and it seemed to operate in the West Palm Beach area.

"Belly up," he said.

"Really?"

"A lot of the players didn't like the guy who ran it. They quit participating." But the reporter said a new tour, called the South Florida Golf Tour, was taking up the slack and enjoyed a good reputation. "The guy who runs it is a former mini-tour player himself— actually, he was on the Big Tour for a while, too—and he puts all his weekly costs up on the board for everyone to see." I said I would check it out.

As we walked out to the course together, I told the reporter about my plans for the Year. "There's the guy you ought to talk to," he said, pointing to a burly pro in the shade of the clubhouse behind the tenth tee. "That's Dick Mast. They call him the King of the Mini-Tours."

Mast appeared to be in his forties. He had dark hair and sun-creased skin and was fully attired for golf: spikes, golf cap, glove sticking out of his rear pocket. This was odd since the last group of the tournament was just then teeing off.

"What's he doing there?" I whispered to the reporter.

"I think he was an alternate. He must not have got in."

In addition to the 190 or so players guaranteed spots in the final stage, a half dozen other players are listed as alternates: first alternate, second alternate, and so forth, the order determined after the second stage by arcane criteria no one fully understands. Most alternates, particularly those who live far away, don't bother to show up because who, after all, would miss their tee time at the most important tournament of the year? As it happened, one player this year *did* miss his tee time—a Texas Aggie named Marco Gortano who read the wrong time on the pairings sheet and showed up at his assigned tee just in time to catch a glimpse of the first alternate striding down the fairway in his place. But this was rare.

Mast was the second alternate, and he had just got the bad news that his services would not be needed. As I watched he began packing up his enormous golf bag—it was the size of an oil barrel—for the long trip home.

I hesitated to intrude on a man at such a distressing moment. But after a few moments of bustle Mast stood up and looked around, as if he were waiting for someone, and I thought, what the hell. Maybe I could take his mind off his disappointment.

"Mr. Mast?" I said cautiously.

"Yes?"

"You don't know me but, well, I was curious and . . . Is this a bad time?"

He shook his head. "No, go ahead. How can I help you?"

"Is it true you're the King of the Mini-Tours?"

I instantly wished I had beat around the bush a little first. Mast seemed taken aback, too. His eyebrows shot to the top of his skull. But then he shook his head and blew a kind of snorting laugh through his nose and said, "Yeah, I guess some people called me that. I was king of the mini-tours because everybody else either moved on to better things or had sense enough to quit."

"We don't have to talk about it," I said. I tried to explain why I was interested, my plans for the Year and so forth.

"I don't mind," he said. "I've got nothing better to do anyhow."

He told me briefly about his career: on and off the Tour since 1974, an unsuccessful attempt to kick the golf habit in the late-seventies with a stint in the business world, years after that mostly on the mini-tours ("I've played every tour but the ladies' "), back on the Big Tour with an intoxicating 82nd-place finish on the money list in 1993, but then some serious backsliding. "The Lord gave me five or six good years up on the Big Tour and there must be a reason," he said. "I don't know what that reason is, but I'm sure He must." Mast had five kids to support, ages five to sixteen.

"The mini-tours are a lot stronger now than they were back in my heyday," he said. "The talent is deeper and the costs are higher and it's much harder to make a go of it without a financial sponsor. Used to be a lot of club pros from up north came south for the winter to have some fun playing on the mini-tours and we regulars were happy to take their money. But now you've got a lot of serious former college golfers on the mini-tours—All-Americans, some of them—who are working hard on their games because the pot at the end of the rainbow is so much bigger. It's a totally different ball game."

He said the main thing I ought to work on if I wanted to be competitive was my short game. "Learn to put the ball in play off the tee and after that it's all chipping and putting. For most guys it takes two to three years to get up to speed. A lot of it's just getting used to the arena. You get nervous, even on the mini-tours. It's like learning to speak in front of large groups of people. At first you're all flustered but once you do it enough, you get used to it—that becomes your norm, and you learn to bring the focus down on your game again. But still, I would say if a guy can't make things happen in two or three years, he's probably better off looking for something else to do."

"Two to three years?" I pressed, hoping to hear him say that sometimes players get there faster.

"For most guys, but not necessarily. Sometimes it can take a good player ten years to figure things out. Look at Tom Lehman— he played on the mini-tours that long before breaking out. Which is what makes it so hard to know when to quit. You can't shake the feeling that a turnaround is right around the corner."

We chatted longer, but after a while I could sense his impatience to leave (I couldn't blame him). I thanked him for his time.

MAST HAD BEEN amazingly gracious under the circumstances. I got a kick out of his assumption that I was a bona fide *player*. Since I was about to set forth on the mini-tours, ipso facto I qualified as something of an equal. He talked to me man-to-man, insider-to-insider, as one pro would talk to another. It was thrilling.

After our talk, I was eager to get out on the course and watch some actual golf. It had been months since I'd walked on green, freshly mown grass and felt the warm sun on my skin. The two Bear Lakes courses, designed by Jack Nicklaus, were in flawless condition. Pink birds wheeled overhead. Everything about the moment was golden, and best of all a whole Year of such moments stretched ahead for me.

Near the green of the second hole, a 195-yard par three, I took my seat on a grassy mound and soaked up the atmosphere. The players looked marvelous in their Bobby Jones and Cross Creek fashions (no plaid pants in sight). The threesomes came and went on the green below me like little ballet troupes: briskly stalking onto center stage, pacing and squatting, sizing up putts, the caddies cleaning balls and holding the pin, everyone freezing briefly while someone putted and then bursting into life again, the beloved old motions and routines. For thirty minutes I sat mesmerized by this action, as content as a cat in the sun.

Then suddenly it struck me that I should be learning something. I wasn't here to be entertained. I was here as a competitor to steal secrets, to figure out how it was done, to make shrewd observations. So I sat up more erectly on the mound, squinted my eyes craftily, and took out my notebook.

It took a long time to think of something to write down, because what can you say about a series of nearly perfect swings? All of the players, using what must have been three- or four-irons, were keeping their tee shots *extremely low* into the twenty-mile-per-hour headwind, but I didn't need to write that down because it was obvious: get the ball up into a wind like that and you lose control. I tried counting how many players faded the ball from left-to-right and how many used a right-to-left draw, but the tally after four threesomes was dead even so I gave it up as inconclusive.

Finally I wrote, "Beautiful swings!" Then I inscribed, "They all putt *straight* at the hole—ball goes in!" In retrospect I have no idea what this meant, other than to reflect my surprise at the number of long putts the players holed. In my golf experience, long putts almost never went in, presumably because I wasn't putting sufficiently *straight* at the hole.

And that was all the shrewd observations I could think of.

After a while I got hungry and went back to the clubhouse for lunch. Perhaps, I figured, it would be more productive just to ask the players directly how they do it.

OVER THE NEXT few days, I did exactly that. At first I was shy. As a spectator at Q School—and there weren't many of us—you are constantly aware of your potential to put the voodoo curse on a player. Out on the course you are sometimes the only observer following a group and live in dread of catching a competitor's eye at the wrong time, jingling change while someone putts, standing someplace someone doesn't want you to stand for some reason, or violating some other unknowable taboo that could make a contestant freak out and destroy his entire career. The players are right at the edge, you can feel it at every turn. Many have strange superstitions, such as eating precisely the same big country breakfast at the same booth at the same Denny's before each round, or fluttering their eyeballs or waving their arms in incantatory ways before each shot, all of which make you long to return to planet earth.

I wouldn't dare approach a player with questions before or during a round. But I discovered I could waylay them after their rounds as they emerged from the scorer's tent on their way to the scoreboard. Usually at that moment they were too dazed to resist a little polite chitchat. My modus operandi was to tell them that I intended to turn pro and wanted their best advice.

Some of the pointers I got were eccentric. The sum and substance of one player's advice was to practice five-foot putts. "If you can make every five-foot putt you face, you can also make every three-foot putt you face," he said, "and you'll do better on your ten- and twenty-foot putts, too."

Another guy grew poetic about visualization. "The best players, before they hit, imagine their balls painting beautiful patterns across the sky," he rhapsodized. Another fellow named Jack Steinicke assured me confidently that "the key to winning is shooting really low scores." This actually isn't as dumb as it sounds. He meant something specific by the comment—that you can't prosper on the mini-tours by merely trying to shoot even-par golf, you have to learn to "go deep," to play gonzo, lights-out golf in the mid to low sixties. But this pearl wasn't of much use at my developmental stage.

After several days of conversation, one invariable theme emerged. It was what Dick Mast had told me: work on the short game. Looking through my notes, not a single player failed to mention the short game in one form or another as the key to doing well as a pro. "Everyone out here can hit the ball as pretty as you please," said Scott Medlin, a fifth-time Q Schooler, in one typical response. "The thing that separates the winners from the losers is chipping and putting, who can get the ball up and down the best."

I didn't doubt it. On the other hand, I was not yet one of those pros who could hit the ball as pretty as you please. Like most recreational golfers, I was stuck in the swing phase, whereas most of these pros had been playing golf and taking lessons and competing in tournaments since they were wee lads. Apart from the occasional tune-up, they took their swings as a given.

The only competitor at the final stage I had met before was a guy named Kevin Sutherland. I buttonholed him coming off the course after round three. He had just shot a 66 to go 13 under par for the tournament, one stroke off the lead, and appeared to be in a trance.

"Yeah, I did pretty well out there today," he slowly intoned. I've heard people talk more excitedly about motor oil. "But there's still a lot more golf to go. I take it one shot at a time, that's my attitude."

Sutherland was a lean, six-foot Californian who briefly played minor league baseball. He and his brother David had both reached the final stage of the 1991 Q School, where I had met him. In that school, Kevin missed the cut and David earned a card, although David stayed on Tour for only a year and now Kevin told me David was recovering from a bad car wreck.

Both Sutherland boys learned golf from an amateur instructor back in Sacramento who was a friend of the family, and they have remarkably similar styles. They both stick their butts way out at address, like chimpanzees presenting rearward, and their backswings are unbelievably sloooow. By my clock, Kevin takes two full seconds to move his clubhead back the first three feet.

"People comment, but honestly I don't think my backswing is that slow," he said when I raised the issue. "I try not to think about it, one way or the other. My goal here is just to take things one shot at a time." He was staring in the middle distance as he spoke, as if at a hypnotist's watch slowly swinging back and forth: one shot at a time, one shot at a time, one shot at a time.

If one-shot-at-a-time was Kevin's strategy for dealing with the pressure of Q School, I was impressed with his discipline. Every player had to have some way of coping as the final rounds approached. Each shot carried weight. The previous year seventeen players had missed getting their Tour cards by one or two strokes, and everyone knew it.

ON THE FOURTH day of Q School, I played hooky so as to visit the mini-tour that the reporter in the clubhouse had told me about, the South Florida Tour.

By chance that morning, while perusing the fine print of the local sports pages, I noticed a partial listing of first round scores from the South Florida Tour event. Shooting a 73 was one "Ivan Lendl." Could this be the former tennis great? How many Ivan Lendls could there be?

The tournament was held at a course called Polo Trace, which was not easy to find. It was brand new, built way out in the swamps as part of a real estate gambit, and accessible only through a dirt parking lot buzzing with construction equipment. In the pro shop, housed in a trailer, I asked if I was in the right place.

"South Florida Tour?" the guy behind the counter responded, momentarily puzzled. "Oh. She's in the snack bar."

"She" was Sarah Stevenson, who ran day-to-day operations for the tour. I interrupted her while she was reading a novel, taking a break since all the players were on the course. We yakked a little—I learned she once coached woman's golf at Florida Atlantic University—and eventually she pulled out a walkie-talkie and said, "You gotta meet Tom."

Tom Eubanks was the tour's founder and owner. I found him, as Sarah had directed, in a cart near the eleventh green monitoring the action. He was an appealing fellow—late thirties, square-jawed, dark-haired, sturdily built—and for an hour or more we tooled around the course as Tom talked about mini-tour economics and occasionally stopped to issue a ruling. For instance, he granted a free drop to one player whose ball had landed in a pile of leftover fence posts. But always he returned to mini-tour economics. This seemed to be the subject he figured a prospective player would most want to hear about.

"I lost fifteen thousand dollars on this tour the first year and two thousand last year," he said. "And that's without paying myself anything. This year I'd like to start paying myself two hundred dollars a week. It depends on how many players we get." The field this week comprised only fifty-one pros, but this was December and midwinter was the hot season for Florida golf. He expected to draw more than twice as many starting in January.

The South Florida Tour was a sideline. The bulk of Eubanks's income derived from a company he had started after dropping out of competitive golf a few years earlier. The company sold granite tee markers and fairway yardage signs to golf courses and yardage guides to players. "Frankly, my main reason for starting the tour was to give myself a good place to compete someday. Once it becomes self-sustaining, I want to get out as much as possible." Old golfers never die, I was beginning to learn. They simply find a new place to compete.

In the snack bar after the tournament (the winner shot 66-67 and

took home a check for twenty-three hundred dollars) I spotted
Lendl. He was sitting at a lunch table surrounded by other players,
scarfing down a tuna fish sandwich and listening to gripes about the
high cost of Q School. "A thousand entrants paying three thousand
dollars each comes to three million," one guy calculated. "What
does the Tour need with another three million dollars? Rolls-Royce
courtesy cars?"

Lendl was wearing olive Dockers shorts and a wild, purple golf
shirt. He looked extremely fit—lean and tan with chiseled calves
and forearms—and when he spoke, the consonant-rich accent of his
native Czechoslovakia came through clearly. "Don't the pros
already have Rollses at home?" he asked, deadpan.

This drew a laugh. Part of what made it funny was that Lendl
himself probably had a Rolls at home, or at least could afford one.
No telling how many millions he had stashed away after a tennis
career that included ninety-four professional titles, eight of them
majors. A bad back had forced him to retire at thirty-two.

In the parking lot a bit later I asked Lendl about his round of 83
that day. "What agony," he moaned. "It was one mental error after
another. I hit one club too much on number two, one club too little
on number eleven, a terrible approach shot on number nine. Then
on twelve I three-putted. . . ." He sounded like any other frustrated
linkster.

He said he had become serious about golf only a year earlier—
"Before that I just hacked around some"—and had turned pro last
March to compete in some events on the Celebrity Golf Association
Tour, which he adored. I asked if he had aspirations of joining the
PGA Tour someday. "Don't be ridiculous," he replied. "I'm just
doing this to enjoy and to compete. I can't not compete. I've always
competed. It's either compete out here or sit around the house
all day."

For most of the year Lendl lived in northwest Connecticut. The
previous summer he had played in a dozen events on the North
Atlantic mini-tour—a tour I had heard about and hoped to play on
come spring, since it was the closest one to where I lived. But he

also had a winter home in Florida, which explained his presence at Polo Trace.

I was curious about how much Lendl had managed to lower his handicap in the year he'd been playing seriously. It was not a good question. "I don't believe in the handicap system," he snapped. "Why should someone give *me* strokes just because they practice more than I do?" The idea of accepting strokes seemed to offend Lendl's honor—if he couldn't take on a man head-to-head, well then, it wasn't worthy competition. It was an insight into the mindset of a proud champion. Either that or his handicap was still twelve or something.

But Lendl was quite enthusiastic in recommending the South Florida tour. "Great guys," he said. "It's very friendly." Such was my impression, too. In the snack bar I chatted with three or four players who gave me generous advice about finding an apartment and options for arranging free or discount range balls. The tour had the flavor I was looking for—small, informal, unintimidating to a tournament rookie like myself. I decided that the South Florida Tour would be my winter home.

BEFORE HEADING BACK to the motel, I dropped by Bear Lakes. A crowd was gathered around the scoreboard. With just a few groups left on the course, speculation was furious as to where the 72-hole cut would fall. Only half the field plus ties would survive the ax, and the fateful number looked like it would be three- or four-under-par.

The mood in front of the billboard-sized scoreboard was edgy. Every so often a runner from the official scorer's tent would arrive with white slips of paper bearing the hole-by-hole results of the latest finishers. With mesmerizing deliberation a woman read out those numbers, one-by-one, to a calligrapher on the catwalk that ran beneath the board and he in turn would transcribe them for all to see, using multicolored felt pens. A hush passed through the mob whenever a new total was posted. A 69. With that score, one more player finished four rounds at four-under-par, increasing the odds that three-under-par would miss the cut. A 73 was posted. The crowd relaxed. One more player bound for the bush leagues, increasing the odds that three-under-par would make it.

This drama was cruel to observe. Players stood in small groups, sometimes flanked by friends and family, waiting for destiny to declare its whimsy. From time to time a contestant at two-under- or one-under-par, finally accepting the inevitable, would stalk away. One such player I observed, tall with dark hair, was Stewart Cink, a three-time Georgia Tech All-American who six months earlier had won the Jack Nicklaus trophy as college player of the year. Before Q School the papers had talked about Cink as a shoo-in, but his rounds of 70-75-72-71 came out to even par—not nearly good enough. (A few hours later, by chance, I encountered Cink in the motel parking lot, packing his car for the drive back to Georgia. I asked him what he intended to do next year. "No idea at all," he replied stonily. There was no humor, no perspective yet on what had happened. He slammed the trunk.)

Another tough case was Eric Booker from Michigan. I had chatted with him the day before about coping with pressure. At the time he stood at seven-under-par, with rounds of 71-65-73, and seemed in good shape to make the cut. "The key is putting yourself in positions where you experience pressure," he told me. "The more you play, the more you learn to control your nerves so it's not such a big deal. When you succeed at one level, you graduate to something bigger, tournaments with bigger purses or the Nike Tour where you have to deal with galleries, and so on up the ladder until, hopefully, someday you're on the Tour." He had seemed confident almost to the point of elation.

Now, however, I noticed Booker standing alone at the edge of the scoreboard crowd and asked him how he had done. He shook his head, tight-lipped, unable to respond. I eased away and snuck a look at the scoreboard. A 78. One-under-par total, out of the picture.

My friend Kevin Sutherland continued to do well, however. I

caught him marching like a sleepwalker past the scoreboard to the practice range.

"Did you make anything happen out there today, Kevin?" I asked.

"Today I did okay. I shot a 68."

"That's great!"

"I was hitting it well. But there's a lot of golf left," he said, repeating almost verbatim what he had told me the day before. "I'm just trying to take things one shot at a time."

He was tied for second place at seventeen-under-par: 70-67-66-68. Amazing golf. I wasn't too worried about Kevin, so long as he kept taking things one shot at a time.

AFTER THE NEXT day's round there was a noticeable pickup in extracurricular activities around the scoreboard. Specifically, the Company Men started to appear: slick, hale fellows with expensive shoes and ingratiating manners. You couldn't help but notice the shoes: tasseled Italian loafers, supple calfskin pumps, gleaming cap-toed businesswear. Of the hundred players left in the competition at this point, all were winners. All would play at least on the Nike Tour next year and forty or more would make it to the Big Tour. The Company Men were there to make contact—no hard sell, just a little pressing of the flesh, some extending of congratulations, some building of relationships with vague hints of endorsement deals for balls, clubs, clothes, hotels, rental cars, and business products. For players new to the scene, this was the first whiff of the PGA Tour wealth that could be theirs. If they could just put the Company Men out of mind and think about nothing but golf for one more round.

On a practice green near the scoreboard, I happened to notice a tall, abnormally skinny competitor working on his chipping. Something about this guy intrigued me. For one thing he wasn't dressed at all like his stylish peers. His faded black chinos had obviously been through many a wash cycle and his red-and-white golf shirt appeared much too small. The sleeves came only to mid-biceps, whereas the current fashion called for sleeves to the elbow or below. The most curious thing, however, was the way his golf cap perched impossibly high on the top of his head, as if drawn there by a cartoonist.

I wandered over to the green and watched him practice. From the upslope of a hill he was chipping balls to a hole with what seemed like every iron in his bag, but frequently he would pace off the distance—the same distance each time—and stick tees in the putting surface at various points where he wanted the chips to land. It was an odd drill.

After a while he noticed me watching from behind the rope and said hello.

"I'm Joe Daley," he said. "Would you like a chipping lesson?"

I said no, no, I was just curious about his drill.

"Well then, come on in and let me give you a lesson." He held up the rope up for me to duck under, but I hesitated. I didn't really want a chipping lesson.

"Come on in. I insist," he said. I did as I was told.

"The first thing you gotta figure out is the ratio for each club you chip with," he informed me. Daley dropped a fresh Titleist on the grass and pointed to a tee stuck in the turf about three feet onto the green. "From here to the tee is five feet, right? And from the tee to the hole is another twenty-one feet. That's a ratio of one to four-and-a-quarter. I use my six-iron."

Deftly he chipped with his six-iron so the ball landed on the green near the tee and rolled to a stop within a few inches of the hole.

"Works every time. For the seven-iron the ratio is one to three-and-a-half and for the eight it's an even one to three. Now here, you try a couple."

He handed me his six-iron, dropped a few more balls in the grass and stood back. I couldn't help but notice that Andy Bean, an eleven-time Tour winner, was standing less than ten feet past my target hole. What if I shanked the ball so badly it hit Andy Bean in the calf and unhinged him psychologically to the extent he never played Tour-caliber golf again?

"No, I'll just watch you," I said.

"No, you do it," Daley replied encouragingly.

I really had no choice. He was so damn friendly. So I stepped up to the ball, carefully judged my distance and made clean contact. The ball landed two feet past the hole and hit Andy Bean in the heel.

Bean looked around quizzically. I shrugged apologetically. Bean knocked the ball back without comment. I handed the six-iron back to Daley. "There, I'm done," I said.

"No, that was good," he said. "You've just got to find your range."

He gave me the club back and forced me to hit a dozen more chip shots. Most were all right—only one more got away, thankfully not hitting anyone—but I couldn't understand what impulse compelled Daley to give me a lesson. Did he think I was someone else?

Eventually I managed to explain what I was doing at Q School and I thanked him for his time. He took this as a cue to tell me all about himself. "I'm entirely self-taught myself," he said. He was thirty-five, lived in Orlando with his wife who was a schoolteacher, worked part-time as a banquet waiter—though until recently he had been a credit officer at a savings and loan. This was his first time reaching the final stage and with one round to play he stood at twelve-under par. That put him one shot ahead of the eight-way tie that included the 40th player, and the next day only forty players plus ties would earn their Tour cards.

If I had been in Daley's shoes, perched smack-dab "on the bubble," I certainly wouldn't have been wasting my time with a total stranger on the practice green. I would have been doing something more productive, like hurling into the john back in my motel room. But Daley couldn't get enough of me. He asked about my lessons with Hebron. "There's nothing much to the swing, really," he said. "Just keep your stance all squared up and swing the club down and through. When I stand over the ball, all I'm thinking about is tempo, because that's the only thing I can really control at that point. My swing's my swing, after all." He recommended that I read Hogan's *Five Lessons* nightly, and . . .

Suddenly it struck me that Daley was *petrified*. He was giving me all this advice—jabbering on like a lonely insurance salesman—because he was desperate not to think about tomorrow. Latching on to the first stranger who showed an interest and giving a chipping lesson kept him calm. Once I realized this, I would have stayed there all evening listening—and almost did. Only when dusk started to descend did Daley excuse himself to hit a few more balls on the range. But by then I had decided that he should be my role model: an everyman golfer who had taught himself to play the game—down and through, nothing much to it.

THE NEXT DAY near the scoreboard, there was blood all over. At one point I was standing five feet from a skinny blond contestant who suddenly broke out in a keening sob. He had just learned that he missed earning a card. "Jesus! Jesus! Jesus!" he wailed into the shoulder of a friend and then sagged to the ground. His friend cradled him in his arms on the sidewalk like a Pieta. Another player named Eric Epperson, who started the day at seventeen-under-par, skied to a 78 and missed getting his card by two. Q School always seems to produce a few sad tales like this.

On the other hand there was Joe Daley. Craftily, so as not to be noticed, I followed his final few holes from behind trees and by blending into the few scattered knots of other spectators. He did fine, all pars. With his ball in the fairway on the eighteenth hole, Daley spotted me.

"Look at this!" he called and waved me over. "My ball's in the exact same divot I filled in yesterday!" Some kind of dispute on the green ahead had created a long delay, so I think he welcomed my presence for the same reason he did the day before.

He was elated—walking on air. And when, after a ten minute wait, he finally knocked his approach shot onto the green and two-putted for a 69 to claim his Tour card, I felt as if I'd accomplished something, too. If Daley could make it through this vicious Q School gauntlet with his wrinkled khakis, golf cap worn like a beanie, and homespun game, then maybe there was hope for me.

Down and through, nothing much to it—the game really is so very simple.

5 . *T h e   S n o w m a n*

WHEN I RETURNED TO ORIENT IN EARLY DE-
cember the weather was bitter cold—the first
blast of what would be the Northeast's harsh-
est winter in a quarter century. Polly was ready
to decamp for Florida immediately, but for
various reasons—Christmas in Texas being
one—we couldn't leave until after New Year's.
This forced interregnum in Orient, however,
turned out to be excellent for my golf swing.

For one thing, I was motivated. The week at
Q School had generated intense consumer
desire: I wanted what those guys had, those
silky swings. And I was willing to do whatever
it took to get it. For another thing, during the
week in Florida I had taken two more lessons
from Michael Hebron and he had left me with

lots of good stuff to work on. Every November Hebron moves his teaching operation from Long Island to Florida, and by chance his southern base this winter was at the ritzy Palm Beach Polo Club, less than thirty minutes from the Q School site.

The first of the two lessons began badly. I was running late and the guard at the Palm Beach Polo gate had an attitude. "You legit?" he asked me suspiciously.

"Born and raised right here in America," I replied testily.

Apparently this was not the password. He eyed my rented Geo Metro as Cadillacs with the appropriate stickers whizzed past freely in both directions. I gave him the number I had for Hebron, but no one answered. We waited. Eventually he got someone on the phone at the pro shop and let me through. One more reason to dislike fancy clubs.

Hebron met me near the parking lot in a cart and we motored out to the far end of the driving range. After an insufficient warm-up, I banged six quick scum-sucking drives.

"What's going on!" I asked Hebron, panic-stricken. None of the drives had climbed more than three feet off the ground—and driving was one of the strengths of my game!

"You're just a little anxious," he said. "Remember, this process takes time. I wouldn't worry."

"Time?" I stuttered. Didn't he realize my mini-tour career would begin in a month? Actually, no, he didn't realize that. I hadn't yet told him of my mini-tour ambitions, and I wasn't about to bring up the subject now, not after hitting that bunch of dog-ass drives.

Hebron fiddled with my setup for a while, to no avail. I was tight and quick. With each new attempt I grew increasingly frustrated. After a few minutes he stepped back and addressed me in a kindly tone. "You are a hardworking person, John Paul, and I can tell that your standards are high. I can also tell that you are very analytical. But it's difficult for analytical people to make progress in golf if they are also self-critical. So one of the challenges you're going to face is turning off the left side of your brain, the analytical, self-criticizing side, and learning to just throw paint up on the wall. See what sticks,

see what works. Don't worry so much about results. Do you understand?"

"Yes, sir."

"Good. So forget everything mechanical for a while. You used to
play quarterback, right?"

"Yes, sir."

"Good. So what I want you to do is close your eyes and remember
what it felt like back then as a quarterback when you were throwing
a long pass. Keep your eyes closed and show me what you did. Act it
out right here."

Now we were on familiar turf. As I mentioned before, I wasted
three-quarters of my youth learning to throw a football. I never
really developed into an ace quarterback because I tended to
choke under pressure (not the quality you want in a QB) and for
some reason I didn't seem to care much about winning. In hud-
dles, a center once told me, I had a way of inspiring negative confidence in the troops, mostly because I kept changing my mind
about what play to call. But as far as purely throwing the football,
I had a talent. I could heave the ball eighty-five yards in the air
and drill bullets into the chests of receivers crossing at forty yards.
In all my life I'm certain I have never been as good at any single
task as I was at throwing a football. I was only too happy to
demonstrate this skill for Hebron.

Handing him my driver, I crouched behind an imaginary center,
took the snap, dropped back seven steps into the pocket, hitched,
and threw a long one. It was a beauty. The motions were as natural
to me as getting out of bed.

"Very nice," Hebron said. "Now let's talk about what you felt."

With a little discussion we isolated the sensations of relaxed
whippiness through my shoulders and arm and of rocking back on
my rear foot and throwing *upward*. Then Hebron handed back the
driver and urged me to incorporate those football sensations into
my swing. The first ball I hit was a boomer, boring into the slight
headwind on a perfect midheight trajectory.

"Whaddya know," he said.

I nailed two or three more boomers while the feeling of throwing was still in my body, but then I began trying to analyze what I was doing right and the worm-burners returned. Even so, the experience was exhilarating. I had made a tantalizing connection between my golf swing and my athletic past. Perhaps eventually I could bring the two together on a permanent basis.

At the second lesson Hebron introduced a difficult concept. After observing me struggle for a while and detecting, no doubt, several hundred possible swing defects to work on, he settled on one. In a proper downswing, he explained, the chest should push the left biceps forward.

This was something I had never focused on before and, frankly, it was baffling. I tried to get a feeling for what he meant but when I swung, the chest and biceps seemed to have nothing to do with each other: the chest could gain no purchase with which to "push." After repeated attempts I began to get angry. "It's impossible," I said.

"You'll figure it out," he assured me, nodding. "Just keep trying when you go home."

It occurred to me that maybe this maddening little piece of advice was a kind of koan. In Zen practice, with which I knew Hebron was familiar, masters often pose unanswerable riddles for their students like, "What is the sound of one hand clapping?" and then send them off to think about it for, like, six months. In pondering the question, good students will stumble into other useful discoveries even if they don't come up with an answer to the koan itself. Was this Hebron's strategy? Or maybe it *was* actually possible for the chest to push the biceps.

The second order of business at the lesson was a grip change. The interlocking grip my brother had taught me long ago, in which the little finger of the right hand hooks underneath the index finger of the left, was good for kids and for grown-ups with small hands. Jack Nicklaus used the interlocking grip. But Hebron said a big lout like me could gain more control over the club using the

Vardon grip, in which the little finger of the right hand nestles on top of the left hand, between the knuckles of the index and middle fingers.

The grip felt extremely awkward, but once again Hebron assured me I would figure it out with time. Keep a club nearby wherever I was, he advised, and practice assuming the grip over and over—the perfect project for housebound winter days up north.

DURING MY FIRST two weeks back in Orient the temperature rose into the upper thirties and low forties a half dozen times, which meant I was able to hit balls at the Greenport fairgrounds. By layering in long underwear and standing in the wind-protected lee of a tree line, I could stay reasonably warm.

Indian Joe showed up every time—it was uncanny. On my first day back he snuck up on me undetected again and scared the bejeebers out of me.

"You pulled that one pretty bad," he pronounced loudly in my ear.

When my heartbeat returned to normal, I said, "Good to see you, too, Indian Joe."

Indian Joe did not approve of Hebron's grip change—"Trevino uses the interlocking," he declared flatly, precluding all further discussion—and said that the chest-biceps conundrum sounded to him like a strategy for drawing the ball. He had read somewhere that older players need to draw the ball on a right-to-left arc to compensate for waning strength. For more than a year he had been trying to learn to draw but had not succeeded because, he said, a bum hip kept him from making a full turn. "A man your age oughta be able to draw the ball every time," he said accusingly.

"Trevino hits a fade," I pointed out.

"Trevino can get away with it. You and I need to hit a draw."

On December 14 a blizzard dumped eighteen inches of snow on Long Island and forced me (and presumably Indian Joe, too) indoors. The office I rented was in the garage apartment of a big house overlooking Long Island Sound and I discovered that the garage space itself made a wonderful indoor driving range. Wonderful is in the eye of the beholder, of course, but given the lack of wintertime golf alternatives, it seemed wonderful to me.

A baby-blue Jaguar being stored for the winter filled half of the two-car garage and the other half brimmed with junk: unwanted furniture, recycling bins, lawn equipment, rusting shop tools. By stacking most of it to the ceiling in one corner and suspending two old tennis nets (each folded over several times) from the ceiling above the hood of the Jaguar, I opened up enough space to pound whiffle balls. I hit off of old carpet remnants and an AstroTurf door-mat purchased at the local five-and-dime, and monitored my swing in two full-length mirrors propped fore and aft. I was actually quite proud of my indoor range. The cleverest touch, I felt, was the ball-return mechanism. Using flattened corrugated boxes, I fashioned a tilted platform beneath the tennis nets which caught most of the balls I hit and funneled them back in my direction. A fair number of balls, however, would squirt through the netting and collect under the Jaguar. Retrieving them was a royal pain.

For making fundamental changes to the swing, working indoors has many advantages. For one thing, you don't become emotionally involved with the flight path of your shots, which can be discouraging in the early going. Instead, all your focus is on the swing itself and its many subtle variations. You also develop a heightened sense of where and how solidly the clubface makes contact with the ball, even with a whiffle ball—not unlike the way a blind person develops heightened senses of hearing and smell.

Habituating myself to the Vardon grip was perfect work for these garage sessions. Within three weeks the overlap felt entirely natural and after that I never had to remind myself to use the grip when I picked up a club. As for its effect on control, I sensed—or *believed* I sensed, which may be just as important given golf's kooky mental nature—that the club was simultaneously looser and more secure in my hands.

The biceps-chest pushing business was a different story, however. Try as I might, I could never feel the chest actually pushing the biceps forward. The one always slipped past the other. Through December and into January I worked at the problem, making literally thousands of swings. Some people seek enlightenment from their navels, I sought enlightenment from my armpit— to no avail.

But then one frigid January morning—cold, by the way, was the main drawback of my beautiful indoor range; the garage was unheated and the temperature seldom climbed out of the twenties—I had a breakthrough. For several days prior I had been carefully studying Ben Hogan's *Five Lessons.* In Lesson Two there is a drawing of Hogan holding a club with some kind of weird S&M strap clamping his elbows together close to his chest. For some reason I began to ponder this illustration in connection with the famous illustration in Lesson Three of Hogan standing under a pane of glass representing the ideal swing plane—a pane like the Plexiglas pane Hebron had me poke my head through at my second lesson. And it hit me, in a "Eureka!" moment, that there are actually *two* planes: the "glass pane" swing plane upon which the arms travel back and forth, and the more horizontal plane, or axis, around which the torso pivots.

The reason I could never feel my chest pushing my biceps was because the two parts of my anatomy were moving on different planes—until, that is, the exact moment of impact, when they converged. It seemed I had been interpreting Hebron's directive too literally. Chest pushing biceps was a metaphor, I decided, for how the swing should *feel.* I should *feel* at the moment of impact as if the chest were delivering up all its power to the ball through the agency of the biceps.

Whether this was precisely what Hebron was getting at, I don't know, but for me at the time it was a marvelously fruitful insight. Once I had it, many other pieces of the swing puzzle fell into place, all relating to a concept that is central to Hebron's teaching philosophy: the inside moves the outside.

See and Feel the Inside Move the Outside is the title of one of Hebron's books. The basic idea is that if you can rotate the big central mass of your body quickly enough and under control, you don't have to worry or even think much about what the arms and hands are doing way out there on the fringe. They have no choice but to drag the club along behind on the proper arc—*and at incredible speeds.* An analogy Hebron uses is the ice-skating game of "crack the whip." Skaters link arms and turn in a giant circle like the spokes of a wheel. Those near the imaginary hub don't have to spin very fast for the skaters at the outside to *fly.* Then, when those on the inside suddenly put on the brakes to "crack the whip," the skaters on the outside shoot forward like rocks out of a slingshot. They can't hold on. The golf swing works similarly in that the inside only has to rotate at a controlled, moderate velocity to generate an abundance of speed way out there at the tip of the club—speed that becomes supercharged if the whip can be made to crack at the moment of impact.

"Swing in as small an area as possible," Hebron had told me repeatedly in our lessons. But until my Eureka moment in the garage, I hadn't fully understood the significance of the concept. His injunction to contemplate the chest-biceps nexus—my armpit—may have been a way of getting me to keep my focus close to my body, where all the power in a swing originates.

These discoveries were intellectually satisfying. I would say "intellectually thrilling" except that it makes me sound like a nerd. Although, in fact, I am a nerd. I approached these daily garage sessions with the enraptured monomania computer hackers bring to developing software. Like them, I knew I could get the damn program working properly by simply ironing out a few more bugs. I kept a log of the changes I made in my swing, closely observed the results in the mirrors, periodically retreated to the warmth of my office to consult an array of manuals, and tested all new hypotheses with scientific scrupulosity: Would I gain more control by pushing back off the ball of my left foot or off the heel? Should my left shoulder literally graze my chin on the backswing or just come close? In the quiet privacy of that garage the hours flew past without notice. The tinkering never failed to hold my attention.

OCCUPYING MOST OF my non-golf hours during this period, and delaying our eventual departure for Florida, was the necessity of endlessly rewriting a profile of Tom Lehman for *Reader's Digest*. I thought I had finished this assignment months before, but the magazine demanded a dozen revisions (and then never ran the story). *Reader's Digest* had been intrigued by Lehman's inspiring rise to Tour stardom after so many years on the mini-tours—"From Journeyman to Champion," the editors wanted to title the story— and that was also my reason for wanting to write it.

Lehman had given me a lot of time. A few weeks before the Masters Tournament the previous spring he had allowed me to walk with him during a practice round at Augusta National, an experience any golfer would treasure. Like everyone who meets Lehman, I was struck by his kindness and core human decency. But I was even more impressed by his toughness. He's a nice guy, but on the course his attitude is intense and ferocious. More than once in tournaments he has snapped clubs across his knee in anger.

The most unexpected thing I learned about Lehman was that even back in college he had extraordinary physical talent. Most stories about Lehman focus on his long apprenticeship in the bush leagues and make it seem as if he needed those years to learn how to play the game. In fact, he was a two-time All-American out of Minnesota and easily made it through Q School onto the Tour the first three times he tried. Those early Tour years were the problem: the famous players, the low scores, the whole experience intimidated Lehman. To prove himself, he felt he had to shoot 65 every time out, and when he didn't, he pressed, resulting in disastrous miscues and ever higher scores. After three years his confidence was shot. The mini-tour years, therefore, were not about learning the knockdown shot or other practical matters of golf, but about spiritual recovery. Specifically, Lehman told me, he had to learn that how he performed on the golf course had nothing to do with his worth as a person. "When I got that concept through my thick head," he said, "it was like a great burden had been lifted, and I was finally free to fail or succeed on the golf course as my talents warranted."

The more I worked on the Lehman story, the more I began to relate to his struggles. In sports my problem had never been physical talent per se, it had been choking. I *did* explicitly link my total value as a human being to my performance. "Overthrow this pass, jerk, and you can kiss all self-respect good-bye for the rest of your life!" was the sort of thing I told myself in clutch situations—resulting most of the time, naturally, in an overthrown pass. If I was that self-conscious in the heat of a football game, I could only imagine how self-conscious and self-doubting I would become in the eerily quiet tension of a professional golf tournament. Not to mention how intimidated I would be by the pros around me.

But I did have one thing going for me, if I could only make myself believe it: this Year of mine was an experiment, a lark, not a serious attempt to establish a new career. From a golf point of view, nothing was at stake. The other contestants might sweat bullets at Q School, their professional futures and/or monthly rents were on the line; but I could approach each round with the remote objectivity of an anthropologist, taking notes about the queer things that happen in golf. In that context, it shouldn't be too hard to keep from equating my scores with my sense of self-worth. Right? Lehman would be my lodestar. Lehman and Joe Daley. Down and through, nothing much to it. I was wise and mature now, I had the perspective of age. I could put all that adolescent, everything-rides-on-this-putt crap behind me.

Yet when I lay awake at night contemplating the months ahead, my heart would bolter and my breathing quicken. Underneath I was as nervous as any rank rookie.

IMPATIENT AT THE delay in our departure for Florida, I started hitting golf balls around in the snow. It's actually a good discipline. As with hitting off sand, you must catch the ball cleanly: too fat and the club stops dead. Plus you get experience with uneven lies, as when the ball comes to rest on the side of a massive drift. Bright orange whiffle balls work best.

One day in mid-January, Polly dropped by my office unexpectedly—perhaps to ask whether I'd finished the Lehman story—and found me outside, calf-deep in the snow, hitting balls. She stood beside the car, Anna sucking on a bottle in the rear seat, and peered at me over the roof. She didn't have to say a word.

"This is my work! This is research!" I protested.

"I didn't say a thing," she said.

"Yeah, but I know what you're thinking."

"What am I thinking?"

"You're thinking I look like a fool out here in the snow and that furthermore I *am* a fool and that you can't believe you married a golfer."

"No," she said morosely, "I believe it, all right." She blew me an air kiss and departed.

A few days later a photographer from the local weekly newspaper came by to take a picture of me hitting balls in the snow, which ran with a short feature headlined "Living a Real-Life Golf Fantasy." The article nicely captured the essence of the Year I was planning—three months in Florida, spring and summer roaming the country playing on the mini-tours, Q School in the fall—but the photo was an embarrassment. Artistically it looked fine: me in a thermal vest and cap, a half-second after impact, snow exploding everywhere. The problem was I had caught the whiffle ball fat and my wrists were way behind where they should have been at that point in the swing. To anyone who knew golf, I looked like a duffer. Making matters worse, the caption read, "John Paul Newport demonstrates the swing he hopes will land him a spot on the PGA Tour."

Was this an omen? Was this how the Year would play out? I wanted to curl up under a rock somewhere and die. But luckily only two days after the paper came out we were able to load up the Honda—Polly, Anna, two cats, as much luggage as possible, and me—and flee. In Florida all would be made right. Florida beckoned like a new nine. The competitive part of my Year was about to begin.

F l o r i d a

✣

You may take it from me that there are two kinds of golf, there is golf—and tournament golf. And they are not at all the same thing.

—BOBBY JONES

6 . *The Mini-Tour Capital of the Universe*

BY LEGEND, IF NOT PRECISELY BY FACT, THE first bona fide mini-tour was the Space Coast Tour in Florida. Certainly the Space Coast Tour was the oldest continuously operating mini-tour in the country, but it evolved indirectly, under murky circumstances, from a quickly defunct predecessor tour, the National Tournament Golfers Association. The traditions of mini-tour golf are not exactly royal and ancient.

According to J. C. Goosie, one of the NTGA's founders and later sole owner and proprietor of the Space Coast Tour, the idea for a mini-tour sprang out of a disgruntled lunch at a golf course grill in Tampa, Florida, in 1970. Goosie and three other former touring pros, all by then in their thirties and forties and exiled from the PGA's big money events by their inability to get through the newfangled Q School process, were griping about their lack of good, professional competition. Someone suggested they up and start a tour for themselves and the notion grew into a business plan. The foursome calculated that if even just 10 percent of the hundreds of pros who annually washed out of Q School could be convinced to compete against each other for their own money, a viable enterprise might be born. The NTGA debuted in Tampa a few months later with thirty-eight players.

For some reason about which Goosie is vague, the other three organizers soon booted him out of the business. But no matter. The NTGA folded within six months anyway, and by that time Goosie was helping some other entrepreneurs get a rival tour off the ground on Florida's opposite coast—the so-called Space Coast near Cape Canaveral. Once again, the vital details of these early days in mini-tour history are a bit blurry, but suffice it to say that after a couple of disputatious years Goosie emerged holding the golden egg. He owned the Space Coast Tour outright and moved it to Orlando, which was just then starting to boom with Disney World and a proliferation of new golf courses.

For the next twenty-plus years Goosie presided over his prosperous franchise like a mini sports czar. The tour's brochure included a boldfaced caveat: "Management reserves the right to refuse any application for any reason." This was not idle boilerplate. Goosie often did excommunicate players for a variety of real or imagined offenses: bad sportsmanship, bounced checks, sneaking off to play on competing mini-tours, badmouthing operations. Though Goosie himself was frequently out of town playing on the Senior Tour, he returned often enough to supervise a whole generation of future PGA Tour stars: Craig Stadler, Lee Janzen, Calvin Peete, Mark Calcavecchia, and Bob Tway among others. Paul Azinger was a Space Coast regular for several years; one season Zinger's wife, Toni, ran the scoreboard in exchange for reduced entry fees.

It was natural, therefore, that when I first heard about the mini-tours in 1992, it would be the Space Coast Tour I visited.

"Our operation is simple," Goosie told me. "We want ex-college players to come down here and spend about sixteen to seventeen thousand dollars a year—that's for everything, entry fees, living expenses, everything. If a guy's good, he's gonna make twelve or thirteen thousand of that back. If he's *very* good, he may break even. So for fifteen to thirty cents on the dollar, which is next to nothing, he's gonna get tournament experience he can't buy nowhere else."

The entry fees—three hundred to four hundred dollars for a two-day event—were essentially bets players placed in an open-air casino. The winner might take home three or four thousand dollars if the field was large enough (over a hundred players), but by design two-thirds of the contestants went home empty-handed. Only "the house," in the person of J. C. Goosie, was guaranteed a profit. The house kept 10 percent or more of the purse (grumbling not permitted) and another hefty portion went toward renting the golf course, paying the rules officials, running the back office, and other expenses.

It was a lousy, almost impossible way for players to make a living, but that was not the point. The point was to compete, to experience tournament pressure, and contestants streamed to the Space Coast Tour from all over the country. Most fit Goosie's profile: former college players in their twenties, struggling to make ends meet for a year or two to see if they had what it took—the mind, the magic, the moxie, whatever—to make it to the Big Time.

I found it nearly impossible during my visit to distinguish these young Space Coast cadets one from another. They all seemed to be blond, five-foot-eleven, obsessed with sports and women, and capable of hitting the golf ball 300 yards in the air. Looking back over the roster now, however, I see that a few of these anonymous competitors have since distinguished themselves. Tom Hearn, Adrian Stills, and Mike Heinen, none of whom made a dime in the three tournaments I witnessed, have all gone on to enjoy moderate success on the PGA Tour, while Steve Stricker, another faceless nobody back in 1992, became a genuine Tour star just four years later, in 1996, when he won twice and finished fourth on the money list with $1.4 million. Stricker's rise is the dream that keeps all the young players hopping.

The older players presented a different picture. Anyone in his late-thirties or forties still playing on the mini-tours is not a strictly rational human being, which of course makes for better stories.

My favorite character was Billy Glisson, forty-six, a friendly, lackadaisical mess of a man who had once supported himself on the mini-tours as the night manager of a brothel in Orlando. The brothel operated out of a beauty salon, which gave Glisson a good line to use whenever the subject came up: "There was a lot more going on in those chairs than just blow-dries, I guarantee." Glisson had a broad, blunt nose, longish dirty blond hair that curlicued out the back of his golf cap, and such a monster belly that he never even tried to tuck his shirttail in. He tended to wear the same pair of baggy gray shorts day after day and left a butt trail of Viceroys around the course that Hansel and Gretel would have envied— three packs per round would have been my guess. He also had the disturbing habit of popping his ball in his mouth to clean it between holes despite all the insecticides around.

Glisson claimed to have won more mini-tour events than anyone in history: ninety-one. Some might consider that a dubious distinction, begging the question of why, if Glisson was such a winner, he hadn't taken his game to the next level. But in fact Glisson *had* played on the PGA Tour in the early eighties, and fared pretty well. "Got on TV four or five times," he bragged to me matter-of-factly. Glisson lasted long enough on tour—three years—to make a mark. He is remembered, among other reasons, for confusing the courtesy-car volunteers with his frequent requests to pick up more than one "Mrs. Glisson" at the airport. At one tournament, the real Mrs. Glisson spotted her husband strolling the fairway holding hands with a Mrs. Glisson not herself and stole his Corvette out of spite, leaving only his street shoes in the parking space.

Unfortunately in 1993, Glisson suffered a nearly fatal stroke—"Too much drinking and carrying on, I reckon"—and had to spend a couple of years recovering. Since then he's been stuck in the bush leagues, driving from event to event in a beat-up black Eldorado with an "I'd Rather Be Golfing" bumper sticker in the rear window. Back home in South Carolina he had a new wife and two young children. When I asked Glisson why he continued to play tournament golf, he had a simple response. "It just gets in the blood, I reckon, and you can't get it out."

Another character was Gene "The Machine" Jones, thirty-five. He was the Space Coast Tour's leading money-winner and as different from Glisson in personality as it was possible to be. Whereas Glisson was lighthearted and easygoing, Gene the Machine was introverted, tightly wrapped, and forlorn. He seemed to have few interests outside golf and worked with savage devotion to perfect his game.

As a high school player, the Machine had been a star. He won both the Florida PGA Junior title and the U.S. Olympic Junior Championship before turning pro at eighteen. But a car wreck put him in a neck brace for five years, and after that he drifted. He sold pots and pans in Fort Worth, cleaned swimming pools in Orlando, and mowed the grass at a country club in South Carolina. "I had went as low as I could go," Jones said.

In the late 1980s a friend of Jones's family rescued him from obscurity. Dr. Malcolm McDonald, an Orlando area surgeon, remembered what a phenom the young Machine had been and convinced him to move back to central Florida. To make that financially possible, the good doctor bought Jones and his wife a trailer and a few acres of land and encouraged him to reconcile with his father, a local teaching pro.

The turning point for Jones was qualifying in a Monday playoff for a spot in the Greensboro Open, a regular PGA event. "At Greensboro, you'd hear ten thousand people giving me the clap, and it was really motivating," he said. "I used to get down on myself because I didn't have any money and all, but the insight I had was that the more failures you go through, the higher you can achieve. You can work hard in golf and make it."

After Greensboro, Jones began to work at golf with a vengeance. He set up a video installation and an AstroTurf putting green at home so he could work out swing flaws and practice on his short game deep into the night. He played in tournaments almost every single day of the week, driving thousands of miles a month.

The thing that most impressed me when I followed the Machine during rounds was his raw animal hunger to score birdies. He worked the course like a bulldog: ferociously darting after the ball as soon as he hit it, constantly making practice swings to groove the right feel, pacing during delays like an impending father in a maternity waiting room, sizing up his putts from every angle of the compass. One time, after missing a seven-foot putt for birdie, he stayed on the green for minutes, inspecting the turf around the hole with the disgusted disbelief of a surgeon trying to comprehend a botched appendectomy.

Gene the Machine won seventeen mini-tour events that year, usually with scores in the mid-sixties—"It scares me how well I'm doing," he told me. "Right now I'd be afraid to take a week off"— and in October earned his Tour card at Q School. But alas, in twenty Tour starts the next year he made only a handful of cuts and a total of $24,522, and hasn't made it back to the Big Time since. The pressure at the top of competitive golf is merciless and has a way of destroying any contender who doesn't believe he can walk on water.

THE SPACE COAST Tour would have been my first choice to play in during the Year, but that option disappeared. In the spring before the Year began, Goosie shut down the Space Coast Tour. New competition had driven him out of business.

If Orlando had once been the St. Andrews of mini-tour golf, by the mid-1990s it was the Myrtle Beach. Mini-tours had set up shop on every corner. The main usurper of Goosie's glory was a nice-enough fellow named Terry Fine, who ran the Tommy Armour

Tour. Fine's tour could boast of significant "added money" from the Tommy Armour company, which made playing there a no-brainer for many young pros: the more added money in the pot, the bigger the percentage payout to contestants. In addition, Fine had arranged exciting special deals for his players, like 10 percent discounts at any Wolf Camera store and a five-hundred-dollar bonus to any player quoted in the media talking about how great PowerBars are.

But Tommy Armour wasn't the only competition around. There was a mini-tour exclusively for club pros, a mini-tour for seniors, a mini-tour for guys over forty who hoped one day to play on the Senior Tour, a mini-tour for pros who used certain types of equipment, and a mini-tour for the less audacious who were willing to accept smaller purses in exchange for smaller entry fees. Golf, in the days since Goosie had started his tour with a simple idea, had become big business, and the result was a cutthroat Darwinian struggle even at the grassroots level.

Given the abundance of opportunity in Orlando—the city could fairly be called the Mini-Tour Capital of the Universe—it might have seemed natural to settle there for my winter adventure. But the city rubbed both Polly and me the wrong way.

Orlando is a fabulous town if you're, like, seven. What seven-year-old doesn't crave unlimited access to go-carts, Goofy T-Shirt shops, sideshow attractions like Alligator World and Dome of Thrills, and restaurants where cheeseburgers are served by clowns, medieval kings, superheroes, or giant kangaroos, depending on your mood? To say nothing of Disney World and MGM/Universal. But for grown-ups who aren't also parents of seven-year-olds, the kitsch is soul-destroying. At least it would have been for me after three months. It would have been hard for me to feel good about golf in that environment.

Call me romantic, but my ideal vision of golf involves minimally maintained linksland courses, bunkers burrowed out by sheep seeking shelter from the wind, and pleasing views of wildlife, oceans, forests, or farms—not of sugarplum castles and larger-than-life rodents. I once played a course in Orlando whose water hazards were dyed bright blue like the water in amusement parks and whose greens may have been painted. I suppose if the only purpose of mini-tours is to pit pro athletes against one another on a level playing field, such courses work fine. But then, so would courses made of AstroTurf. I just plain didn't like the aesthetic of Orlando.

The Miami–Fort Lauderdale area, by contrast, at least had an ethnic mix and indigenous style. The kitsch down there was noir, not corporate: pink flamingo lawn ornaments, strip joints out of Elmore Leonard novels, speedboats à la Crockett and Tubbs. And some of the golf courses where the South Florida Tour staged tournaments actually had history. Inverrary had been the site for many years of the Jackie Gleason PGA Tour event. The Links at Key Biscayne was still a regular Senior Tour stop. Plus, you've got the beach and the weather was warmer. Midwinter in Orlando can sometimes get frosty.

Though Orlando does have its uses. For one week each January the PGA Merchandise Show hits town, and that week coincided with our arrival in Florida.

For the uninitiated, the PGA Merchandise Show is the golf industry's annual orgy. Inside the mammoth Orange County Convention Center, the best and the newest of the world's golfing goods are on display. Even the booths themselves are dazzling: oak paneling, lush carpets, recessed lighting, high-quality signage, and pulsing multimedia presentations. For golf gearheads, which includes most of us, the show is almost pornographic: brightly lit racks of drivers made of exotic metals, endless variations of the latest muscle-backed irons, sleekly sculpted putters, pyramids of gleaming balls, row upon row of fine leather golf shoes for those whose fetishes run in that direction, samples of creamy linen slacks and nubby silk-cotton sweaters, swing-improvement gizmos and teaching gadgets of all description. One wanders the halls in a daze.

And the best part, for a savvy fledgling mini-tour player, is that people are willing to give you stuff for free. The golf industry takes in *eight billion dollars a year*. A little spillage into the hands of needy young players who might one day grow up to become big-time endorsers is seen as a trivial cost of doing business.

But you have to work at it. Which is why Polly, Anna, and I had to stay in a massive tourist hotel for an entire week.

The previous spring I happened to have written a review of Taylor-Made's then-new bubble-shafted irons for *Men's Journal*. In the course of dealing with the company's public relations man, I mentioned my book project and he said, "Why don't you let us fit you out with clubs?"

Given that I was still using my original $325 set of off-the-rack Dunlops, how could I refuse? The review was already written. Perhaps there was a slight conflict of interest involved (though I rationalized that the review was written before the offer was made), but I didn't care. I needed new clubs. A few months later at a Tour event I spent fifteen minutes with Steve Mata, the company's Tour representative, being fitted at the Taylor-Made van. Twice our session was interrupted by Tour pros Mark O'Meara and David Duval, requesting minor adjustments to their own clubs and I nodded at O'Meara and Duval, colleague to colleague. As I left the van a few minutes later, a kid asked me for my autograph. I gave it with guilty relish.

Mata had written out some specs for me, which I sent to the PR man, but nothing happened. Then I received an engraved invitation to Taylor-Made's corporate outing during the Merchandise Show. This, I figured, would be my chance to speed things along, and I was right. Everyone who simply bothered to show up—some three hundred of us—was given a brand new Titanium Burner Bubble driver with head cover, two sleeves of balata balls, a cap, a shirt, a towel, two lavish meals, and a free round of golf that included a couple of holes with either O'Meara or LPGA star Helen Alfredsson (I drew the gorgeous Alfredsson, thank you). At the cocktail party afterward, Taylor-Made announced that its ad budget for the following year would be forty million dollars which—to put things in perspective—equaled roughly two-thirds of that year's entire PGA

Tour prize purse. We tend to think of the Tour as rich, but it's nothing compared to the manufacturers.

In this context, I felt no hesitation about pushing the PR man and Mata, who was also present, for a little more responsiveness to my request. Sure enough, two weeks later, a big box of custom-fitted Taylor-Made clubs, both irons and woods, showed up on our front doorstep in Fort Lauderdale.

My next task at the Merchandise Show was to procure a year's worth of free golf balls. This proved more difficult.

The obvious first stop was the Titleist–Foot Joy booth, easy enough to find in the precise center of the hall. Dozens of Titleist salesmen were running around in bright white blazers, but no one seemed to know whom I should talk to. It was actually rather awkward phrasing my request. Boiling things down to their essentials, I was an amateur golfer who had just arrived in Florida for a few months of golf and wanted Titleist to give me a truckload of free balls. Finally, however, a sympathetic white-haired salesman with a Boston accent pointed to a sleek female vice president on the other side of the booth and said she might be able to help me.

The vice president, however, was occupied with Ian Baker-Finch, who was signing autographs. Since winning the 1991 British Open, Baker-Finch had been mired in one of golf's worst-ever recorded slumps. Most of the fans who presented themselves were intent on offering Baker-Finch advice for pulling out of his tailspin. The primary job of the vice president, stationed nearby, seemed to be to keep the fans moving on when their advice became too detailed.

In sporadic bursts between her intercessions, I tried to explain what I was after. "The publicity Titleist might get from being part of this Year . . . ," I explained.

She shooed along another customer. I started again. "The basic idea is that most amateurs like me *know* they can play golf a lot better than they do. . . ."

She intercepted a putting tip to thank the next fan for his interest.

I continued, "It's not that I claim to be a great golfer. I'm only a three handicapper, but . . ."

"You're a three?" Baker-Finch interrupted, looking up from the table with a perky grin. "I'm a three, too!"

I didn't quite know how to respond to this, but luckily I didn't have to. Baker-Finch finished signing the next autograph and pulled up the long sleeve of his shirt to reveal a rubber band around his wrist. "Shouldn't have said that," he groaned, and snapped the rubber band, hard.

"My psychologist . . . ," he explained to me sheepishly. "Punishment for negative thoughts."

Eventually I made the sleek vice president understand what I wanted. In Titleist lingo, I wanted to "participate" in the "product support program" for the "developmental tours." But unfortunately, she informed me, Titleist had recently suspended its product support program for the developmental tours. Sorry.

At the Maxfli booth things were more promising. Without having to do too much awkward groveling, I was ushered into the cubicle of Robin English, an Englishman who was Maxfli's director of tour promotions. We chatted for twenty minutes and it seemed that English rather took a fancy to my project. He told me to come back the next day.

Which I did.

Finally, when I came back the third day running, he gave in. I would become the newest member of Team Maxfli, along with Jack Nicklaus, Greg Norman, Fred Couples, Tom Watson, and fifty mini-tour players. As far as I could figure, the deal was a one-way street. Maxfli would supply me with all the balls I could possibly need for a year—the first shipment of six dozen would arrive within two weeks, English promised—as well as all the golf gloves and visors I needed and a Maxfli staff bag complete with high-quality umbrella. In return, the only thing I had to do was . . . use the stuff.

"Sounds good to me," I told English. We shook hands.

I had made some preliminary inquiries at the Nike booth about getting shoes, clothes, and maybe even a little cash sponsorship, but after snagging the Maxfli deal I decided not to push my luck. I was impatient to leave Orlando, and I knew Polly, back at the hotel with Anna, was, too. Two hundred miles south, my mini-tour debut awaited. By that afternoon we were speeding down the Florida turnpike.

Perhaps I should mention that Maxfli makes really great golf balls. I use the XS 100 brand myself.

7 . *T h e   D e b u t*

I WAS STANDING ON THE FIRST TEE OF THE
Golf Club of Miami, in my first mini-tour
event, trying not to think of a white polar bear.
This proved difficult. I was also trying not to
think about Polly, who was standing twenty
feet away watching and who until ten minutes
before at the practice range had never seen
me hit more than a whiffle ball. Or about
twenty-month-old Anna in Polly's arms, who I
felt sure would cry out "Daddy!" or "I'm
bored!" or something equally cute at the top of
my backswing. Or about the possibility that I
would be so distracted by trying not to think
about all these things simultaneously that I
would miss the ball completely, a blow to my
ego from which I might never recover.

Altogether, it was a lot of things not to think about.

The two other players in my threesome, John Putt and John Press—someone obviously had a sense of humor, pairing me, John Paul, with these two guys—had both already hit beautiful drives in the fairway and were standing calmly to the side watching my every move with what I interpreted as mild derision. They were predisposed to derision because I had asked so many panic-tinged questions of the starter (Who determines when a rule has been broken? Where will I find bathrooms on the course?) that I was clearly a rank rookie.

Another fifteen or so mini-tour competitors and tour officials were also standing near the tee watching, not because they were interested in seeing my drive or had any sense of the moment's historical significance for me, but because, in the case of the officials, they were paid to do so, and because, in the case of the other players, they had been caught walking nearby on the cart path in their noisy steel spikes and etiquette required them to halt when a fellow competitor stood over his ball. Which of course gave me one more thing to try to not think about: the unified impatience of everyone nearby for me to hit the damn ball.

I had already taken about a dozen practice swings, so I approached the ball and waggled my club five or six times as a stalling technique, desperately trying to regain my composure. Eventually this happened. I grew still in a posture of address, as if I were actually going to make a pass at the ball.

There I remained, lock-solid frozen, for probably the ten longest seconds of my life. And then finally, somehow, I found the courage deep inside to let out a deep breath, releasing tension, and back away from the ball altogether.

Through the whirling din of my internalized panic, I heard a rush of cleats on the pavement scurrying to get away and Anna's bell-clear voice asking Polly, "Did he miss it, Mommy?"

"Not yet, dear," my wife replied. "Now hush."

TO THIS POINT in my golf career I had participated in six other tournaments, and this might be a good time to review my record.

The first, in 1980, was for employees of the *Fort Worth Star-Telegram*, where I worked at the time. It took place at the municipal Z. Boaz Golf Course, regularly listed as one of the ten worst courses in the country and the site of an annual, ironic Dan Jenkins charity event. I shot 92 and won an enormous trophy because there were only three players in my "C" flight and the other two shot 125 and 143, respectively.

I played in my second tournament while reporting on the Space Coast Tour in 1992. J. C. Goosie allowed a few groups of amateurs to append themselves to the pro field because, well, he could make a little more money that way, and I couldn't resist. During my practice round the day before the tournament I played one hole with some members of the host club and actually birdied it. They mistook me for a pro.

"Yeah, I'm playing tomorrow," I replied, suavely, when they asked. That night I didn't sleep so well. My head was filled with fantasy.

Up until about five minutes before my first round began the following morning, I remained reasonably calm—a bit jumpy, perhaps, nothing more. But then, abruptly, when our group was called to the tee, everything changed. My breathing got quick and shallow, my forearms started twitching as if they were attached to high-voltage wires and I could feel my blood smashing against the inside of my temples. In a misguided attempted to calm myself, I checked my pulse: 140 beats a minute. I yearned for some emergency reason to have to excuse myself, such as an attack of appendicitis.

Somehow I managed to hit the ball on my first swing. It sliced wickedly into a lake. I made contact on my do-over swing as well. The ball popped one hundred feet into the air and landed just short of the women's tees. My sixth shot on the hole died in thick grass near the green, from which point, on my seventh shot, I advanced the ball two inches. My eighth shot was more successful—the ball dribbled onto the green—but my ninth was an outright miracle. I curled the ball into the cup from twenty-five feet, avoiding double figures.

For the rest of the round, with no dignity left to lose, I played reasonably well, finishing with two freak birdies in three holes for an 80. In the second round I also played well—at least through the twelfth hole. On the thirteenth I knocked two drives into the water, became completely unglued, and lost thirteen strokes to par over the final five holes for a 91.

You would think that after such a beating I would have learned some humility. But I did not. That night in my motel room I made a few calculations. Take away that ridiculous nine on the first hole and the equally preposterous eight I scored on the same hole the next day, eliminate three or four other dumb mistakes, discount the meltdown at the end, and give myself a few putts that should have fallen but somehow didn't, and—hell, I could have *won* that tournament. I remember reading in a survey somewhere that half of all American men believe that, if things had just worked out a little differently in their lives, they could have been successful professional athletes. That's me, I blush to admit.

The other four tournaments on my pre-Year résumé were one-round amateur events run by the most excellent Metropolitan Golf Association in the New York City area. In none did I play admirably—I was always tight, always overthinking—but in the last of them, at least, I got off to a good start.

I was paired with a fellow named John Baldwin. Older than most of the other players in the field, he was perhaps in his late forties, and though he wore short pants like everyone else and carried the skinniest golf bag I had ever seen, he commanded respect. I figured him for a boardroom hotshot, perhaps a CEO.

On the first green I rolled in a long, birdie putt. The surprised, slightly patronizing look on Baldwin's face betrayed that he considered this a fluke. On the second hole I outdrove Mr. CEO by twenty yards and, though I duffed my second shot, we still matched pars. We both parred the third, a short par three, and on the fourth I pounded my drive a good thirty yards past Baldwin. One up after three, in the catbird seat on four, I began to think how satisfying it would be to dust the guy. When Baldwin then hit a weak approach shot into the greenside bunker, I thought: "Uh-huh. True colors, Mr. Big Shot. Watch this!" If I snuggled my approach shot next to the pin, I projected, Baldwin would have to start pressing and would probably soon fall apart.

So naturally, I bladed my approach shot over the green into deep woods. Baldwin saved par from the sand and I scored a six. Furious with myself, I bombed not one but *two* drives on the next hole dead out-of-bounds. Baldwin birdied. I took a nine. And so on and so forth. As the round progressed I became increasingly annoyed at his ability to score pars despite, quite obviously, not having a golf game. His drives were to laugh at: 240 yard bunts down the middle of the fairway. His tedious, low-flying approach shots possessed none of the drama of my towering, big-swing affairs. And his short game consisted almost entirely of cowardly little bump-and-run pitches, none of the daring flop-shots and tight-spinning check shots that I attempted. When all was said and done he had beaten me by twenty strokes: 73 to 93.

I did not realize it at the time, but this was my first exposure to a truly excellent golfer. In the clubhouse after the round I noticed a dozen players and tournament officials clustering around Baldwin. I made inquiries. It turns out he was a former New York State amateur champion and two-time MGA player-of-the-year.

My comeuppance was complete. I didn't know enough about golf back then to understand exactly what made Baldwin so much better than me, but in my gut I was aware that a vast gulf separated our games.

WHICH BRINGS US back to my debut on the South Florida Tour. I knew a lot more now—in theory—about what makes a golfer good, but this was my first tournament attempt since the round with Baldwin to put what I had learned into practice.

After backing away from my tee ball on the first and letting the crowd thin out, I realized that my best chance of successfully putting the ball into play was the approach I used when entering a cold lake: the running start. In golf, unless you're Happy

Gilmore, this can only be done metaphorically. I took my stance, held my breath, closed my eyes, and swung.

The ball rocketed due left, straight at the trees. But then, as if steered by a drunk with a remote control, it veered violently to the right in a wicked pull slice. The net result was a drive nestled in deep rough on the right some 140 yards from the tee.

"How did it go?" Polly asked when I walked over to where she was standing with Anna. Unaccustomed to anything having to do with golf, Polly had been unable to track the ball visually.

"It's down there on the right," I said. "It went more than a hundred yards."

"That's great!" she said enthusiastically. "Now Anna, let's tell Daddy good-bye." I was touched that Polly and Anna had come to see my first shot, but none of us was eager for them to follow me around the course.

The round, to put it mildly, did not go well. By the fourth or fifth hole it was clear that I was up against something large: virtually every full-swing shot I attempted sliced villainously. I'm not talking about controlled fades, which would have been strange enough given that my customary shot-shape was a draw. No, these were full-out slices, some rolling to a halt in a direction fully ninety degrees off the initial heading. It was inexplicable and embarrassing. My mind raced to find solutions at mach one speed: hood the club, close the stance, strengthen the grip, slow the downswing, aim to the left, aim to the right. But nothing I tried worked better than merely morphing the slice into a feckless banana ball. The only one of my drives that didn't slice was an amazing heel shot on sixteen. The ball squirted due left, practically between my legs, into some pretty flowering bushes.

John Press and John Putt were no help at all, though I don't know what help I could have expected. Press, a recent college graduate, was apoplectic about his own dismal performance, while Putt, a visiting upper-class amateur from Britain (a member of ritzy Sunningdale west of London), simply couldn't be bothered. For five hours the three of us coexisted in an incommunicado snit.

My score for the round was 88—much better than my actual play warranted. In the second round I improved to 85, for a tournament total of 173. This put me 39 strokes behind the winner, Adam Armagost, who shot 68-66 and took home three thousand dollars; thirty strokes behind the last pro to earn a check (worth $81.25); and thirteen strokes behind my nearest competitor, Ivan Lendl.

Excuses and/or explanations for my rancid play were not hard to come by: a) The pressure: it was my first tournament, the routines were unfamiliar, I was counterproductively self-conscious; b) The clubs: the new Burner Bubbles from Taylor-Made had arrived only three days before and I wasn't used to them yet; c) The rust: since the previous September, I had played only four rounds of golf on an actual course, primarily because of d) The new swing: I had been devoting my time to incorporating the new elements from Hebron, most of which still felt awkward.

As excuses go, these were top-of-the-line. Even so, my ego needed many days to recover from the beating. My main consolation was that Polly and Anna didn't know enough to share in my shame.

"You still love me, don't you?" I asked Polly several times in the succeeding days.

"Of course I do," she replied. And as far as I could tell, she did. She had no idea that a man who shoots 88-85 in a mini-tour event doesn't deserve to be loved.

In gingerly reviewing the tournament, I decided that my main problem had been tension. On the drive home immediately after the second round, I had stopped by the Blockbuster Driving Range and Family Fun Center to hit a few balls. I wanted to figure out why I had been slicing. But at Blockbuster, I didn't slice. I boomed drive after drive, long and straight. People stopped to watch. "Check out this guy," a teen told his pal. They probably thought I was a mini-tour pro.

The difference was, at the range, I let it all hang out. I didn't give a shit. The "fairway" was seven hundred yards wide. I used reverse pivot, broken sticks, loop-the-loop backswings, and Comanche yells—whatever it took to feel free. And the freedom, I realized after a while, primarily expressed itself *in my forearms.* On the range, I was letting loose through the ball with my fore-arms. In the tournament, out of fear, I had kept my forearms clenched, I had tried to *steer* the ball, I had *held on* through impact. One of the main things I had learned over the winter was that most of a swing's power comes from "cracking the whip," which requires loose arms. But in the tournament my whip never cracked. It was as if I had been using a stiff board to hit the ball. As a result the clubface stayed open through impact and imparted that wicked slice spin.

Okay, so I had figured out what happened. But the cause of my tension had been fear, and fear is tricky to fix.

After a day off for self-flagellation, I returned to the range and found that the slice had returned. Not as bad as in the tourna-ment, but a slice nonetheless. By force of will I could relax my forearms and shoulders at address, but the instant I pulled the clubhead back from the ball the premonition of a certain slice flashed into consciousness. The muscles of my arms and neck clenched. Involuntarily, to compensate for the slice I knew was coming, I jerked each shot to the left. To some extent this system of compensating errors worked—the further left I pulled the ball, the bigger my right-veering slice—but at a cost of nearly half my former distance. Apparently those terrifying images of slices from the tournament had burned themselves deep into my cerebral cor-tex, or wherever it is nightmares reside, and my body could not ignore them.

By the end of the week I had sweet-talked the slice into becom-ing something more like a controlled fade, but this worried me. I did not want to be a fader. My preference for shot-shape had always been the right-to-left draw, which I considered more manly. Draws knife aggressively into the wind and shoot forward when

they land like energetic pups; fades tend to lose interest and plop
to earth like exhausted shoppers. Since beginning my lessons with
Hebron, I had lost all consistency as to shot-shape. Hebron said
this was normal: my swing was a work in progress and sooner or
later my natural shape, draw or fade, would declare itself. Was this
that declaration? I hoped not. This fade seemed like an artifact of
fear. There was nothing natural about it.

ONE OF THE side benefits Tom Eubanks had arranged for members in good standing of the South Florida Tour was a month-by-
month, full golf membership at the Palm-Aire Country Club in
Pompano Beach. The Palm-Aire, which was only about ten minutes from the house Polly, Anna, and I were renting, is maybe not
Florida's most exciting place to spend the winter. Most of the regular members are retirees who live in the mausoleum-like condo
complexes scattered about the property. But for $150 a month I
had full access to Palm-Aire's four regulation golf courses, an executive course, a topographically varied short game practice area,
and two driving ranges *with unlimited balls*. To me this was
heaven.

Surprisingly few mini-tour players took advantage of Palm-
Aire—some had working arrangements with other courses, such as
use of the facilities in exchange for driving the range tractor once
in a while—but there were always a few around and they were
easy to spot. Their sweet swings were one clue; an average age
forty years younger than the typical Palm-Airian was another.

One of the first fellow players I got to know was Scott Yancey,
the son of Bert Yancey, a seven-time PGA Tour winner who for
several years had been Palm-Aire's official representative on the
Tour. Yancey had died only the year before, of a heart attack at
fifty-six, while practicing in Utah for a Senior Tour event. The
obituaries had been prominent because Yancey had struggled pub-
licly and courageously for many years with manic depression. By
his forties, with lithium and psychotherapy, he had gotten his condition under control and became a national spokesman for patients

with the disorder, but some commentators wrote that professional golf was simply too stressful for Yancey, citing as examples the several times he had taken substantial leads into the final round of the Masters, and once at the U.S. Open, only to fall apart.

Scott, twenty-seven, was an affable blond marshmallow of a guy who was powerfully confused about whether to pursue golf as a profession. He had moved to Florida only six weeks before to compete on the mini-tours but hadn't yet entered a tournament. Much depended on whether Arnold Palmer, a friend of his dad, would come through with some sponsorship money. Meanwhile he was working at Palm-Aire in a teaching capacity to save up money for an unspecified, non-golf business opportunity. On the other hand, he had just used some of his savings to purchase an enormous, expensive, black leather Yonex staff bag with his name emblazoned on the side.

One afternoon Scott and I played a practice round and he was generous with advice. A lot of it had to do with putting: how to practice, how to focus. "Dad called putts between five and fifteen feet *things*," he told me. "Dad said that the key to scoring well is to make a lot of *things*. If you can make your share of *things*, you'll win some tournaments." I liked this concept. It seemed like grade-A advice.

But I was surprised to discover during our round that Scott was not that much better a player than I was, and neither were the three guys from the pro shop, two of them occasional mini-tour players, who joined us on the second hole. Or maybe they were better, it was just no one except me took the round seriously. I played one ball only and earnestly kept statistics on every hole: fairways and greens hit in regulation, number of putts, up-and-down attempts converted, and so forth. The other guys basically kept dropping balls until they hit one they liked and hopped in their carts. We had five carts in the fivesome and swerved down the fairways like an army of clowns at the Big Top. Had there been alcohol involved, the round could easily have ended in tragedy.

Such was the general level of hilarity that after nine holes everyone wanted to quit. But finally I convinced Kennard, a forty-eight-year-old army vet who was trying to get into the PGA apprentice program for club professionals, to join me on the back nine. He was an interesting case: a lean, muscular black guy with a deep, gravelly voice who told me over the next couple of hours that for many years he had been down and out. Then he had found religion. Now his goal was to pass the apprentice program's playing test: two consecutive rounds of 78 or lower under tournament conditions. In his two attempts thus far, he hadn't come close.

Filled as I was with bold ideas for my own golf improvement, I decided to give Kennard the benefit of my wisdom. "The first thing you've got to do," I advised him, "is stop playing goofball rounds with the guys from the shop. You need to approach practice rounds as seriously as you do tournament rounds." I suggested that he might also benefit from more goal-oriented sessions at the range. And of course the short game was key. Plus, a lot of top tour players were big visualizers. Nicklaus supposedly never hit a shot, even in practice, without first seeing the ball land and roll in his mind's eye. Also, a balanced diet was important.

"How do you know so much about golf?" Kennard finally demanded.

"Well, I . . ." I had to think. "I've been reading up on the subject."

"Oh, I see. I see," Kennard said. His hearty, basso profundo laugh echoed through the condo canyons.

THE NEXT TOURNAMENT was at a tight, water-lined course called Cobblestone. According to the stats I kept from round one, I hit a respectable eight of thirteen fairways, got up-and-down from near the green eight times in ten attempts (including once from the sand), did not miss a putt under five feet, and holed three "things" from seven, eight, and fifteen feet.

Even so, I scored an 86.

In the second round, despite similarly decent stats, I scored 86 again.

How was this possible? I was proud of the way I had kept my new fade under control and my short game—the key to scoring!—had been superb. In two days I had needed only fifty-two putts, or twenty-six per round, an excellent average.

The answer was bonehead plays.

Bonehead plays are not to be confused with simple bad shots. Bad shots you can live with. Bad shots you can chalk up to lack of native talent, ignorance, inexperience, the ordinary, everyday limitations of being a human.

Bonehead plays are inexcusable. One could argue that a drive which sails out of bounds by thirty yards is not a bonehead play, it is a bad shot. But when you instantly reload and nail your next shot 270 yards down the center of the fairway, you know the first shot was a bonehead play. The distinction can be subtle. The only viable standard is the "we know it when we see it" approach the Supreme Court took in defining pornography. Bonehead plays engender the same, intense feelings of regret and self-loathing that killing a friend in a hunting accident does.

To capture this phenomenon on my stat sheet, I invented a new category for the second Cobblestone round: "BP (for Bonehead Plays) X-Y," where X represented the number of discrete acts of boneheadedness and Y represented the number of strokes such acts added to my score. Thus, the aforementioned out-of-bounds drive on number three earned a "BP 1-2" bonehead rating because it resulted in two lost strokes. My bladed pitch shot on four earned a "BP 1-1" rating because I managed to stop the next shot on the green about where the first shot should have stopped. But my bladed pitch shot on number eight rated "BP 2-4." I foozled that one so extremely the ball landed in a hazard, but rather than take a drop I tried unsuccessfully to hit the ball out of the hazard (the second discrete act of boneheadedness), resulting in two more lost strokes. For the round my final bonehead tally was "BP 7-11." Take away the bonehead plays and I shoot 75. Not too bad.

Some of my bonehead plays at Cobblestone involved unwitting violations of the rules. The most galling occurred in round two on the fourteenth hole. My drive came to rest about fifteen feet from a creek running up the right side. So far as I could tell the ball was in the fairway; it had a clean lie on closely mown grass. But Daniel Levesque, my French Canadian playing companion, advised caution because my ball lay within the painted red line demarcating the water hazard. Or so he claims he said. I can't swear he did because his heavy French accent was difficult to understand. In any event, after taking several practice swings that grazed the grass—illegal when standing inside a hazard—I punched a sweet shot onto the green and Daniel said I would have to assess myself a two-stroke penalty for grounding my club in a hazard.

This was a hard penalty to swallow. It seemed so patently *unfair*. For all intents and purposes, my ball was in the fairway, not even in the rough! But Tom Eubanks told me later, over beers in the clubhouse, that getting used to the rigid application of rules was a stumbling block for many.

"The amateurs we get, a lot of them *say* they have handicaps of two or four, like you, but when they get here they can't break 90. They're not used to playing by the rules. The kids out of college programs are, but not the club guys. Back home they give each other three- and four-foot putts, which you'll find under pressure are incredibly easy to miss, and if they can't find their ball in the woods they just drop another ball somewhere and maybe they add a stroke to their score. But that's not what the rules call for. With a lost ball you're *supposed* to go back to the tee and re-hit with a two-shot penalty, stroke and distance."

I considered my knowledge of the rules decent, but having to apply them in the heat of competition quickly exposed my ignorance. It wasn't the overall concepts that posed problems, it was the details.

Consider, for instance, a seemingly simple procedure like taking relief from a cart path. No penalty is involved, you just pick up the ball and drop it on the closest patch of grass no nearer to the hole. Right?

Not quite. The first step is to determine precisely where the nearest point of relief is. By definition only one such nearest point exists—you can't just choose one side of the path or the other. To determine the nearest point you sometimes must take trial stances at various spots near the path and stick a tee in the ground where the ball would be if you were to hit it *using the club you intend to use for that shot* (that is, you can't manipulate the point—to get a better sight line, for instance—by taking your stance with a forty-five-inch driver if the shot calls for a wedge). Whichever tee in the ground is nearest where your original ball came to rest is the mandatory nearest point of relief. When you drop, the ball must hit the ground within one club length of that point no nearer the hole, though in determining one club length in this case you *are* allowed to use your driver or any other club in your bag or in anyone else's bag. If the ball rolls back onto the path, you repeat the drop twice and if the ball still rolls onto the path, you then *place* the ball where it hit the ground when you dropped. If a dropped ball rolls under a bush or behind a tree, you're stuck with that lie and may proceed under "Rule 28: Ball Unplayable," which has its own complicated set of codicils, subsections, and official interpretations. Use of sextants, graph paper, and the Navstar Global Positioning Satellite System is allowed, time permitting.

Rarely do these fine points make a practical difference, but once or twice is enough. At Cobblestone, for instance, I became so discombobulated when it appeared I would have to drop off a cart path directly into a bush that I requested a rules official. With his blessing I decided to hit the ball off the gravel where it lay, but the wait caused our group to fall behind by more than a hole, which got me rattled and led, on the very next hole, to the grounding-my-club-in-the-hazard miscue.

To return to that fiasco for a moment, I want to assert I do not blame Daniel Levesque for calling the penalty. Not for a minute. "Every competitor owes it to the rest of the field to assess any penalty he sees," a rule book I own states. On the other hand, Daniel (pronounced the French way, dan-*yell*) wound up beating me by exactly those two strokes. He was thirty-two strokes behind the winner (Adam Armagost again) and I was thirty-four.

That far back in the pack, it's easy to feel overlooked, as if one's hard effort is pointless. But now I had a purpose: the next time out I wanted to beat Daniel. And this surge of competitive pride—the first nonabstract stirring of desire I had had since the Year began—felt awfully good.

THE WEEK AFTER THE COBBLESTONE TOURNA-
ment, the Celebrity Golf Association Tour
came to town. The CGA, which has since
evolved into the Celebrity Players Tour, is
basically an excuse for big-time professional
athletes and a few coordinated stars from the
entertainment industry to compete against
each other for real money in a PGA Tour–like
atmosphere. Boys who never grew up—that's
how pundits often describe pro athletes. Well,
more power to them. The CGA is an off-
season, postretirement extension of the franchise.

Miami Dolphins quarterback Dan Marino
was the host of the $125,000 CGA tournament
in Fort Lauderdale that February, and I

attended. Not only did I attend, I got press credentials and spent the better part of three days schmoozing with the likes of Marino, John Elway, John Smoltz, and Roger Clemens about how they learned golf. The level of their play was amazingly good; the top twenty-five players on the CGA had tournament stroke averages under 76. And most of these players, like me, had not played much golf as kids. They had been too focused on their primary sports.

The biggest surprise was the grace of their swings. I suppose I had imagined that brawny, athletic superstars would go about golf in a brawny, hyperathletic way, but this was not the case. One of the first players I observed on the course was Elway. He is a big guy— six-three, 215 pounds, thick-thighed—and when he dug in near his ball preparing to hit, he reminded me of one of those crazed Scottish sportsmen in a kilt bracing to heave a large stone on *Wide World of Sports*. But once he assumed the correct posture, he relaxed and swung his club as effortlessly as a fairy princess waving her wand. The same was true of Lawrence Taylor, the New York Giants' former mammoth linebacker. It almost made me laugh, he was so fluid: an elephant on point.

From reading Hebron's books, profusely illustrated with photos of athletes from other sports swinging bats and throwing balls, I was curious to see which sports the CGA players would think were most similar to golf. The consensus was hockey and baseball. In hockey, the basic movement of the slapshot and the hand-eye coordination required to produce it are very golf-like. In baseball, sluggers produce leverage by clearing the hips and staying behind the ball, as golfers do.

Beyond that, though, the mechanical/physical connections grew more tenuous. Joe Namath, the former New York Jets quarterback, told me he thought the visual experience quarterbacks got watching footballs arc through the air helped in visualizing golf shots. But Broadway Joe—looking a bit like a bedraggled Gilligan, humped in the shoulders and deeply tanned—also saw many negative connections. "In football, as a quarterback, guys are trying to kill you. When I saw my target, the trigger went off and—zap!—I threw the ball instantly. But in golf that same instinct works against you. It makes you jump at the ball. I fight it, but it's a lot tougher to break an old habit than to start a new one."

The main thing the CGA players wanted to discuss, when comparing their sports to golf, was the mental game. The tournament was like a psychologists' convention: all the talk concerned fear and psyche jobs and strategies for overcoming mental dysfunction.

"I don't know how the PGA Tour players do it, playing thirty tournaments a year," said former Atlanta Falcons quarterback Steve Bartkowski. "I'm beat to death by six of these tournaments a year. It's a major grind. In football you could come off the field, have a Gatorade, and let the defense go at it for a while. Here, the pressure is constant. And the nature of golf is that you hit more bad shots, or at least *unsatisfactory* shots, than you do good shots. It wears away at you."

"What prepares you for golf?" asked Pierre Larouche, the former hockey great. "Nothing. Absolutely nothing. Golf is the hardest, most mentally taxing thing I've ever done." Larouche, a nine-handicap, was especially agitated because earlier that day he had shot a 99.

Al Del Greco, the Oilers (now Titans) All-Pro placekicker and one of the CGA's best players, opined that 80 percent of making a field goal depended on thinking the right things. "And that's about right for golf, too, only more so."

Del Greco's pre-shot and pre-kick routines are almost identical. He takes a precise number of paces to the ball (in golf) or away from the ball (in football), lines up the target, takes a couple of deep breaths, and then looks at the target one final time. "After that, my only thought is to make good contact without overswinging. In golf or football it's the same—stay in rhythm, nice and easy." Del Greco had no doubt that his mental routine was the key to his success on both fronts.

Even John Smoltz, that most macho and aggressive of baseball pitchers, admitted to psychological tribulation on the golf course. "A competitive round of golf exhausts me far more than pitching," he said, "but otherwise the two things are so much alike it's scary." He ticked off the similarities: Both are target-oriented and require visualization. In both, the spin deliberately imparted to the ball causes it to curve in the air. The pitcher and the golfer both initiate the action rather than react to what others do, which allows time and space for fear and doubt to fester. In Smoltz's opinion, the key to both golf and pitching is learning to leave mistakes behind. "In baseball, you're going to throw bad pitches. In golf, you're going to hit bad shots. But if you can recover, you'll succeed. You can't be afraid to fail, that's what it boils down to."

In the second round of the tournament I watched Smoltz on the eighteenth hole yank a five-wood into the lake. "I couldn't overcome a negative thought," he deconstructed the moment later. "The day before from the same position I splashed my five-wood, too, and I couldn't get the thought out of my mind. It was like facing a batter you haven't had success with in the past, and I blew it." He said he might have overcome the negative vibes if he hadn't been aware that a par on the hole would give him his first sub-seventy tournament round. "Shooting 69 is just not an area I'm comfortable with. It psyched me out. But next time I'll be ready. Now I know what it takes."

I was gratified to hear Smoltz, a Cy Young Award winner, talk about choking under pressure. It made my own tournament miscues seem more excusable. On the other hand, I could tell Smoltz couldn't wait for the next chance to prove himself, firing into another eighteenth green with 69 on the line, whereas for me the mere thought of such a challenge created heart palpitations. I was envious of his animal self-confidence. Even just the way he stood there on his feet—poised, aggressive, in control—was inspiring.

But Smoltz's way was not the only way. One of the things that most impressed me about the CGA athletes was the widely varying routes they had each taken to get good at tournament golf. Smoltz was all about will. Bartkowski was almost entirely self-taught, and trusted his swing in the clutch because he'd built it himself. Del Greco put his faith in the routine: putting all thoughts aside except "swing easy" and "stay in rhythm." Another player I talked to, former NBA star Truck Robinson, said that for him golf was primarily a battle of self-control: avoiding anger, limiting frustration, trying not to worry.

But of all the players I spoke with, Ken Harrelson, the former Boston Red Sox star and now a broadcaster with the Chicago White Sox, had the most idiosyncratic approach to golf: the use of an alter ego. And his ideas were the ones I came away most curious to explore.

"Ninety-eight percent of athletes choke under pressure," Harrelson assured me. "That's the norm. Jack Nicklaus told me once that anybody who tells you they don't choke is full of shit. 'I choke with the best of them,' he told me. So the key is finding some way to take the pressure off yourself. Pressure is the biggest killer of talent and performance in sports. The only difference between superstars and the rest of us is they know how to control their mind and their emotions better. That's the *only* difference."

Back in his baseball days Harrelson was known as The Hawk, but he said The Hawk was more than a nickname, it was his secret weapon. "Do you think *I* was the guy pulling off all those heroics? Me, Ken Harrelson? You gotta be kidding. Ken Harrelson is a choking son of a bitch. No, that was The Hawk. The Hawk was great. My only job as Ken Harrelson was to try to get out of The Hawk's way. Sometimes The Hawk wouldn't come out, but when he did, man, I just sat back and watched him perform like everybody else and had a ball."

There are two possible responses to talk like this: a) To regard the speaker as a schizophrenic lunatic and b) To think, "Hey, maybe this guy's onto something."

By a close margin, I chose the latter. I love a good theory, especially one that promises big rewards with minimal effort. The notion of developing an alter ego was intriguing—why not turn over all the stress-producing stuff to a third party? Born-again Christian golfers did something like this, I had noticed. Doug Weaver, a journeyman born-again pro, once described the process to me. He did all the prep work for a shot—deciding on a strategy, choosing the right club, checking his setup—but before he actually swung, he off-loaded responsibility for the results to the Lord. "That way I'm less anxious," he said. "The outcome is beyond my control, so I can just concentrate on making a smooth stroke."

In contemplating possible alter egos for myself, the first that sprang to mind was "The Horse." This harkened back to my days as a runner, before my left knee went bad. I often fancied myself as a horse: strong, tireless, indomitable, sprinting with long loping strides. Sometimes on long runs through the woods I neighed. Frequently I had the sensation of hovering over my body, watching myself gallop along.

But I wasn't sure this metaphor would work for golf. Running actually changes one's chemistry; the body releases morphines into the blood. For golf I would need a more neurotic, cerebral alter ego. Perhaps "RoboPro" or "The Machine," something that connoted control. Or something fanciful to guard against overseriousness, like "The Shack" (with homage to both *Caddyshack* and Shaquille O'Neal) or "Studebaker Hawk" or "Mr. Smooth." Or maybe something Smoltzian like "The Intimidator." Or something rhythmic like "Fred," as in Astaire with a nod to Couples.

Despite a great deal of thought on the subject in the week after the tournament, I couldn't settle on an alter ego. The problem, I think, was that I didn't yet know who I was as a golfer. I still didn't have a functioning golf swing, much less a sense of what personality characteristics would work best for me in athletic competition. The CGA players were all proven winners. They had developed bulletproof athletic styles in other sports and transferred that self-knowledge, in one way or another, to golf. By contrast, I was an adolescent when it came to athletic pressure, just beginning to find my way.

It occurred to me that I might simply wait for my alter ego to identify itself. But what if it never did? At the celebrity event, former 49ers quarterback John Brodie had told me he thought of golf as an expression of who you are. "If you're in a pretty good space with the rest of your life, you're likely to do well at golf," he said.

This had impressed me at the time, especially since Brodie went out the next day and won the tournament. But now I focused on the flip side. If you couldn't get into a "pretty good space" with your life, did that mean your golf game was doomed? What if, in the course of the Year, I got worse, not better? This was something I hadn't considered. What if my alter ego turned out to be, say, The Bunny instead of something cool like The Hawk?

To Polly I sometimes half-jokingly defended golf as "psychoanalysis by other means." The difference, I explained, was that with golf you can't fake it. The truth shows up on your scorecard after every round. Was I ready for the truth? Did I really want to push my limits? The connection between golf and character, which had always been one of the sport's appeals, was now beginning to scare me a little.

MY SWING, WHEN we first arrived in Florida, was an unnatural mess. Two months of garage-bound practice in Orient had allowed me to work hard on its individual pieces—the spine-tilt, the swing plane, the weight transfer to the right side, the leaning stick business—but without watching real balls fly through the air, it was hard to know what all these efforts had wrought. The hard part of making a swing change is knitting the various components into a seamless piece of magic.

During my first few days of hitting on real turf in Fort Lauderdale, strange things happened—outright shanks, divots that began two or three inches behind the ball, a fear that the club might fly out of my hands on the backswing. Everything felt tentative. Once at a range, when the ball I hit (or tried to hit) slammed loudly into the wooden barrier separating my bay from the next, I told my alarmed-looking neighbor not to worry, I was just being ironic.

But within about a week the swing started coming together. Every once in a while the ball sprang off the clubface with a startling new authority. The most notable difference was trajectory. Before the changes, I hit my irons sky-high, and was proud to do so. It was part of my Big John game. Now my best shots bore through the air on a low arc similar to that of John Baldwin, the New York amateur champion who had so effectively put me in my place a few years earlier. With my hands leading the clubhead (thanks to the leaning-stick effect), the clubface was de-lofted at impact. This not only produced the lower trajectory, but also imparted more backspin. For the first time, I began to understand what Tour pros must feel when they spin balls into the greens, begging for them to bite. Spin and the control of spin for those guys is as much a part of a shot as distance and direction.

As I began to work these changes into my swing, I noticed another change—in my attitude. Previously, when I hit a good shot it seemed like an accident. I was *glad* for the accident, of course, but deep inside I knew I didn't deserve it. I had no more idea what had gone right than what had gone wrong with the previous swing, when I hit a knuckleball. Now when I pulled off a good shot, I usually understood why and felt inordinately proud. It was like finally knowing enough about wine to appreciate a pricey Bordeaux, after years of just gulping down grape juice. Even when I hit a bad shot, there was a subtle new richness to my exasperation. Mistakes were a puzzle to solve, an intellectual challenge.

At least I felt that way some of the time.

Other times I raged as much as ever. Take my efforts to solve the hip-turn enigma—after my first few weeks of work in Florida, this was a puzzle that defeated me. How much hip turn was too much? When I turned the back of my shoulders to the target, I knew that my hips were not supposed to turn equally far—that way leads to the dreaded reverse pivot. And I knew they weren't supposed to stay still. Somewhere in between. But how was I to get a feel for precisely where to stop the hip turn? I spent countless hours at the range, and attracted countless stares, wiggling my hips in a kind of deranged tribute to Elvis. No insight. Someone somewhere, I felt sure, had invented a $189 training device specifically to solve this riddle, but I decided to pay a visit to Hebron at the Palm Beach Polo Club instead.

It was my first lesson since moving to Florida, and he solved the mystery in about two minutes. "Try not to turn your hips at all," he said. "Just concentrate on making a full shoulder turn over your right leg and on keeping your right knee bent. The hips will have to rotate some, and they'll stop in the right place by themselves." But the less turn the better, he said. The coiled tension between the fully turned shoulders and the partially turned hips (which I should feel in my left lower back) was the main major source of the swing's power. It was the tension in the slingshot before letting the stone loose.

I tried it a couple times and instantly felt what he meant. "Well, duh!" I thought. Why, in two months of winter captivity and with countless instructional books to consult, hadn't I been able to figure this out for myself?

But Hebron wasn't surprised. "The swing is a complicated thing," he reminded me. "That's why you have a teacher."

I felt much more comfortable and relaxed with Hebron than I had at earlier lessons. Partly this was because I had been a good boy over the winter and made some genuine progress. He complimented me. But also, I think, I had come to accept that my progress would not be as rapid as I originally hoped. Psychologically, I had settled in for the long haul and that made me less sensitive about my failures and limitations. Hebron was there to help me, not to judge me. If I made good progress he would be pleased, but if I didn't— well, he'd told me from the start that improving was hard. And when I accepted this, his lesson tee became a safe place, the way my psychiatrist's office had been a safe place where I was free to experiment, to be who I needed to be without fear of repercussion.

Toward the end of the lesson I finally confessed to Hebron my plans to play on the mini-tours and that, in fact, I already had played in a couple of events and performed dreadfully because of my nervousness. He seemed to know it already.

"The tightness you feel when you get excited or distracted comes because you are asking more muscles to get involved in the swing than are necessary for the task at hand," he explained. "It's like leaning over to pick up a box that you think is real heavy, but it's not. You almost get jarred. So next time, if you're tight, don't tell yourself to *relax* or *get focused,* because you won't be able to. Be more specific. Say, 'Hey, I'm using too many muscles to dig this ditch,' and find a calmness that way."

He added that he would expect a three- to five-handicapper like me to shoot scores around 80, as I had. "Playing away from home, on unfamiliar courses, under tournament pressure—I'd be amazed if you did much better than that anytime soon."

I wasn't prepared to accept that analysis lying down, if by "anytime soon" he meant by Q School in October. But I could live with shooting 80 for the time being, as I learned the ropes of tournament play and pulled my new swing together. In fact, I was grateful for the comment. It took some pressure off.

TWO WEEKS AFTER the Cobblestone tournament I teed off in another South Florida Tour event at Inverrary Country Club, former home of the PGA Tour's Jackie Gleason Golf Classic. My foursome included Daniel Levesque, the French Canadian who had called the club-grounding penalty on me.

It wasn't surprising to be paired with Daniel again. He and I were among only nine amateurs in the field of 130, and Tom Eubanks, like most mini-tour organizers, lumped the amateurs together for the first round. In succeeding rounds the players were grouped by score, which meant the payoff for an amateur playing well was a pairing with pros in round two. Amateurs and pros played the same course from the same tees, but our entry fee was "only" $175 whereas the pros had to pony up $575, the extra $400 going into the pro purse. When pros heard you were still an amateur, they always tried to talk you into turning pro. That way you could pump $400 extra into their pot as well. (Pros who never won any money had a nickname: "donators.")

On the first tee at Inverrary, I was nervous—*appropriately* nervous, I felt. This resulted in a pulled drive into the creek, out-of-bounds. Over the next fifteen holes, however, I played quite well, thank you—even par, except for a bonehead double-bogey on thirteen, when I finessed a thirty-yard pitch-and-run shot into a lake. The swing felt solid. I felt like I was taking my new car out for a spin and liked the way it behaved. That opening drive into the drink loosened me up, I think: What else could I do but laugh about it, go out, and have some fun?

On the tee of the par-three seventeenth, however, we encountered a twenty-five-minute wait. (This is another hard fact about mini-tour life: play can be excruciatingly slow.) I tallied my score: four over par. Casually, as if a matter of trivial consequence, I asked Daniel where he stood.

"I zam standing zright here," he joked, knowing full well what I meant.

"No, I mean your score," I said.

But he wouldn't tell me! I couldn't believe it. He was gaming me. With nothing more at stake than pride in a two-bit amateur competition, Daniel was playing head games.

"And yeeeeew?" he said. "Zee score?"

This I doubly couldn't believe, that he would have the gall, after refusing to give his score, to ask for mine.

"Four over," I blurted. I was so proud of my score I had to tell him, but instantly regretted it. It was as if I'd divulged having three queens in a game of five-card stud, simply because the sharpie across the table had asked. What a patsy!

Perturbed, I topped my two-iron tee shot into a lake about fifty yards in front of the tee.

This I triply couldn't believe. My face flooded with humiliation. Stalking to the drop area, black fumes streamed from my ears. Daniel, the cur, had gotten the better of me again. With double-bogeys on seventeen and eighteen, I finished with 79. Daniel, after parring both holes, carded a 78.

In the second round something similar happened, though not involving Daniel. I played well again (after my de rigueur out-of-bounds drive on number one) and was told on the fifteenth tee that I stood just one stroke behind the amateur leader, who happened to be a member of the Danish national golf team. To me this seemed like big-time stuff. I finished the round triple-bogey, double-bogey, triple-bogey, par, for an 85. Even Daniel beat me, by three.

But I wasn't as furious with myself as I might have predicted. Like John Smoltz, maybe I just wasn't comfortable yet being in contention, and next time would be different. In the meantime I could congratulate myself for having played stretches of fine golf in each round. In only my third tournament with the new swing, I had briefly been an amateur contender.

That afternoon I took the city bus home from Inverrary, joining a crew of busboys from the dining room. I sat huddled in the rear with my clubs and golf spikes on the seat beside me, going over my scorecard.

"You play golf?" one of the busboys asked.

A wealth of smart responses occurred to me, but then I remembered that late-night subway ride a few years earlier, when the teenage girls had laughed at my golf clubs and pathetic muttering, and it hit me how much better I felt about myself and my game now than I had then. I was making progress. I was finding my way.

"Greatest game in the world," I replied.

9 . *The Zippo Lighter*

BY THE MIDDLE OF MARCH OUR LIFE IN
Florida had settled into an agreeable routine.
Polly's biggest apprehension had been that
somehow we would be forced to live in a gated
golf community surrounded by Bermuda
shorts–clad retirees—"I want reality, not virtual reality," she said—but this didn't happen.
Instead we rented half of a small bungalow in a
working-class enclave of Fort Lauderdale
called Oakland Park. The house had an actual
producing orange tree in the back.

The neighborhood was straight out of an
Elmore Leonard novel, which pleased Polly, a
fan of all things noir. Our neighbor to the rear
was a surreptitious young man with no apparent job, except that he received frequent short

visits, often late at night, from all kinds of people—a rogue's gallery of ethnicity, gender, and income levels. What he was selling we could only guess. The house next door belonged to a fifty-year-old woman, her thirty-year-old son, and his three-year-old daughter. The girl's mother, we learned, was a stripper and lived elsewhere. Anna loved playing with the girl—she had a swing in her backyard!—and most of the time the girl couldn't have been sweeter, though when she got angry she could spew a stream of obscenities that would make a sailor proud.

Within a few days of moving in, Polly and I both felt our nerves untangle for perhaps the first time in our life together. Our relationship had been a blind leap over the waterfall: courtship, marriage, a baby, three horrible months of colic, three (now four) changes of residence, constant money worries. The sojourn in Florida was an escape: three months of unpressured, uncomplicated retreat. One of the best things was our relative lack of possessions: we had brought with us only what we could squeeze into our Honda. Our life was lean and our social obligations nil, except for a pleasantly spaced stream of visitors from New York. Polly fixed up an acceptable painting studio in the carport, and once or twice a week we sampled one of the many small ethnic restaurants in Oakland Park. Twice we ventured to Miami's South Beach for an infusion of glitz.

In addition to all this, the beach was only ten minutes away. Polly and Anna went almost every day while I played golf. If my golf game required being in a "pretty good space" with my life, this was that place.

SOME GOLFERS LIKE to practice and some don't. I always have. Since I essentially learned the game in a big open field rather than on a course, the range is my natural habitat. I'm sure that more than half the time I've spent with golf has been in practice rather than play. Partly this is because I've never belonged to a club and, in the New York area, getting onto decent public courses is time-consuming and expensive. But partly it's because I simply love hitting balls.

The South Florida tournaments were on Tuesdays and Wednesdays of each week, and the day before I usually played a practice round at the tournament site. But my favorite part of the week was after the tournament. When I woke up on Thursday, Friday, and Saturday mornings, I practically had to pinch myself. My job for the day, my *duty*, was to head over to the practice facility at Palm-Aire and goof all day with clubs and balls.

After a few weeks of this regimen I began to notice that I looked forward to short-game practice more than my full-swing drills. This was a switch. Always before, the sheer animal fun of hitting balls as far as I could was the most compelling aspect of practice. But now, for one thing, I was beginning to creak a little. Months of repetitive swinging had produced mild, chronic soreness in my left lower back, my right elbow, and my often-operated-upon left knee. Nothing disabling, but enough discomfort so my body groaned rather than tingled at the prospect of another hour on the range. For another thing, when I wasn't in the groove, the *psychological* pain was much greater than it had been before. Watching ball after ball slice sickeningly into the trees is not just frustrating, it is dispiriting. The sheer physical magnitude of long-ball errors—forty yards to the right sometimes, and forty yards short—mocked my whole project.

Short-game practice, on the other hand, was always a relief. I could be off my long game but still stop the ball reassuringly close to the cup or the green or whatever I was aiming at. Furthermore, short-game practice was almost entirely intuitive. Hip-turn, wrist cock, swing plane, follow-through—I never thought about these things consciously. I simply focused on distance and direction and tried to *will* the ball to go where I wanted it to.

And Palm-Aire had an excellent practice area. The putting green was spacious and nearby was a separate, elevated green complex surrounded by slopes and sand for practicing pitches and chips. For hours at a time I happily worked on low runners and high spinners, buried-lie sand blasts, uphill pitches and downhill chips, pitches from the rough, and hacks out of divots. As my confidence improved I got more ambitious. I learned to do things that amazed even me: flop shots that went twenty feet straight up and five feet forward, controlled bouncies off the cart path, bouncies into a garbage can from thirty feet, extrications from beneath the lip of the bunker. It was mindless activity to the point that I sometimes felt I was in a yogic trance. The world was reduced to three things: the target, the ball, and the angle of the clubface as it made contact with the ball. Utter bliss.

These sessions were also where I mastered one of the most crucial skills a mini-tour competitor can possess: picking a golf ball up off the turf using only the face of a wedge. The key is to make this feat look effortless, and then for good measure to bounce the ball a half dozen times on your club face. After several weeks of concentrated practice, I became fairly accomplished.

THE DAY AFTER my meltdown at Inverrary in late February, I holed up in the extra bedroom of our bungalow and removed two files from my briefcase. They were labeled "GolfPsych" and "Mental Golf." I figured it was time to re-boot my mental game. There had to be *some* way to eliminate, or at least alleviate, choking on such a scale.

The first file, GolfPsych, contained a profile of my golfing personality prepared by Dr. Deborah Graham, a psychologist who has worked with dozens of Tour pros. I had met Graham and her husband, John Stabler, at the Q School finals in December. She was a warm, attractive woman with short dark hair, around forty, and was circulating among the players after the fourth round cut like Scarlett O'Hara among the wounded troops at Atlanta. Golfers who had just missed the cut were weeping and gnashing their teeth. Essentially, she was drumming up business.

The profiles Graham does for golfers are based on a study she conducted in 1988. More than one hundred Tour and Senior Tour regulars completed an hour-long personality questionnaire, and she compared the responses of frequent winners—the champions—to those of everyone else. Graham found eight personality characteristics, out of many others that did not correlate, which the champions shared. When her clients complete the same 187-item questionnaire, they can contrast their chart with the composite champion's profile. "If you know which areas you are weak in compared to the champions," she told me at Q School, "you can work at making changes in those specific areas. That's the starting point for the work we do with golfers."

I told her about my project and she agreed to work up a profile of me for free. I completed the questionnaire in December and got the results in January.

Graham presents the eight characteristics on scales that stretch between opposites: cool vs. warm, abstract vs. concrete, and so forth. The champions do not occupy the extreme end on any scale—they are not, for instance, the iciest characters on earth, David Duval to the contrary—but they do have marked tendencies. They tend to be more cool, more abstract, more dominant, more emotionally stable, and more self-sufficient than the general run of golfers.

In three of the eight key traits I was spot on with the champions: cool, dominant, and self-sufficient. In three other areas I was close: abstract, unstable, and tense (in each case I was slightly more so than the champions). But in two of the eight championship characteristics I was *way* out of line. Whereas champions are self-assured, I was at the most extreme opposite end of the scale, right next to the defining word "apprehensive." And whereas champions are tough-minded, I was once again at the far opposite end of the scale: tender-minded.

When I first got these results, I looked them over with the same amused skepticism I do when reading astrological charts. Graham's computer-generated analyses seemed correct, but so do my charts. Of course my natural enthusiasm and inner beauty will win the day! But now, burrowing into the material a little deeper, especially in light of my performance in three real-world tournaments, I found Graham's approach more compelling. The elaborations of my deficiencies in the accompanying fifty-page workbook were disturbingly on the mark.

"You are very likely hard on yourself and prone to feel guilty for a wide variety of things," read the section on apprehension. "This leads to negative self-talk, negative imagery, and self-doubt on the golf course which can make it virtually impossible for you to be competitive. Low self-esteem can even subconsciously leave you feeling you don't deserve to play well." That was me, okay.

As for my tender-mindedness, the workbook acknowledged that this could be an advantage in "maintaining close and caring relationships with others." On the golf course, however, it made me prey to gamesmanship (I thought of Daniel) and easily distractible by issues from my non-golf life, such as those selfsame close and caring relationships when things weren't totally peachy (I thought about how poorly my practice sessions went when Polly and I parted with even a little tension). The goal is to have it both ways: "True Champions can be altruistic, loving, and caring at home while being tough, and self-absorbed during competition," Dr. Graham wrote.

The workbook was packed with corrective procedures: tips about using positive self-talk and "thought checks" and various visualization tricks on the course. There was a bibliography of works on self-esteem and suggestions for how to keep a golfing life in balance. Most of this advice seemed solid, if similar to the suggestions most self-help books make (determine priorities, set goals, be realistic). I had no doubt that, if rigorously followed over time, Graham's remedies could help me with my tendency to choke. But I was forty-one. These suspect personality traits had been hardening like arteries now for decades. How much deep-down change could I expect in the next eight months, change of the type that would stand up in a crisis situation, which was how I was already beginning to think of my Q School showdown in October?

THE SECOND FILE from my briefcase, "Mental Golf," contained notes from an intensive three-and-a-half-day seminar called "Experts Only" that I had taken eighteen months before. The guru was Chuck Hogan (no relation to Ben), a charismatic, bushy-eyebrowed golf coach (he denies the title "golf psychologist") who specializes in the mental side of the game. Peter

Jacobsen, Johnny Miller, and Raymond Floyd are among his former clients.

A magazine had paid my $1,495 tuition in exchange for a story about the experience, which I wrote under the title, "You Are a Plus-Four Handicapper." Plus-four means you're four strokes *better* than scratch, for me an incomprehensible concept but one which Hogan insisted should not be.

"Don't come here to understand stuff," were Hogan's first words at the seminar. "Understanding is the booby prize. *Experiencing* is the point." And this did get right to the heart of Hogan's central message: in golf, the conscious mind is your enemy, not your friend.

In Hogan's view, most golfers obsess over their golf swings in neurotic and counterproductive ways. He doesn't deny that sound mechanics are important—he started his career as a traditional PGA swing teacher—but believes that anyone with a single-digit handicap (a requirement for enrollment in the course) already has a good enough swing and would benefit from spending less time tinkering and more time nurturing the sensory imagination. Reviewing my notes now, this put me in a bind, since all I did was tinker. Still, I read on.

"Your brain is capable of processing only two words a second, but it can process ten thousand bits of other sensory information in that same time," he asked. "Which would you rather have working for you as you prepare for a critical shot?"

On the first day of the seminar Hogan had demonstrated the power of the visualizing mind with the help of Al Richards, a burly, sunburnt, fifty-year-old pro who happened to be sitting next to me. Al aspired to play on the Senior Tour, but had confessed to the group that he was intimidated by the prospect of competing against so many legendary players.

Hogan called Al to the front of the seminar room and told him to close his eyes. "Now pick out one of those legends and imagine him standing naked in front of a mirror," Hogan said.

Al did this, though not without a little protest.

"Now picture yourself standing next to him, fully clothed, ready to hunt bear. Which one of you seems bigger, brighter, more colorful, more vivid?"

Al said that he seemed much bigger and more powerful than the legend.

"Good. Now keep your eyes closed and hold out your arm. You are Al Richards, golf professional, and I'm going to try to push your arm down. Resist me." Despite manful exertion, Hogan barely managed to budge Richards's arm.

"Now imagine that you are Elmer Fudd. You are Elmer Fudd. Get that image in your mind and resist me again." This time Hogan easily pushed Richards's arm down with one hand.

"Mental, huh?" Hogan said as Al took his seat beside me. "If you believe that, you're cooked. It's much more than mental, it's biological, mental, physical—it all happens at once."

I whispered to Al, "Were you faking it?"

He shook his head. "That was unbelievable."

Later that first morning the class did an exercise which was the first step in Hogan's system. I remembered it well. He exhorted each of us to close our eyes and form a specific, crystal clear vision of ourselves playing golf at our best, like champions. How did we walk? How did we talk? What sounds did we hear? Were the colors we saw vivid or muted? What did our forearms feel like?

In the seminar I had no difficulty calling forth such a vision. In it I was focused, confident, and tension-free, as I had been during my round of 69. I walked slowly, in perfect balance and control, and brimmed with vigor. "If you want to *be* a champion," Hogan intoned as we all held our visions in mind, "you have to *act* like a champion. Remember, you are the living projection of yourself. Champions *are* their vision, and it's a very concrete vision. Wanna-bes merely *have* a vision, and it's abstract."

Now, however, in the bedroom at our Oakland Park bungalow, I found I couldn't conjure up a vision of myself as a champion. On the first attempt I casually made a little joke to myself, throwing up the image of myself after the first round at Inverrary, slinking away stoop-shouldered and humiliated toward the city bus. "There's your champion," I said, laughing. And that spoiled the whole deal. I tried again several times in deadly earnest to create a more positive championship image, but this choker image was the only one that stuck.

Clearly I needed work on the vision thing.

UNDERLYING BOTH DEBORAH Graham and Chuck Hogan's approach to golf is classic American bootstrap individualism: the power to succeed resides within, you only have to tap into it. Simply by controlling your own thoughts and attitudes, you can vault to a new level of play. I love that message. It's intoxicating. And so, over the next few weeks, I worked hard at implementing some of their practical advice. At Graham's suggestion I compiled a list of the things that made me such a wonderful human being and tried to think about it daily. I can't say my self-esteem shot through the roof, but one time on the range after a series of malignant shots I did catch myself thinking, unbidden, that my mother loved me.

Another tip of Graham's which I followed was staring at a golf ball. She contends that contemplating some neutral object in the middle of a round can blank the mind and distract it from pressure. One does occasionally see pros on TV, such as David Duval, staring at their balls and I, too, found the practice to be relaxing. Sometimes, contemplating my bright white Maxfli, my mind would wander back to an essay I once read called "The Whiteness of Evil." It was about the Nazi concentration camps. This really took my mind off the game.

From Chuck Hogan the main thing I learned to work on was developing a consistent pre-shot routine. Virtually every golf teacher stresses the importance of a rock solid routine before each shot. The familiar motions—typically involving visualization, a deep "cleansing" breath, a designated number of steps to the ball, and a precise waggling sequence—calm the soul and establish a Pavlovian cue to hit away. But Hogan carried the concept further, encouraging us to picture ourselves inside a fantastic bubble of safety. The world outside with its stresses and concerns could not permeate the bubble's skin. Inside we were immune, we were in heaven, we were liberated to play our best golf. It was embarrassing to practice the simple routine I had developed at the range; I felt too conspicuous parading back and forth repeatedly like the famous neurotic polar bear at the Central Park Zoo. So I did it furtively back at the house. Whenever Polly drove off with Anna somewhere, I dashed into the backyard with a golf club and paced in and out of my imaginary bubble.

It would be nice to report that these efforts paid off immediately, but the fact is my next tournament, at my new "home" course, Palm-Aire, was a mental game disaster. Too many tricks and injunctions were swimming around in my head. The pre-shot routine, designed to free my mind to concentrate on nothing but the golf shot, had precisely the opposite effect: all I could think about was performing the routine itself correctly. When the moment of truth arrived, I was so focused on the routine I had to remind myself to swing.

Ironically, my short game suffered the most from this surfeit of thoughts, particularly lag putting, which is almost all feel. I had no feel whatsoever, only insistent, all-too-conscious thoughts about becoming one with the ball. Usually we remained two.

Things came to a head in the second round, on the fourth hole, when I missed a one-foot putt. My jaw dropped. Missing a one-foot putt is very hard to do. Then, on the next hole, I missed an almost identical eighteen-inch putt. My mind blew a fuse and basically shut down. I was stunned.

On the next tee I announced to my playing companions, "Okay, that's it. Time to stop the insanity." I flipped my hat around backwards and decided to quit caring. For the rest of the round I played with a scuffed-up ball, eschewed practice swings, muttered dark, nihilistic insults against golf, whistled insipid show tunes while sauntering down the fairways, and drank a beer I bought off the beverage cart though this was against tour policy. Naturally my play improved dramatically. I could do no wrong. I scored three birdies, one of them a hole-out from the sand. Only when I realized on the sixteenth tee that I had a chance to beat Daniel, who was in my group, did I start screwing up again. I immediately reinstituted the pre-shot routine and ripped my drive deep out-of-bounds, into the branches of a palmetto outside Palm-Aire condo 421.

But I did not interpret the results of this tournament as a repudiation of the mental game, only as a sign that I needed more work. I had stumbled upon an important truth: thinking about the mental game during a round can be just as detrimental as thinking about swing mechanics, and maybe more so. The goal is to make both so thoroughly a matter of habit that conscious thought is unnecessary.

And despite everything, I beat Daniel that day by a stroke, 80 to 81.

As I GOT comfortable with the other amateur regulars, the tournaments became more fun. A few of these novices, the best of the group, were recent college golf team graduates tuning up their games before turning pro. They typically shot in the low seventies and were burdened, week after week, with having to redeem the one-hundred- and two-hundred-dollar pro shop gift certificates awarded to the top amateur finishers; there are only so many ugly golf shirts one can stand in one's closet. The rest of us were more closely matched in ability but could hardly have been more diverse: snowbirds like Daniel from the frozen north, Europeans in Florida on extended business or vacations, college kids skipping classes, local club members hungry for better competition.

To give you an example of the diversity, in the group with Daniel and me for the second round at Palm-Aire were Michael the Dapper Danish Diver and Mr. Excitability, a hyperenergetic local real estate broker. Michael the Dane made his living working four hundred feet beneath the surface of the North Sea on giant oil rigs. He had to spend ten days at a stretch submerged with one other diver in a tiny capsule. To pass the off-hours he visualized playing the courses of the South Florida Tour over and over, and as soon as he resurfaced (a process which itself took the better part of a day) hopped the first jet to Miami. He was a calm, methodical player who usually shot in the upper seventies and low eighties.

Mr. Excitability, by contrast, usually showed up at the course about five minutes before his tee time and needed most of that time simply to remove and stow his jewelry: rings, heavy watches, gold necklaces. He was deeply tanned, sported a pencil-thin mustache, and bragged about having played golf for the University of Miami. When I later discovered the University of Miami didn't have a golf team, he denied ever having made the claim. On the golf course Mr. Excitability had no fear. He attempted recovery shots no one in his right mind would consider—hitting a driver off a cart path, for instance. With amazing frequency he pulled the shots off, but when he didn't he went postal. After a few successive bungles he would simply walk off the course. "Bad back," he explained one time. Another time he said he'd been up all night partying with his mistress in South Beach.

At least a third of the amateurs, by my reckoning, played only once and were never seen again, presumably because they were embarrassed by their play. One guy I was paired with, an alleged three handicapper, shot 96 the first round and was dumbfounded. "I told my girlfriend about it last night," he mentioned to me before the second round, "and she wouldn't believe me. I guess I was more nervous yesterday than I thought." In the second round, he shot 104.

It was harder to get to know the pros. They were segregated from the amateurs not just by tee times but socially as well. Most of the hundred-plus pros in the fields were transients, in Florida just for the few hard winter months, and they typically hung together in small roommate clusters. There was, however, a hard-core nucleus of two or three dozen pros who lived in South Florida year round and played the mini-tours full-time. They won most of the tournaments (over the years they got to know every hazard and every subtle break in the greens) and remained aloof not just from the amateurs but also from the transient pros (who were, essentially, their "donators").

The best player in this pack, though not its leader owing to almost pathological shyness, was Adam Armagost. Of the twelve South Florida tournaments I played in, he won four and finished worse than ninth only once. On Thursday and Friday of each week he played on another new mini-tour in the area, the Sunshine Players Tour, and did just as well there. Sarah Stevenson, the South Florida Tour's manager, estimated Armagost won more than one hundred thousand dollars a year.

I tried to talk to Armagost once by hovering near the scorer's table after a tournament, waiting for him to sign his card, and then practically trapping him in a corner of the clubhouse snack bar.

"Congratulations," I said (he had just won four thousand dollars), extending my hand. I introduced myself and explained that I was both playing on the tour and writing a book and would love to sit down and chat a bit. His eyes went wide with terror.

"That's interesting," he said, shuffling sideways toward the exit. "There's a lot to say about the mini-tours. Sure, we should talk sometime, and . . ."

Poof! He was gone. It was incredible, a magician's trick—he vanished into thin air.

The only top pro I got to know even semi-well was named Michael McNearney. He was a tall (six-foot-six), skinny native of Chicago with reddish blond hair, sunburnt skin, and pale blue eyes. In high school he had been a basketball phenom and won a scholarship to Depauw, but once there quickly realized he would never make it to the NBA and so switched to golf. The transition was not difficult. He had been playing in tournaments since age five. After college and a four-year stint in the real world, McNearney turned pro.

"Those first two years I learned more than I did in my previous twenty years in golf put together," he told me one night over dinner. "You can get David Leadbetter to give you all the lessons in the world, but the only way to learn how to *really* play is from the other pros, the guys who have to earn a check every week or else they go hungry."

What kind of things did he learn, I asked.

"Okay, I've never seen you play, but one shot I'll bet you don't have is a 110-yard six-iron." He was correct. Six-irons typically carry from 165 to 180 yards. "But there are times you need half-swing six-irons, like into a heavy wind or in a critical situation when direction is the only thing that matters. I've got that shot now." The local veteran pros also taught him how to absolutely, positively block a shot from going left or right, as needed, and how on certain holes at certain courses (the thirteenth at Cobblestone, for instance) the tee boxes were deceptive and caused most golfers to align themselves incorrectly.

McNearney had an abundance of energy for golf and high confidence. "The difference between me and the other guys out here is that I *know* I'm going to get through Q School this year," he told me. I could easily believe it. He had the kind of "big" game Tour courses favor—his average drive was over three hundred yards—and also seemed to thrive on pressure. He loved the *gamble* of golf and was rapidly acquiring experience. On the other hand, experts once said the same, on the basis of more evidence, about pros like Bobby Clampett and Gary Hallberg and their careers fizzled. I wasn't sure anyone really knew what it took.

THE ONLY TIME that most of the South Florida Tour players assembled in one place during my tenure in Florida was at a seminar in early March that Eubanks organized with a golf psychologist. I attended, naturally, being a whore for advice, but I was surprised that so many of the pros showed up, too. Even the wiliest, most hard-core locals apparently sensed that they were missing some magic—or else, presumably, they would be out there making millions on the Big Tour.

The expert turned out to be none other than Dr. GolfPsych herself, Deborah Graham. She was relaxed, funny, and impressively knowledgeable about tournament golf. The pros ate it up. When she described the eight personality traits of champions, they asked earnest questions. When she detailed a few specific techniques for diffusing pressure, they hung on to every word. "Yes, yes," one of the regulars said excitedly. "I do something like that already, but I'd never thought of it as being so important." The session was almost like an Alcoholics Anonymous meeting: confession, openness, and vulnerability such as I had not suspected these hardened scrappers would be capable of.

At one point I flashed on the image from an old movie of a pretty, pith-helmeted explorer amazing a murderous band of spear-carrying warriors with her Zippo lighter. She flicked it on and off, making fire, and the natives were mesmerized. They feared the sorcery, but they also desperately wanted it for themselves.

All of us in the room felt like that, I think. We craved what Deborah Graham offered. It didn't seem like too much to ask, to be able to flick a Zippo. Golf was that simple, too—or at least it seemed like it ought to be. As a golfer, it's hard not to believe that someone out there has the answer, a magical solution that will reduce the game's complexity to the elegance of a Zippo's simple white flame.

IN THE PARKING lot after the seminar, I reintroduced myself to Graham and her husband and told them I had been working on my champions' traits. She asked how the Year was going. "I'm not sure," I said. "I've found it harder to make progress than I hoped. I feel stuck at the level of just learning to swing correctly."

She nodded sympathetically and advised that, even so, I should start preparing mentally for Q School. "Q School is tough, no matter why you're there. You'll have a lot of stress and anxiety. You owe it to yourself to start getting ready mentally already."

In my heart I knew she was right, but frankly it was hard to focus on something so far in the future. Right now I was obsessed with just making a proper hip turn. Golf is not just mind or just body, I knew that—it is both, a duet. But working on the purely physical side of the equation—mechanics, alignment, solid contact, and so forth—seemed so much more urgent right now. It was also more satisfying, more concrete. The mental side was slippery and ambiguous. How did you know your efforts would pay off? Beyond establishing a reliable pre-shot routine, I wasn't even sure how to proceed. It seemed easier to avoid the subject altogether.

10 . *The Big Tour Comes to Town*

OVER THE YEARS I HAD ATTENDED MAYBE A dozen PGA tournaments and had always been duly impressed by the pros. I remember sneaking into the Colonial in Fort Worth as a kid and being flabbergasted primarily by how *far* the pros could swat the ball. In later years it was the pros' implacable *rhythm* that stayed with me; they never hurried their shots, never lunged, even when trying to unload for maximum distance. An aura enveloped them as they set up for a shot. We in the crowd looked on in awe, as if a sacred ritual of vital importance to our culture was about to unfold.

In the first week of March the PGA Tour began its Florida swing with the Doral-Ryder Open in Miami. I went, and after five months

of concentrated work on my own game, was more impressed by the
pros than ever. For twenty minutes I stared slack-jawed as Phil
Mickelson and Steve Elkington, a lefty and a righty respectively,
stood back to back on the range hitting balls. They were mirror
images of each other, the two most sumptuous swings in golf.
"Beautiful" is a much overused word. A college pal of mine argued
that people should be limited to three uses of the word "beautiful"
in their lifetimes: once at their wedding, once at the birth of their
first child, and once at a time of their choosing. I could settle for this
as the time of my choosing

But what was the source of this beauty? I puzzled. One part of it,
easy to ignore, was simply that Elkington and Mickelson were
themselves such healthy, athletic animals—strong men in the prime
of life. They weren't grotesque pituitary cases like basketball or
football players; they were in most ways rather ordinary, only more
physically proud than usual and extremely well-structured—exem-
plars of the species. On television Tour pros seem like actors, their
near perfection of a piece with all the other unattainable images of
perfection that our TV culture dishes up. But up close you realize
they are merely people like yourself, which simultaneously makes
their athletic accomplishment more marvelous and less abstract.
One rarely sees acts of near perfection performed repeatedly an
arm's length away.

Beyond that, though, a good golf swing has an aesthetic quality
with no "meaning" outside of itself. Like music, it simply gives pleasure. Elkington and Mickelson are famous for their grace. Their
swings had nothing to do with effort, yet somehow they generated
enormous power. Kapow! The ball explodes off the clubface and
launches into the ether. There was an ecstasy to their swings which I
yearned to imitate.

When I came to my senses after thinking such thoughts, I tried to
examine their swings for clues and noticed two things in particular.
The first was seamlessness. It was impossible to isolate the elements
of Mickelson's swing—the moment of transition from backswing to
downswing, the limit of his hip turn. This was not a swing of parts, it

was a whole. But how did he get there? Surely he must have built the swing from pieces originally; it didn't just descend upon him from heaven, did it?

The other thing I noticed, not unrelated, was that these swings seemed so *free* not because they were loosey-goosey, but because they were tightly controlled and mechanically perfect. Watching one after another, I realized they were as repetitively precise as numerically controlled assembly line tools. Elkington in particular was meticulous, especially in his setup. He screwed his legs into the earth as if erecting a platform upon which to perform laser surgery; then he tested the balance and limits of this structure with calculated waggling; then he arranged his upper torso exactly so; then he zeroed in on the target and handed over the operation to his software systems. In action, however, each swing seemed as free as a whim. This balance between ease and power, freedom and control is surely part of golf's great appeal, especially for men. In this country men are taught to maintain control at all costs, to keep a tight rein on emotions. In golf you can do that, but also let loose and play. The central idea is to knock the cover off the ball, but under control. It's a nifty trick.

I spent two days at the Doral tournament and was freshly dazzled by many other things I saw. At one point I stood near Jim Furyk when he hit a five-iron from an uneven lie in the rough to the closely bunkered back portion of a green 185 yards away. He left himself a twenty-five-foot putt for birdie, but was visibly disgusted—stabbing his club into the turf—because he hadn't nailed it closer. Before the Year began, I might have reflexively empathized with Furyk's disappointment: "Too bad he didn't get it close." Now, realizing that from a similar lie I probably wouldn't have even attempted to put the ball on the green, I could only shake my head. If I ever naïvely assumed a Fine Green Line existed between me and someone like Furyk, I knew better now.

By MID-MARCH, after two months of weekly tournament competition, my game had developed a certain consistency. Unfortunately, it wasn't the consistency I had hoped for. My scores ranged from 78 to 82, except when I shot 85, which I seemed to do every third or fourth time out because, well, I lost control. I let a bonehead play get to me, or I hit two or three shots in a row making the same mistake (most often a pull) and either my equanimity melted or my confidence shattered, sometimes both.

I also began having a miserable time with three- to five-foot putts. These are the worst. Missing a three-foot putt is inexcusable, so the pressure to make it is intense. The meagerest nervous twitch at impact is usually enough to skate the ball right past the hole, and three-footers are not immune to break and the effects of Florida's bristly Bermuda grain. Once you miss a couple of short putts in a round (or in a week, or in a year), all subsequent short putts become even more of a booby trap. There was nothing I dreaded more in life—not out-of-bounds left, not Anna's 5 A.M. wake-up call, not the sound of a dragging muffler—than facing a five-foot putt.

On the other hand, I was playing often enough now to recognize a pattern to my mistakes, which gave me concrete objectives to work on. A consistent pattern of mistakes was at least better than my old, unpredictable pattern of mistakes. Most of the time now I faded the ball, and my bad shots simply tended to be more pronounced fades or slices. As long as I made sure not to pull the ball (which, of course, I could never guarantee but which was rare), I could aim at targets with trouble on the left and feel fairly confident that I wouldn't end up in that trouble. When water or sand or out-of-bounds loomed on the right, however, the challenge was tougher, but at least I understood what I was up against. Before the Year, every shot was something of a blind man's gamble.

As for my swing, it and I were becoming joined at the hip. I could scarcely stand still anywhere anymore—waiting for the bus, in line at the bank, washing dishes at the sink—without carefully placing my feet shoulders' width apart and practicing my hip turn or follow-through. This was occasionally embarrassing, especially at fast-food restaurants, when I sensed that most people had no idea what I was doing. It occurred to me that the relationship between me and my swing was like that of a ventriloquist and his dummy: I was putatively in charge, but the swing had a life of its own and sometimes sassed me back, as for instance when, in the tournament after the Doral, it seemed to balk at the notion of following through and pushed shot after shot to the right.

About this time I had my sixth lesson with Michael Hebron. It had been nearly a month since my previous visit, and despite my constant work on the swing I was aware that certain messy attributes had snuck in. It felt looser than it ought to, and I had no idea where the problem lay.

"Your swing plane is off. That's the main thing I see. It's too flat," Hebron analyzed after I'd hit only two or three shots. He had me poke my head through the slanting, Plexiglas swing plane device he had introduced at our second lesson and corrected the problem. We also worked on balance, which is often a problem with taller golfers like me. He suggested a trick ice skaters sometimes use: scrunching my toes a bit as I took my stance. Sometimes this results in greater stability.

I told Hebron about seeing Elkington and Mickelson and being impressed with their rhythm, so this became the second focus of the lesson. "There's probably nothing more important but less taught than rhythm," he said. He suggested I work at making my backswing and my throughswing last the same amount of time no matter what club I was using, driver through putter. "Count the next time you're watching the Tour pros and you'll see it's true. Nine times out of ten, if a Tour pro hits a bad shot it's because his rhythm is off."

It was a useful lesson. But I found, as I drove home, that my enthusiasm for working on mechanics was not what it had been. I knew my swing was a long way from perfect. It had changed substantially since the start of the Year, but was still only "pretty good" at best. Deborah Graham's comments at the seminar made me doubt for the first time whether working on incremental improvements in my swing mechanics was the best use of my time and energy.

Curiously in the past few weeks, I had begun to notice a change in the way I thought about bad shots. Previously, whenever I bungled badly, I had immediately sought a mechanical explanation: Had I turned my wrists over too soon? Failed to complete the backswing? "Held on" after impact? My ability to make these analyses had greatly improved since I started studying with Hebron, but pinpointing exactly *what* had gone wrong didn't eliminate the problem. I knew that "holding on" was a no-no even before I made the mistake.

Now when I messed up, the more important question seemed to be *why,* and I could almost always find a mental-game explanation: I had been distracted by a bug on the ball, my forearms had tensed up for no good reason before the takeaway, I had hurried my pre-shot routine because the marshal was giving me a dirty look, or at address I had sensed that my ball position was off but did not make the necessary adjustment. If these really were the main causes of my miscues, now that I at least in theory knew what my swing should look like, wouldn't it make more sense to channel the bulk of my energy into the mental-game agendas proposed by Graham and Chuck Hogan? Wouldn't eliminating a few more bonehead plays per round be a surer way to lower my score than to continue focusing on the minutiae of mechanics?

Though to be honest, my thinking in this regard may have been influenced by Hebron's $125-per-lesson fee. Polly and I had already exceeded our $9,000 budget for our three months in Florida, and we still had six weeks to go.

"TEN TO ONE it's going in the water," Jay Slazinski whispered in my ear.

We were standing on the fifth tee at the PGA National Estates course north of West Palm Beach and there was indeed a formidable body of water running down the left side. One of the other players in our group, a black-haired, twenty-three-year-old newcomer from Kentucky, had just backed off his drive and announced, "Jiminey Cricket, that lake over there's got me spooked. Anyone know how to block a shot left?"

He didn't actually expect advice in the middle of a tournament, he was talking to calm himself. To further calm himself he took five or six more practice swings, then a deep breath, and walked tentatively toward his ball. This was the point at which Jay had whispered his prophetic words.

The Kentuckian made a mighty swing and the ball flew straight in the water.

This might have been more comic to me—Jay could hardly stop chuckling—had I not psyched myself into dunking a ball in almost precisely the same way two holes earlier, though without announcing it to the crowd. On that tee I had warned myself not to yank the ball left into the marsh. I had been specific: "Whatever you do, don't hit the ball left into that marsh." Naturally I had.

I am proud to report, however, that I did not let this botch job spin me into a state of psychological despair. For three days before the tournament I had repeated several mantras suggested by Hogan, the relevant one in this case being, "Let each mistake serve as a cue to prove my mental strength on the next shot." The Kentuckian's water shot served as an additional cue: he had flown his ball into the water precisely as I had on the third hole. The situation was tailor-made for me to follow suit—but I didn't. I proved my mental strength to myself by punching a short, cautious drive onto the fairway.

In retrospect, I consider that weak-ass drive my first significant mental victory of the Year. I had told myself not to think about a white bear and more or less succeeded.

I played in a state of semi-confidence for eight or nine holes after that. As our group waited on the thirteenth tee, a marshal drove up with a grease board upon which were scrawled, in smudgy red ink, the scores of the leading contenders. Most of the board was reserved for the pros' scores, of course, but at the bottom he listed the low three or four amateur scores from the groups ahead of us—there were nineteen amateurs in all—and my total of five-over was good for second place. The marshal seemed as surprised as I was.

I was actually tied with the aforementioned Jay Slazinski, a ponytailed former computer programmer who was one of my best friends on the tour. We were two behind the leader and one ahead of Daniel—a delicious situation, as far as competition went, and one I felt certain I would blow.

But amazingly I birdied the thirteenth, a short par four, by sneaking a twelve-foot putt into the back right corner of the cup. I didn't know where this left me in relation to the leader, since the marshal had disappeared never to return, but I did know I was one ahead of Jay and two ahead of Daniel. Furthermore, I knew something about the upcoming fourteenth hole that they almost certainly didn't.

The day before during my practice round I had picked up on the back nine with a vacationing PGA pro from Michigan who often competed in tournaments on the course. He gave me some general tips about dealing with the pronounced grain on the greens and, regarding the par-five fourteenth, some specific advice. "I don't know what it is about this hole, but everybody ends up long," he said. "No matter what the conditions—dead into the wind, even— balls tend to roll to the back of the green and that leaves you with a very tricky downhill putt." He said I should take at least one club less than I normally would on the approach shot.

At the time I didn't think twice about this little nugget, but now in the thick of competition I realized its value—the kind of trick Tour pros learn when they play the same courses year after year.

On the tee-box my heart pounded: if I could just put my drive in the fairway, I would have a decided advantage on the lay-up. For once my desire to succeed was greater than my fear; I aced a perfect drive.

The lay-up, 142 yards to the pin, would normally have been a nine-iron for me. But this time I pulled out my sand wedge. I was jazzed totally into the thrill of the moment. I had tunnel vision. My arms felt light and tingly. Was this how the Big Guys felt coming down the stretch at the Masters? The ones who didn't fall apart, that is? Because this time I knew I wasn't going to choke. The shot and I were *one*. There was cosmic convergence going on.

I hit it pure, a knock-down wedge that sailed precisely at the dark spot in front of the green which was my target.

Even as the ball arced through the air, I was elated. I had *done* it: I had combined my new skills with my special knowledge and pulled off a fine, wily shot under pressure. Unfortunately, the dark spot which was my target turned out to be an oozy patch of mud. *Thwat!* The ball plugged. I ended up bogeying the hole, like everyone else in my group. But this disappointment was minor compared to the kick I had had executing the shot.

I finished the round with two pars and two bogeys. Jay Slazinski and I split the hundred-dollar fourth-place gift certificate, and Daniel took fifth.

I did not rejoice, but neither did I mope. I had actually *won* something—fifty dollars—on the golf course. I felt, just a little bit, like a player.

A COUPLE OF days later I paid a visit to the PGA Tour's second stop in Florida, the Honda Classic in Fort Lauderdale. On the putting green after the first round I collared Kevin "One Shot at a Time" Sutherland, my robopro acquaintance from Q School. He hadn't exactly set the Tour on fire thus far in his rookie year, but he had made the cut in five tournaments and picked up a few checks. He said it was tough as a rookie, getting used to new courses each week and finding decent places to eat and stay, but he was sort of having fun. He missed his wife, who was home in California, working.

"Well, you must be busy. I don't want to interrupt your practice,"

I said. As a reporter I had learned that with PGA Tour players, you didn't hang around chatting unless you had something specific to say.

"No, not at all," Kevin replied. "Actually it's pretty boring out here. I got nothing else to do." So he gave me a brief lesson about making short putts ("Emphasize smooth, think 'accelerate' through the ball"); described his own pre-shot routine in detail (he counted out his steps to the ball, one-two-three); and explained how he hums or sings a song to keep his mind from racing under pressure.

"Getting over a bad shot is maybe the toughest thing about golf," he said. "If I hit a bad shot, that doesn't mean I'm playing bad golf. It just means I hit a bad shot. The worst thing is to obsess about it, because that keeps you from thinking about what you need to do right the next time."

"That's easy for you to say, because you're a great golfer," I pointed out. "But when I hit a bad shot, sometimes I really *am* playing bad golf."

"Yeah, well," he shrugged. "It's a tough game. Hit the ball, go find it, and hit it again—that's the way I look at things."

What is it about golf that makes inane formulations like this seem so profound? Over the next few months I found myself thinking about Sutherland's innocent pearl often: hit the ball, go find it, and hit it again. It seemed to capture something essential about the Sisyphean struggle of golf. The quest never ends.

Probably the reason clichés have such power in golf is because the game *is* so simple. It's the unneeded complications that mess everyone up; clichés return the mind to what matters. It may also be true, however, that this simplemindedness is what makes golf pros seem so boring.

Joe Daley, the pro who had given me another lesson about chipping at Q School, was also at the Honda. I located him on the range, at the far end, all by himself, wearing what may have been the same pair of oft-washed chinos he had worn at Bear

Lakes and the same cap, perched characteristically way up on top of his head.

"Congratulations on the 68!" I told him enthusiastically when we greeted. I'd noticed his score on the scoreboard.

"Thanks. But that was John Daly—D-A-L-Y. I shot a 78."

"Oh, right." I was mortified. I may have been one of the few people at the tournament who actually knew something about Joe Daley, and I'd muffed it. But he took it in stride. He asked about my Year and whether I used his chipping system (I told him I didn't, I'd stuck with my own method, which didn't surprise him), and described his life on Tour as "great, the real thing." But I must confess, he seemed even more out of place at the Honda than he had at Q School. The pro nearest us on the range was Mark O'Meara, a close age contemporary of Daley. But O'Meara, with his graying sideburns and costly clothes, had a palpable aura of confidence and success that Daley couldn't touch. I found O'Meara intimidating. I wondered if Daley did.

Driving home, I questioned whether O'Meara's confidence was the product of his success or its cause. Had he been born of confidence or was the Fine Green Line that separated him from Daley primarily a matter of physical talent? O'Meara had already won the U.S. Amateur Championship and three Tour titles when Daley was still working as a bank credit officer. Whatever difference in physical talent there may have once been between them, surely by this stage the confidence gap must be more crucial.

I had reason to think about this more a few days later when I drove forty miles to watch Adam Armagost play a round in a tournament on the Sunshine Players Tour. Because of our different tee times, I had never been able to watch him play on the South Florida Tour, where he was winning most of the tournaments.

For the region's dominant player, Armagost was not an imposing physical specimen. He was around thirty, shorter than average, with receding hair, a receding chin, and the early signs of a middle-age paunch. There was also nothing immediately impressive about his game. At most he drove the ball around 250 yards, maybe 260, with a swing that was bouncy and unorthodox. He seemed somehow to punch up at the ball. On the other hand he just plain didn't miss fairways, and around the greens he was a genuine wizard. Twice during the nine holes I observed he chipped in for birdies, and none of his lag putts left him more than a tap in for par. He did, however, bogey the final hole by failing to get up and down, and lost the tournament by a stroke to a young European pro.

Deconstructing Armagost was a favorite pastime among his peers on the South Florida Tour. His doubters said he would never make it on the Tour because he lacked length and strength, but I was not convinced. Lots of Tour pros who don't hit the ball long but place it in the fairways and putt like demons are successful: Corey Pavin, Mike Reid, even Nick Faldo. Armagost regularly shot Tour-like scores on courses that weren't any easier than those the Big Boys played.

More convincing to me was the comfort zone argument. Year after year Armagost tried to get through Q School, but despite his abundant talent he never made it. Here in Florida he knew every course, every hazard, every blade of grass, and made a lot of money while living at home. I wondered whether at some level he simply didn't want to face the challenges of life on the Big Tour.

The skills required to make it on the PGA Tour go way beyond simply being able to play the game well. Mark O'Meara's family, for instance, moved around a lot when he was a kid: nine homes in seven states before he was a teen. Who's to say that early training in the nomadic lifestyle wasn't as big a factor in his later success as his ability to strike a golf ball? But, of course, if you're a young player with talent, you can't know if you have just the right blend of skills until you give it a whirl. That's why the mini-tours are filled to overflowing with contenders.

OBSERVING THE BIG Boys and Adam Armagost was all well and good, but I was impatient to get on with my own game. I'd had a taste of the high of competition, and I wanted more of it right away. So in preparation for the next tournament at the Westchester Golf Club in Boynton Beach, I intensified my practice regime. I played my usual practice round at the host club three days before the tournament, so I would have more time to visualize the holes and work on specific shots I might need. I also spent more time than usual at the range. The main thing I tried to work on was rhythm.

One of my secret pleasures in Florida was occasionally being mistaken for a real-life pro. A few days before the Westchester tournament this happened for maybe the third time in my life at the American Golf Center, a range near our house where I sometimes went after dinner. A rumpled middle-age guy who had been practicing a few stations down from me sauntered over, plopped on a bench, and watched me hit three or four balls.

Eventually, casual-like, he said, "We've been getting some fine players through here lately."

"Yeah, I guess so," I replied absently, finishing a shot. "What do you mean?"

"Quite a few of you fellows."

" 'We fellows?' " I led him on. It briefly flashed in my mind that he might be a gay pickup artist.

"You know, guys like you—pros."

I was flattered, even though the compliment had been more or less induced. Also, I suspected the misconception had been created as much by my manner of practice—I had been working systematically through my bag and was clearing a compact, little square of black dirt with my divots rather than the random pattern most golfers do—as by the elegance of my swing. In any event, we chatted a bit about how tough it is to make a living on the South Florida Tour (I fudged about still being an amateur) and when he asked for some swing advice I equivocated, afraid of doing harm, and taught him instead how to flip golf balls up off the turf using his sand wedge. This little trick had "pro" written all over it.

After a while, with him still watching, I returned to hitting balls. After a couple of nice ones, I pull-hooked a three-iron. Then I pull-hooked a few more—no matter what I tried I couldn't straighten things out. This incensed me. Then I topped one. Then I caught one clean but hit the next one horribly fat, plowing up a full foot of turf behind the ball. From the corner of my eye I noticed my admirer tiptoeing away.

After another few minutes of livid whacking, I had achieved a state of Range Rage.

Range Rage often begins, as now, with a few innocently bad shots. A quick bloom of fury follows, then irreversible frustration, and finally an all-out massacre of range balls. When my supply of yellow balls was depleted, I bought another large bucket at the pro shop and went through that in about five minutes, as fast as I could, like Sam Kinnison on a rampage. All the careful work I'd been doing on spine-tilt and hip-turn flew out the window. This was not about golf, it was about violence. All I desired was the satisfaction of nailing *one measly shot* dead on the meat. Though, of course, when this actually happened, I wanted to nail one more. There's no winning at Range Rage.

Range Rage has ruined many a tranquil afternoon for me, but never so many in a row as that week before the Westchester tournament. I had felt that I was on the verge of a breakout—in my golf journal I had postulated a "Great Leap Forward" in my game—but instead, there I was, frightening blameless strangers on the range. The pull-hooks grew worse day-to-day and were supplemented by an ignominious mixture of other flaws, all straight out of the duffer's handbook. With every miscue, my determination to fix the problems with redoubled effort grew insanely.

By tournament day I was spent.

My Westchester experience was ugly. I incurred fourteen penalty strokes from veering out-of-bounds or into hazards, three-putted four times, four-putted once, and almost hit a fellow competitor standing in the tee box with an outright shank. That was the first round, a 94. I didn't play round two.

What had gone wrong? Why had my game, slowly but steadily improving all these months, impishly decided to go haywire? All I knew was that suddenly, three weeks before my Florida finale, I felt very, very tired. And for the first time all Year, I was genuinely discouraged.

My first response to the disastrous performance at Westchester was to contact
Hebron. If I'd had a shrink or a priest, I would
have called him instead, but Hebron was the
best I could come up with. From a roadside
pay phone immediately after leaving the tournament I placed a call to the Palm Beach Polo
Club, hoping for a last-minute cancellation in
his schedule and an emergency infusion of
advice. But the woman at the pro shop said he
was booked solid that afternoon and also for
the next three days, so I drove home.

When I woke up the next morning, I had
second thoughts about summoning Hebron.
My swing had been execrable in the tournament, this was true: herky-jerky, tight, and

wild. But I knew the 94 wasn't the result of some technical flaw Hebron could fix in a couple of lessons. My swing *had* such flaws, many of them, but they weren't the proximate problem. The problem, I decided, was burnout. I was listless. Lining up a putt, I tried to envision the ball rolling across the green, but I just didn't care enough to follow it all the way into the cup. It was my spirit that needed fixing, not my swing.

So I decided to take the next tournament off. A few months earlier, this would have been unthinkable. This was Florida! I was in golf paradise! Too tired to play golf? I remembered smirking when I heard the Tour pros talk about fatigue and their need to take a break: "Right. It must be tough having to play golf all the time." But now that didn't seem so far-fetched. For six months now I had been practicing golf almost every day. Since moving to Florida I had played at least four rounds a week. In theory, I suppose, one could even grow tired of photographing *Sports Illustrated* swimsuit models.

For the first two days I basically stared into space. I leafed through magazines, watched an amazing fight sequence on *Jerry Springer,* and went shopping for flip-flops with Anna. Whenever I noticed my golf bag sitting in a corner of the living room, it beamed guilt and pain in my direction.

On the third day I picked up one of the self-esteem books Deborah Graham had recommended in the GolfPsych manual. It suggested that I systematically examine the barriers I had erected to success as a first step in dismantling them. Having nothing better to do, I made an attempt.

According to the Freudian psychoanalyst to whom I paid more than $20,000 in the years immediately after my first marriage, my biggest fear in life was that my father wanted to chop off my penis. This is boilerplate stuff for Freudians: we men all want to sleep with our mothers, so we work hard to succeed to attract their attention, but if we do succeed our fathers will become so enraged by jealousy that they will chop off our penises. Hence, we fear success. Luckily, I didn't believe this argument for a second, so I quickly moved on to secondary considerations.

Perhaps, it occurred to me, I had deliberately chosen golf to become obsessed with because, of all the sports or activities I could have chosen, failure in golf was the most assured. That's because golf is impossible. Nobody succeeds. The best you can do is fail slightly less often than you used to or than others. Also in golf, you can fail nobly, which was a concept dear to the hearts of Southerners. My mother's family came from the Old South—Mississippi—and bittersweet nostalgia about losing the War Between the States hung over the family's reunions like the perfume of wisteria. Not only that (now that I got going on the subject), but the whole Baptist-Calvinist concept of Original Sin was about the noble certainty of defeat. We are born as slugs and doomed to a life of failure, but so long as we believe correctly and make a decent effort we will get to heaven anyway. Put all this together and it's a wonder I hadn't become obsessed with golf much earlier in my life. The sport is unusually rich in providing opportunities for self-hatred.

The idea in the self-esteem book was that after making these helpful analyses of why you failed, you held them up to the bright light of rationality and saw how silly they were. But this didn't work for me. The more I thought about why I failed, the more persuasive the arguments became.

So I decided to shift my focus to just how plain tuckered out I was. It wasn't physical fatigue. It was mental fatigue, from all the pressure I put on myself. Unlike genuine mini-tour pros, at least I didn't have the pressure of seriously trying to make a living as a player. For this I was grateful. But I was more than making up for it by loading the Year with all kinds of subsidiary purposes. My primary goal was Q School, but along the way I also hoped to decode the mystery of golf, define the Fine Green Line, change my life with golf-related insights, and write a worthy book about it all. Anxiety about the eventual book was constant. Was I getting enough material? Was I taking enough notes? I couldn't just play lousy in a tournament and forget about it, I had to devise something meaningful to say about having played lousy.

All this, in addition to simply working on my game.

THE WEEKEND AFTER the tournament, Polly, Anna, and I spent two nights at The Breakers in Palm Beach. The Breakers is a ridiculously expensive pink resort surrounded by palm trees, Rolls-Royces, and people in pastel. We were fundamentally unsuited for this place—I was broke and Polly usually wore only black—but a golf magazine had offered to pay our expenses in exchange for a review, and we are not fools. I looked at it mostly as free food.

I mention the visit because of an incident with Anna. In the late afternoon one day she and I set up shop on the beach. Polly, as I recall, had gone off to spray-paint "Workers of the World Unite!" on the hotel's pink facade. Anna, in her tiny pink bathing suit, had a bucket and a shovel and instantly set to work moving a pile of sand from somewhere near my right foot to somewhere near my left foot. I lay back on my towel and watched. She was babbling merry nonsense and could not have been happier or more absorbed in her urgent task.

Yes, I thought, she was in the zone. She was in precisely the mental place I wanted to be in when I played golf. But why was she able to sustain her absorption and I wasn't?

She felt safe, for one thing. The reassuring bulk of her father an arm's length away guaranteed absolute security (so far as she knew). By contrast, I never felt secure on the golf course, at least not in tournament competition. For another thing, her task was interesting and challenging, yet not beyond her abilities. She had a high probability of success and knew it. At the same time, her work wasn't so simple as to be boring: the shovel sometimes bent, the sand hill eroded. I, by contrast, was beginning to feel overmatched by the challenge of competing on the mini-tours.

A final thing Anna had going for her was an absence of existential doubt about the sanity of her project. This was not true for me.

But maybe I just think too much. When you're in a golf slump, you grasp at whatever straws you can.

THE NEXT WEEK—my week off—I reopened Chuck Hogan's bag of tricks. It was literally a bag. At the seminar Hogan had given each of us a small canvas briefcase in which to tote home his material: books, pamphlets, videotapes, audiotapes, photocopied handouts, our individual notes.

Leafing through my notes, I happened upon a suggestion I had forgotten about. It involved "filling the image banks." Each time you hit a good shot, he advised, discipline yourself to pause for a moment and savor the sweet sensations. Call to mind all the delectable details of the shot and then "anchor" them with a distinctive gesture or phrase. The process is supposed to "emotionalize" the good shots. Most golfers, Hogan contended, ignore their good shots—they tend to think of them as their "usual game" and therefore nothing to make a big deal about—but give enormous psychic weight to the bad ones. They curse, berate themselves, hurl their clubs, and otherwise succumb to Range Rage.

I remember after the seminar settling on an "anchoring" gesture something like the violent arm pump Tiger Woods is famous for, coupled with an enthusiastic "Yeah!" But I found, frankly, that during a round I was usually too furious about my last bad shot to be in any sort of mood for "anchoring" a good one, and on the range it was simply too embarrassing to pump my arm all the time. I thought about altering the elements of my anchor, but before I could get around to it my interest lapsed.

Now, however, anchoring seemed like a promising antidote to Range Rage and the other murderous thoughts that sometimes popped up during rounds. With a little work I developed a more subtle anchor—a sibilant, smiling, through-the-teeth rendering of "Yes!"—and tried to remember to anchor as often as possible. Emphasize the good, forget about the bad: this would be my new policy.

Digging deeper into Hogan's bag of tricks, I discovered two audiotapes still in their cellophane wraps.

The first, "Exercises for Golfing Excellence," guides the listener through some general breathing and relaxation exercises ("Associate a color with the fresh energy coming in as you inhale. Let this color fill your lungs bottom to top.") and then proceeds to visualization drills. The fifth selection, for example, was "Peel an Orange." In it a sultry female voice invites the listener to imagine stripping an orange and eating it. "Take the section to your mouth, bite it in half, and let the flavor stimulate your palate," she coos slowly. "Notice its fragrance. Taste the juice as it squirts into your mouth. Is it sweet? Or is it tart? Now take a clean napkin and wipe the juice from your hands, your lips, and your chin." One afternoon as I listened to this tape on the couch, eyes closed, Polly burst into the room unexpectedly and asked what I was doing. I felt like I'd been caught with the baby-sitter.

The second tape, "Mindshapes: Images through Sound," consisted of subdued, electronic tones waxing and waning like wind through the trees. In theory, the sounds increased the number of beneficial alpha waves coursing through my brain, which in turn were supposed to facilitate better imaging and make me a better golfer. In practice, they usually just put me to sleep.

Even so, I had a good instinct about the tapes. They were pleasant to work with and seemed to help me channel my mind toward positive images of golf, rather than to the potent negative images my mind tended to fixate on by itself. "Weight lifting for the mind," Hogan called these exercises. I started listening twice a day. It was hard to detect any immediate change in my golf, but I can say that I began enjoying oranges more than I ever had before.

Also my dream life was more vivid. In one dream, for instance, Nick Faldo and I were chatting in a locker room after playing a round together. He was friendly and told me the key to success was rhythm. "Try not to hurry the backswing, that's the whole secret," he said. I was in a hurry to leave so as not to bother the great pro, but the laces on my spikes kept knotting. "Don't be in such a hurry,"

Faldo said. "I want to hear how you're doing on the mini-tours." Then we were in a pro shop and he insisted on buying me a shirt. In the dream we were equals, talking pro-to-pro. It was very encouraging. But then I woke up.

ONE EVENING AFTER dinner during the off week, I had a cosmic experience at Palm-Aire. I had been assigned to pick up Polly's visiting niece at the airport and decided to drop by the course for a little short-game practice on the way. The sun was beginning to set and the sky was magnificent: pink, gold, and magenta clouds above the palms. I wore a flowery Hawaiian shirt and my new flip-flops, and my only goal was to relax and enjoy myself for thirty minutes or so.

After a few minutes of putting I noticed that I was visualizing well—too well. If I read a putt to break two inches from right to left, I aimed at a spot two inches to the right of the hole and made my stroke. With uncanny accuracy, the ball would roll right over that spot: two inches to the right of the hole. Obviously, this was not my intention. It was my visualization, not my aim or my stroke, that had been off. Once I changed the visualization and started imagining the ball breaking toward the hole instead of the spot, I started making putts right and left. I sank three fifteen-footers in a row and then two twenty-five-footers.

It was so scary I quit putting and played with my sand wedge for a while. Here my visualization was similarly acute. From fluffy lies near the chipping green, I lobbed a half dozen balls in a row over a steep face bunker onto the fringe of the green and watched the balls trickle downhill to within a few feet of the hole. These were tricky shots but I nailed every one.

Then I got careless and lobbed one short. It buried deep into the sand about eighteen inches under the bunker's overhanging lip. "I wonder if I could make that shot?" I thought.

Basically the answer was no. It was virtually impossible. The hole was only twelve feet away on a steep downhill slope. But *in theory* it was possible. Some precise combination of force and clubface angle and the right amount of sand could theoretically cause the ball to pop out of its crater, land softly, and roll into the hole.

As I stood thinking about what it would take, I could literally feel my mind changing modes. It was as if some elixir had entered my bloodstream carrying warm, positive thoughts to replace the sense of impossibility. This transformation took only a few seconds to complete, but now I was totally convinced that I *could* make the shot.

For quite a long while, maybe two or three full minutes, I stood next to the ball sizing up the necessary physics. It was not easy, this mental process. It took energy. But I did it.

Finally, when I had the image securely in mind, I dug my feet into the sand, waggled the club briefly, and made my swing without hesitation. The ball did just what I had imagined it would. From a shower of sand it plopped gently onto the fringe, rolled slowly toward the pin, and then . . . glory of glories . . . tumbled into the heart of the cup.

As you can imagine, I was ecstatic. This one shot seemed to prove correct everything Chuck Hogan and Deborah Graham had been telling me. The power of the mind *is* extraordinary.

I knew I couldn't pull off shots like that regularly—this had been a special situation. The sun was setting, the stars were in alignment, I was unusually relaxed and had taken the time to work myself up into a state of absolute conviction. In real competition this would never happen. But it showed what *could* happen, it showed what was possible when one worked with the mind. On the way to the airport I had to laugh. Anna had had her moment in the sand, now I had mine.

THE NEXT TOURNAMENT was at Palm-Aire again, and I felt ready. My goal was to think about mechanics as little as possible—maybe one simple swing thought per round such as "stay in balance" or "take the club back slowly"—but otherwise, zilch. To enable this, following a recommendation in the GolfPsych material, I made a short list of things *not* to think about during the round. These included my cumulative score, any previous shot, and any white out-of-bounds stake. I then compiled a list of positive things I *should* try to think about between shots: the weather, my good fortune to be playing golf full-time, Anna on the beach.

I had a good tournament. My first round score was 78, second among amateurs. Off the tee I felt unusually confident, convincing myself most of the time that the fairways were actually quite wide (they weren't) and that, anyway, the drive is only a positioning setup shot for the approach (that's true). In the second round I continued to play well from tee to green, and as my confidence grew I noticed that my pre-shot routine took less time: I simply visualized the shot, took a deep breath, stepped up to the ball, and fired. On the front nine, however, I yipped two three-foot putts and subsequently lost my nerve around the greens. Even so, I hung in there—I listened to birdsongs as a distraction—and carded an 80, which earned me a small gift certificate.

All things considered, I was proud of my performance. The second round felt like work, but I had toughed it out.

MY LAST TOURNAMENT in Florida, in the first week of May, was the Miami Open at Key Biscayne. This was not a regular South Florida Tour event, though Tom Eubanks happened to be running it. It was a bona fide regional open with 140 competitors—sixty of them amateurs. I had been looking forward to Key Biscayne as a kind of midterm exam for the Year and a dry run for Q School. And the Links course at Key Biscayne, the site until recently of a PGA Senior Tour event, was a challenge: it was long (more than seven thousand yards), windswept, and fraught with water hazards.

In preparation I played the course twice, the second time with three local single-digit handicappers who would also be in the tournament. They were happy to share tips. On the par-three third hole, for instance, they advised me to use one or two clubs more than the scorecard distance indicated. The wind was always against you, they said, but you didn't notice it because trees shielded the tee box.

I kept careful notes during these rounds, creating a small, spiral-bound notebook with a diagram of each hole. In particular I mapped out the humps and plateaus of the greens, which were quite pronounced, and determined how I had to play my approach shots. I also marked areas where it was safe to bail out. It can give you a lot of confidence—hitting into a back, right pin—to know that behind the green to the back and right is open rough rather than, say, a swamp.

In the days leading up to the tournament I continued listening to the Chuck Hogan tapes and practicing rhythm on the range. And I'll admit I became a bit anal. I went so far as to write out a script for my activities starting the day before the event. "Friday: buy snack food for bag, clean grooves of clubs, visualize playing holes one, three, and eleven (the three toughest holes, in my estimation), stretch in P.M., Mindshapes tape before bed." My agenda for Saturday, the day of the tournament, was a minute-by-minute log starting when I arrived at the course ninety minutes before my tee time. My theory was that by sparing myself the horrible indecision of whether, for instance, to work on my chipping or putting first, I would be able to stay calm. Minutes zero to ten called for me to register, organize my bag, and put on suntan lotion. At minute thirty-five I would find a suitable tree, as Buddha had found his Bo tree, and sit beneath it visualizing to a Hogan tape for fifteen minutes. From minute sixty-five to minute seventy, I would practice short pitches. And so forth.

Owing to my respectable performance at Palm-Aire and my new, positive mental strategies, I was excited about the tournament. And bizarre as it may seem, the meticulous schedule I had drawn up for myself actually worked. I arrived at the first tee for round one feeling relaxed and confident. Frankly, my confidence had gotten a boost from inspecting the competition during my warm-ups. "I can beat *these* guys," I told myself. They were not the usual, recent-college-golf-team-graduates who dominated the amateur portion of the South Florida Tour. For the most part they were simply recreational golfers who could not possibly have played in as many rule-bound tournaments as I had recently. By comparison to them—or what I imagined them to be—I was a battle-hardened veteran. I had a *game*. I would be turning pro soon. *They* were the ones who ought to feel intimidated in this tournament, I thought.

From the opening drive I felt sharp. My rhythm was impeccable. I easily parred the first two holes, a par five and a par four, and on the par-three third I pulled a three-iron from my bag even though the distance was only 187 yards. I felt smart doing so—this was the hole the locals had told me always played into the wind. My boring shot came to rest four feet below the hole and I converted for a birdie. I also managed to birdie the next hole, a monster 642-yard par five, and after that I felt like a god.

I was also lucky in my playing companions. One was Jonas, a college kid I had played with once on the South Florida Tour. I *knew* I was a better player than he was, which gave me confidence. The other player, John Kent, was in his late twenties and said during one of our frequent long waits that the best mental game advice he'd ever heard was to be your own best friend on the course. On this day, however, he treated *me* like his best friend. He sensed that I had a special round going—I was one-under-par at the turn—and gave me every encouragement possible. After my lone double-bogey of the round, on eleven, he told me, "Slow down, slow down. You've got a great round going." On the next hole, a par three, he dumped his tee ball in a bunker but then told me, "Well, I know where *you're* gonna put it. Right by the cup." And I did, too. The golf course during a tournament can be a lonely and vulnerable place, especially when you feel you're about to fall apart. It's rare for another competitor to come through with just the right level of moral support, but Kent did and that was a big reason I did as well as I did.

The final six holes of the round were iffy. It was hard not to worry about spoiling a good round, and my swing became tentative. But I saved par a couple of times with good chips and made only one real bonehead play. That was on the eighteenth, when I missed my three-foot cleanup putt for par simply because I was so excited about finishing with a good score. So I lost a stroke there but still posted a 75.

Walking off the course I knew it was the best round of my life. The course rating at Key Biscayne from the back tees we played was 75.2. The wind had been blowing steadily at over twenty miles an hour all day, with stronger gusts. And unlike my leisurely, long-ago round of 69, I had earned this 75 under tournament conditions.

Since our group had gone out in the middle of the field, I did not wait around to see all the day's scores come in. Only the next morning when I returned to Key Biscayne did I learn that I was tied for the amateur *lead*, news that hit me like a blow to the gut. A man named Dan Bradley had also shot 75 and another amateur 76—we three would be paired in the last group for the final round. Altogether only ten amateurs from the field of sixty broke 80, and my 75 beat more than a quarter of the pros.

Preparing for the round, my stomach was jumping like a sackful of horned toads. I grew even more nervous when Tom Eubanks, after congratulating me on my score, showed me the trophy I stood to win. It was beautiful, made of crystal and inscribed with the words: "1996 Miami Open Amateur Champion." I stared at the thing dumbfounded, particularly the word "Champion." A month earlier when I had tried to envision myself as a champion, all I could conjure up was an image of myself as a slump-shouldered joke. Now here I was in contention for a title with a trophy! My heart started banging. For a second or two my vision dimmed and I grew light-headed.

In a daze I wandered back to the parking lot to fetch my clubs. I had parked next to a blue van whose side door slid open just as I popped my trunk and Mike McNearney, the tall skinny pro from the South Florida Tour I had gotten to know, hoisted himself out. He had been sleeping inside after a night of partying—till 3 A.M.!— at Miami's South Beach. He looked as rumpled and drowsy as a bear after hibernation.

He asked how I'd done the day before and I told him excitedly, and he offered his congratulations.

"How did you play?" I asked

"Not so great. I screwed up the back nine pretty bad."

"What did you shoot?"

"Sixty-nine."

Just in case I had any illusions.

Given how well my round had gone the day before, I tried to follow the same typed-out, pretournament activity schedule, but it wasn't the same. I was too distracted by random thoughts and quickly fell behind. Beneath the Bo tree, for instance, instead of envisioning myself conquering the three toughest holes, I fantasized shooting a 64—the way champion wanna-bes do, not real champions like Jack Nicklaus.

Then on the first tee I met the competition, and this drove a stake through any presumptions I may have had. Dan Bradley was about fifty, with soulful brown eyes and immensely strong forearms. Both he and the guy who shot 76 had made it more than once to the finals of the U.S. Amateur. They were *players*, not the recreational patsies I had condescendingly imagined everyone in the field to be the day before. Though I had played as well as either of them in round one, suddenly I felt out of my league. And that, of course, is death.

"I *do* deserve to be here," I started telling myself in a panicky tone. "I'm as good as these guys. I really am. The advantage is all mine. I'm tournament-tough from the mini-tours. I'm a really good golfer. I swear I am, I really am."

But I didn't believe it. That's the problem with positive self-propaganda: You have to genuinely believe it, or else it's just words.

The round started out shakily with a weak par and a weaker bogey. But on three, the par three I had birdied the day before, I got mad at myself and pulled off a great shot. It wasn't the tee shot—I botched that into a bunker short of the green. But when I stepped into the bunker I recalled my cosmic sand session at Palm-Aire the week before. I did study the shot with close to the same intensity I had then. It would not be easy. I had to get the ball up quickly and carry it eighty feet in the air. But after a few moments I felt I understood what had to be done—a very hard swing, for one thing. Swallowing hard, I stepped up to the ball and had at it. The ball lifted magnificently out of the trap, like a rocket rising through smoke, and settled softly on the green four feet above the hole.

"Well, that's as good as *this* cowboy can hit a sand shot," I told my competitors. It occurred to me that this was just the sort of shot that could turn a match around. Dan Bradley was also four feet from the hole, albeit *below* the hole and lying only one. If he should miss and I should make, we would tie and the game would be on.

But that did not happen. Bradley made, for a birdie. I missed, not once but four times. In my defense, the first putt was not easy. It was slick, both sidehill and downhill, and I made a good stroke. The ball just missed the high edge of the hole and kept rolling and rolling downhill. As for my next three putts, I guess you could say I choked. Triple-bogey.

The rest of my round was not the worst golf I've ever played. I hung in reasonably well, considering the degree of my deflation after that four-putt triple. I birdied eleven and held the honors for the rest of the round. But my final score was 85, seven worse than Bradley, who won the tournament by two.

In the clubhouse bar afterward, thirty or so amateurs hung around to watch Bradley accept the crystal championship trophy and make an impromptu speech. The room was as quiet as a church.

"Golf's a hard game," he started out, communicating as much with his eyes as with his voice. It was a strangely emotional moment—not just for Bradley, but for me. I felt proud of the guy. He was divorced (he had mentioned this during the round) and judging by appearances didn't have much money. But he did have golf, and he had learned to play the game well—solidly, at close to his full potential, even under pressure. And his game was for real, an authentic accomplishment.

"Anytime you win one of these things, you've done something," he continued. "I don't care what level you play at, a victory means a lot. I feel very humbled."

We clapped when Bradley finished. We all understood what a commitment of heart and soul it takes to win even a minor tournament like this. Competing successfully at golf is not just a matter of learning and executing skills. The skills only get you to the table. The hard part is discovering how to integrate those skills into your character, with who you are as a person. My hat was off to Dan Bradley. He seemed like a man who had learned a lot about golf and through golf about himself.

As for me, I left Florida satisfied. I had played one round of golf, the first round at Key Biscayne, which seemed genuinely accomplished. Now, if I could build on that round in the months ahead, learn to repeat it at will, I might actually have a chance of making it through the first stage at Q School.

· SECTION THREE ·

On the Road

The least thing upset him on the links. He missed short putts because of the uproar of butterflies in the adjoining meadows.

—P. G. WODEHOUSE

WHEN I WAS A BOY GROWING UP IN FORT Worth, our route to church each Sunday morning wound past the golf course at Colonial Country Club—Hogan's Alley, so-called because Ben Hogan won five PGA tournaments there. Stiffly stuffed into my coat and tie, I might easily have envied the golfers their fun and sworn to myself that someday I would return to Colonial as a great champion.

But I didn't.

For one thing, I didn't give a fig for golf at the time. For another thing, I was convinced that every one of those golfers was headed straight for hell. No one told me this, I had figured it out entirely by myself. It was only logical: they weren't going to church, therefore they were heathens and going to hell. And frankly, I was disturbed: How could anyone be so shortsighted as to risk eternal damnation for a diddly-squat sport like golf?

This memory flashed through my mind during a lunch stop on my drive back from Florida to New York in early May. Polly, Anna, and the cats had already returned by air, so I was by myself. Near Florence, South Carolina, I found a good old Southern-style cafeteria and settled in for meat loaf and overcooked green beans. Suddenly the dining room began to fill: men and scrub-faced boys in coats and ties, women and girls in pretty dresses. I had forgotten, it was a Sunday. The churchgoers' presence made me uneasy. I was wearing shorts, flip-flops, and the same ratty golf shirt I'd had on for two days. I hadn't shaved in a week. Furthermore, I was reading a suspect book: *Creative Visualization* by Shakti Gawain. The cover depicted a gowned Far Eastern woman praying to a lotus flower.

To make myself less conspicuous I slunk down into my booth, but across the way I noticed a towheaded boy of eight or nine staring at me goggle-eyed. I knew just what he was thinking: I was a heathen, headed straight for hell.

Was this true? Was my soul in jeopardy? Had golf become a kind of secular stand-in for the religion of my youth? God and golf. Golf and God. The words sounded so similar. Both were stern masters. Both demanded all you could give, yet you still fell far short of the mark. Both reached back across the centuries. It wasn't hard to think of golf as a kind of historical church: every Sunday morning since the late Middle Ages believers have assembled in natural sanctuaries (think of fairways as aisles, greens as altars) to prostrate themselves before the game's inscrutable mysteries. Simultaneously humbled and elated, they vow to improve, pray for atonement from past subpar performance, and beg for grace.

Even the way I had stumbled onto golf as an adult smacked of a conversion experience. My life was a mess, I was in the midst of a divorce, I was aging. I longed for something to believe in and golf answered the call. It was suffused with familiar moral qualities: the certainty of personal failure, the possibility of redemption, the occasional vouchsafed glimpses of perfection, the imperative to carry on no matter what misfortunes befell. It even occurred to me that golf itself was a kind of salvation, a release from the madcap pointlessness of everyday life.

These half-baked notions drifted through my head as the boy across the way, that version of myself thirty years ago, continued to observe me. After a while I became annoyed, by both his attention and the burdensome thoughts his attention triggered. And so slowly I turned my unshaven face in his direction—I was the Devil incarnate!—and mouthed the word "Boo!"

The boy quickly looked away, clearly frightened, and started shoveling cubes of red Jell-O into his mouth.

BACK ON THE interstate, heading north, I asked myself an important question: Was I some kind of fool? Did I really expect golf to deliver metaphysical solutions to my vexing life questions?

I had to admit that in conceiving the Year, I had murkily hoped so. One friend, when I described my projected quest, suggested I title the book *The Adventures of John Paul Quixote.* "But instead of misinterpreting everything in terms of chivalry and knight errantry like Don Quixote did," he said, "you'll misinterpret everything in terms of deep thoughts and midlife crises. It'll be hilarious."

Well, this guy happens to be a wiseass, but I took his point. I did have a tendency to overinterpret. But looking back over the three months of total golf immersion in Florida, I was gratified to note how seldom my mind had actually wandered into transcendental realms. Many of the things about golf I had formerly suspected of being "mystical" now seemed more earthbound. My twilight revelation in the bunker at the Palm-Aire, to take one example, didn't seem magical so much as simply a demonstration of the power of confidence.

Many years ago when I first read Norman Maclean's wonderful book *A River Runs Through It,* I copied out a favorite passage and taped it to the wall beside my desk. The book is about fly-fishing, which Maclean learned from his father, a Presbyterian minister, and the passage was about his father: "To him all good things—trout as well as eternal salvation—come by grace, and grace comes by art, and art does not come easy."

Substitute "birdies" for "trout," and that's about where I was now. Maybe, with all the hard work I had put into developing my skills, "art" would begin to happen in my game. My first round at Key Biscayne had contained a little art, I wanted to believe. And if I kept working hard, maybe my art would improve to the point where I could experience grace on a semi-regular basis.

As for eternal salvation, I'd leave that for another day.

MY PLAN FOR the rest of the spring and summer was to compete in a full schedule of professional tournaments—mini-tour events, state opens, USGA qualifiers, whatever I could find—without giving up my thrifty status as an amateur. I had not yet decided when to turn pro.

Refining one's schedule is a year-round preoccupation for itinerant mini-tour players. It is a constant topic of conversation at the range. There seem to be two distinct strategies.

The first is Show Me the Money. The objective here is simply to enter those tournaments with the biggest purses. Big-field state opens, events with added money from sponsors or local communities like the fabled Dakotas Tour, and sponsored USGA or local PGA section events headed the list. The pros most likely to pursue this approach are those most serious about making it to the Big Time. They figure if they can't learn to win in these types of events, they'll never win on Tour.

The second strategy is Show Me the Odds. This requires more sophisticated analysis. State opens are popular to the extent that they attract more local club pros than touring pros. Coming down the stretch with real money on the line, the theory goes, club pros are more likely to fade. Small-field events are another possibility. The overall purses are smaller but most organizers pay the top one or two spots an outsize portion thereof. Depending on a player's confidence and his assessment of the competition, small-field events can be an attractive financial option.

For me, of course, none of these considerations mattered. My main concern was sampling a variety of tournaments within a reasonable driving distance of Orient. In putting together my schedule, one of the snowbird pros I had met in South Florida, Eric Coultoff, was particularly helpful.

Like me, Eric lived most of the year on Long Island, but unlike me he was meticulously organized. He toted a black, hard-sided briefcase jammed with files—brochures, fact sheets, and applications—about dozens of tournaments in the Northeast. He maintained a list of useful mini-tour phone numbers and regularly printed out an updated version of his own schedule, projected six months in advance, which he bound between plastic covers.

Eric strongly recommended that I make the North Atlantic Tour the heart of my summer schedule. He showed me the tour's brochure, which featured a picture of the owner, Buddy Young, wearing a sporty fishing hat. "You'll get a kick out of Buddy," he said. "Buddy's like no one else." The North Atlantic Tour staged tournaments from May through September across New England and in upstate New York.

I was eager to continue competing and would have entered a North Atlantic event the week after returning from Florida, but unfortunately I had sustained an injury. During my practice sessions for the last tournament at Palm-Aire, I developed a niggling pain in my lower right rib, possibly due to banging on the course's unusually hard fairways. The pain grew worse through the tournament at Key Biscayne, but I thought a week of abstinence during the move back to Orient would take care of the matter. It didn't. A few days after unpacking, I hit a few easy wedge shots at the Greenport fairgrounds (no Indian Joe!) and the following morning could barely get out of bed. Bending, twisting, reaching—each of these movements tripped a pain switch at the bottom of my rib cage and in my back beneath the scapula. The doctor, after probing my pain with what felt like a machete and taking X-rays, diagnosed either a hairline fracture of the rib or a pulled muscle. Treatment in either case was the same: rest until the pain went away.

I happened to talk by phone a few days later with an old neighbor of my family from Fort Worth, Jim Grubbs. Jim was a superb and avid golfer—he had been to the U.S. Amateur finals twice—and had suffered a similar rib problem for two summers running. He said I should expect to keep my clubs in the garage for three to four weeks.

"I can't lay off for a month!" I howled.

"I know, it's a hard pill to swallow," he said.

"I've got momentum. I'm making progress."

"Work on your mental game."

Jim was a psychiatrist who often treated golfers, although—disappointingly—not with the objective of lowering their handicaps. Rather, he used his patients' golf experiences as a tool to help them get their non-golf lives together. Even so, he knew a lot about the mental game and I sought some free advice.

One thing he warned me about was the potentially negative effects of the self-hypnosis techniques Chuck Hogan preached. A young mini-tour player from Jim's club in Dallas had had bad luck with visualization. "He went to Hogan, too, and became very proficient—too proficient. Because after a while he stopped being able to visualize good shots, he could only visualize bad shots, and couldn't get those horrifying images out of his mind. And that was the end of him as a golfer. He never could recover."

Jim applauded my work on rhythm. To enrich his own rhythm, he said he sometimes listened to waltz tapes on his drive to a tournament and hummed popular songs during rounds. We talked on and on—about overcoming childhood fears, about curing the yips, about the thrilling percussive plunk the ball makes when it falls into the cup—for over an hour. And this was a guy I hardly knew. He had been my brother's friend, six years older. To the extent he had paid me attention back in those days, I was just "The Babe" or "The Punk." But here we were years later, two virtual strangers, talking about our childhood anxieties and the songs we hummed under our breath. What else but golf could have brought us together in this way?

When we hung up I realized that somewhere along the line, without my quite knowing it, I had ceased being an oddball, isolated golf dilettante, riding the subway to ranges and hiding my obsession from most of my acquaintances. I was now a member of the fraternity. It pleased me to think I was not alone anymore. There would always be men out there—and women, too—with whom I could share this passion, down to the silliest details.

As FRUSTRATING AS my little injury was, I didn't lack for things to do as the rib healed. For one thing I had to buy a car. Over the next six months I anticipated driving more than fifteen thousand miles, and my current car, a 1966 Chrysler with roughly 170,000 miles on it (the precise mileage was unknowable since the odometer had broken years before at 138,770), was clearly not up to the task. Our good car, the nine-year-old Honda with 110,000 miles, would obviously have to stay with Polly and Anna.

Over the years I had had good luck with used cars. The Chrysler, for instance, had served me well as a summer car for a decade, despite my only having paid $16.50 to buy it. (The seller and I had actually agreed on fifteen dollars, but in consummating the deal we discovered I had nothing smaller than a twenty and he had only $3.50 in change.) So I wasn't looking for anything fancy. And that's what I found in the parking lot at Island's End one afternoon: a pitiful-looking 1988 Olds Cutlass with a For Sale sign in the rear window. My heart leaped. The owner, I knew, could not possibly be asking much for this heap: the finish, formerly black, had half disappeared, revealing the white undercoating; upholstery sagged from the ceiling; the hubcaps were missing. Just as I had my face pressed to the window to read the odometer (123,000 miles), the owner walked up. He was a New York City cop who had used the car daily for his 120-mile round-trip commute from Long Island where he lived to his station house in Fort Apache, the Bronx. I drove the car, detected no major problems, and bought it for five hundred dollars even.

Something about the Olds made me supremely happy. Its disreputable paint job bespoke danger, yet the car rode as smoothly and decadently as a good American car should. A friend of Polly's who had once owned a similar vehicle bestowed the gift of a name: Mr. Lucky. He said he had always felt lucky to get where he was going in his old car, and so should I.

I also busied myself with putting during the interregnum, which I could do without pain. In fact, the time off gave me a chance to radically alter my regime. I had read somewhere in a book that practice strokes over the ball interfere with the intense pre-shot visualizations of a putt going into the hole. So I tried dispensing with my practice strokes over the ball and found I made more putts. The change required working out an entirely new pre-putt routine (I now took a few practice strokes while visualizing the line from behind the ball) but I had plenty of time to do so.

Other than that I spent my time doing painless tasks around the house and yard, in a (probably vain) attempt to accumulate a backlog of brownie points with Polly for the time I would be gone, and sitting around my office thinking up harebrained schemes for getting better at golf.

One scheme of which I was particularly fond—just to give you an idea—grew out of a profile I read in *The New Yorker* of the concert pianist Alfred Brendel. Brendel, it seems, still gets extremely nervous before each performance. To overcome his fear, he works himself into a lather of conviction that each performance is a *gift* he is giving the audience. He interprets the music for *them*, not for himself, and therefore he owes it to them to stay composed. But of course! I thought. I could approach golf the same way. Rather than wallow self-indulgently in my own petty anxieties, I could view each tournament round as something I was doing for others, a performance for their pleasure, a gift. The only unresolved detail was who might possibly want such a gift. Polly? Not bloody likely. The other guys in my pairing? God? Soon I was imagining myself playing golf for the same ecstatic reason the imbecile in *Chariots of Fire* ran cross-country: "to feel His glory!" Visions of myself winning tournaments with the *Chariots of Fire* soundtrack echoing down the fairways filled my imagination.

BY EARLY JUNE my rib had healed. So early one Sunday morning I piled my clubs, a duffel bag of golf shirts and spare pants, and a suede briefcase crammed with waltz tapes and meditation books into Mr. Lucky and headed north to Vermont.

Marring the departure was a tiff with Polly. Nothing serious—I couldn't even remember the ostensible subject by the time I was on the auto ferry that sails from Orient to the Connecticut coast—but it was a sure indication, I knew, of the stress my travels would put on our family in the months ahead. I intended never to be gone more than two or three weeks at a time, and usually just four or five days at a time, but that was a lot. Meanwhile Polly would be left alone in Orient with a two-year-old to look after. This was an aspect of the Year we had anticipated, but neither of us knew how things would pan out, emotionally speaking. The argument left me feeling dejected and uneasy. How did Tour pros with families do this year after year? It must be hell on the wives, but also on the pros.

But the human mind is resilient, and golf so seductive. By the time I pulled into the Lake Morey Country Club in tiny Fairlee, Vermont, my concerns had been displaced by zeal.

The three-round Vermont Open always attracts a full field of 220, mostly pros, and it wasn't hard to see why. The course, though not wildly challenging, was charming. It fills most of a small mountain valley, threading beneath towering firs, hard by a two-hundred-acre lake. For forty-five dollars a night I stayed in a simply furnished wooden cabin that belonged to the Lake Morey Inn, and took a swim each afternoon off the dock. The people who run the tournament, from the rules officials to the brassy woman who announces the players' names (often incorrectly), make everyone feel at home. Several times over the years, while hiking in the New England mountains, I have looked down on a distant golf course in a white-steepled village like Fairlee and thought to myself how beneficent civilization sometimes is. Now I was preparing to spend four days here.

I arrived in time for my practice round on Sunday, which was actually a one-day tournament unto itself, with modest prizes for the pros. By chance I was paired with a redheaded pro named David Ladd, whom I knew slightly from the South Florida Tour. He had been one of the frequent money-winners there, but on this day his driving was abysmal. On every other hole, it seemed, he had to pitch back into the fairway from the woods. Nevertheless he finished with a 69 and won some money.

He did it with putting. On the greens he had no fear. On the front nine he rammed most of his lag putts five feet or more past the hole, but made every comebacker. By the back nine he'd figured out the speed of the greens and rolled in three lengthy snakes for birdies. I didn't see him miss a putt of less than ten feet all day.

"So that's how they do it," I thought. No question about it, the short game rules.

My round, by contrast, deeply sucked. Before the round I sat on the dock contemplating how I would interpret the Lake Morey course with wit and grace, à la Alfred Brendel, for the pleasure of David Ladd. But Ladd, I immediately noticed, was not paying attention—and why should he? I hit my opening drive into the street and followed that with a stubbed chip and three putts for a quintuple-bogey. Had I been Brendel, at this point I would have smashed my palms on the keyboard and stormed off the stage.

That evening and the following morning, I counseled patience for myself. My expectations of doing well had grown irrationally during the month of quarantine, but first I had to get back into the tournament swing. This did not happen during the first nine holes I played in the tournament. I scored a 45, my anger rising with each hole to near Range Rage proportions. But then on the eighteenth hole (my ninth), the anger suddenly expired. Maybe I was exhausted, but it whooshed out of my system like air from a balloon. I visualized the tiny rubber bladder that had contained my anger fluttering harmlessly to the turf, a trivial and inconsequential thing.

In an instant my mood and my body altered. I felt bluesy and subdued, like the morning after a regrettable alcoholic bender, but positive.

I easily parred eighteen with a smooth wedge and two putts, and birdied the next hole, number one. The tee shot on this hole, a 205-yard par three with out-of-bounds tight on the left, was darn near perfect. I can still see it soaring high against the backdrop of dark green mountains and braking to a halt two feet from the pin. The shot drew applause from the spectators around the clubhouse. I took a theatrical bow.

I toured this nine in 34, which gave me 79 for the day, and I posted an even better 75 in the second round. This 75 didn't compare to the 75 at Key Biscayne—the course was much easier—but I was pleased. My 154 total made the amateur cut for the tournament's final round.

ONE OF THE pros I played with in the second round was Don Robertson, a driving range instructor from Dallas and a frequent caddie on the PGA and Nike Tours. He was about my age, with blue eyes, curly hair, and a droopy mustache, and I had never seen anyone make golf look more like blue-collar work. On the next to last hole, needing to finish with two pars to make the cut for pros, Robertson plopped his approach shot into a bunker. When he saw the ball's lie in the sand—partially buried, on a downslope—he said "Shit," but with no self-drama or panicked sense of alarm. This was just another fix to get out of, another task in the day-to-day life of a golf pro. He stepped into the bunker with the world-weary air of a coal miner lowering himself into the pit, figured out what needed doing, and then did it. He splashed the ball satisfactorily onto the green, ten feet from the hole, and made the putt for par.

"Nice up and down," I complimented him as we walked to the next tee.

He shook his head. "Tough way to make a living, huh?"

That night I had dinner with Robertson and a pro friend of his, Kerry Johnston, who now mostly works for a golf course design company in Palm Springs, California. They dished a lot of skinny on the world of minor league professional golf.

"It used to be you could slip into tournaments like this and win five hundred, a thousand, fifteen hundred dollars pretty easy," Johnston told me as we waited for steaks. "Things like the Waterloo Open in Iowa—now there you have a pretty good purse, a hundred thousand dollars I think, and it used to be you could count on taking home a good share of it. But now you show up and run into twenty guys you know—twenty guys who are *players*. The fields everywhere you go nowadays are definitely much better and much *deeper* than they used to be. You've got to bring your 'A' game every time if you want to make money anymore."

Robertson said that he'd been to seventeen or eighteen Q Schools, the last in 1981, and was unsuccessful every time. "Who needs that anymore. It's expensive. The entry fee is up to, what, three thousand dollars now, plus hotel, food, and a caddie. I'll tell you another good place to lose a lot of money fast—the Nike Tour. Fifty grand a year at least to play the Nike Tour, if you play every week. There aren't many guys on the Nike who earn that kind of money."

Robertson and Johnston now play almost exclusively in state opens and lucrative once-a-year regional events like the Waterloo or the Queen Mary Open in Long Beach, California. They don't have much use for the mini-tours. "Playing for your own money week after week, against the same guys on the same courses—those aren't real tournaments," Robertson said dismissively.

But their favorite tournaments to play in were "invitationals," which I had never heard of. These are small, local events sponsored by individual clubs. One to two dozen pros, selected as much for their ability to flatter as their ability to play, get invites to compete with three amateur partners—club members, usually—for purses that are often decent, given the small number of pros competing. A pro lucky enough to draw a sandbagging amateur (that is, a player significantly better than his posted handicap) can sometimes win checks on both ends, the pro and the team competition, and clear five thousand dollars or more. Coupled with a few winning side bets, which amateurs are often eager to make, it can make for a lucrative week. Johnston, in fact, was helping organize a small invitational for later that month in the Catskills. That was one reason he was here, to issue invitations to guys he ran into at the Vermont Open.

I asked the two about cheating. Pros desperate to meet expenses must be awfully tempted to cheat, I speculated.

"It *can* happen," Johnston said, looking to see if Robertson wanted to handle this question. Robertson didn't.

"The most common method is the old eraser, especially in the pro-ams. The pros usually keep the score, and the amateurs tend to be too involved with their own games to notice a few strokes disappearing here and there, or else too intimidated to say anything if they do notice."

However, he said, cheaters and scoundrels don't last long. Robertson told a story about a guy—he wouldn't divulge the name— famous for bouncing checks and borrowing money without repaying it. "Generally, he just nickel-and-dimed you to death—five bucks here, twenty bucks there—but it was annoying." One time this guy and another pro shared a rental car for a few weeks while touring the New England state opens and when they were done, the scoundrel volunteered to return the car to the rental office. Which of course he didn't for about three months. The rental was on the other guy's credit card, so he got a bill for thousands of dollars in unexpected charges.

"But the crazy thing is, this guy had the balls to show up in New England the following year," Robertson said. "He was acting friendly and all, but I wouldn't speak to him. For one thing, he'd bounced a check to Kerry here, as well as screwing the other guy. So after a couple of days he comes up to me and says, 'Don, are you avoiding me or something?' and I gave him the what-to for three or four minutes—I mean, putting my finger in his face and telling him off. 'You're screwing my friends, you're a snake,' and on like that. He listens and then walks away without saying anything. But then he turns back around and says, 'Yeah, I knew it was *something*. . . .'"

Johnston laughed. "It was unbelievable. The guy had no sense of right or wrong. But the thing is, that's one joker who can't ever show his face in golf anywhere again. The word is out on him. And a reputation like that is what keeps there from being too many cheaters around."

THE NEXT MORNING I got to the course at daybreak and had coffee while watching the pretty mountain valley fill up with golfers. What a playground this was. A lodge by a lake, guys without women (for the most part). It was like summer camp for grown-ups. I could understand why men like Robertson and Johnston find it hard to quit this life. From here many of the pros would be going to the Massachusetts Open, the Cape Cod Open, the Maine Open, the New Hampshire Open, and other, more minor events. Not a bad itinerary for summertime fun. Packs of males, swarming across the land, having a ball.

These lovely thoughts evaporated as my tee time approached, however. That's the pity of competitive golf: inside the game it's agony and hell. At least it was for me that day.

I was paired for the final round with a young French Canadian named Stephane Lavoie. We were the first two out—the dew-sweepers, in golf tour parlance. Lavoie sprayed his drives left and right, often into neighboring fairways, but still managed to beat the socks off me with a 73. He hit one miraculous recovery shot after another—high slices around doglegs, low knockdowns under tree limbs, pitches deliberately bounced off cart paths over bunkers, chips that rolled fifty feet into the hole. It was exasperating, particularly since I was bunting safe little three-woods down the middle of the fairway like a good boy and still lost hole after hole. Until the final three holes I actually scored fairly well, but then I made two double-bogeys by hitting wedge shots absurdly fat—for no reason at all, total blunders. My score was 82. It could easily have been 75.

After signing my card I threw myself sullenly into a booth in the clubhouse and ordered a beer. On the table I noticed a newspaper someone had left. The front page featured a photo of two men in a river over the caption: "Despair."

"Yeah, I'll tell you something about despair," I said disgustedly and tossed the paper aside. I wanted to fume some more about my 82.

But after a while, once the beer came, I grew curious and picked up the paper again to read the caption. "Two men, one a state trooper, comforting each other after trying to save a baby tossed off a bridge in Alabama. The trooper briefly had the baby in his grasp before losing it."

I was stunned. My heart broke into a thousand pieces, right there on the table. To lose a baby like that. Suddenly the despair I felt about the 82 seemed absurd.

When I got home that night, after a long drive and trip on the ferry, it was after eleven o'clock. Polly met me at the door.

"How did you play?" she asked.

"Not bad," I said. "The course was in a lovely valley."

And together we snuck into Anna's room to watch her sleep.

13 · *Playing for Buddy*

I FIRST MET BUDDY YOUNG, SOLE OWNER OF the North Atlantic Tour, on the putting green at the Willimantic Country Club in Connecticut. It was twilight and I was squeezing in some last-minute chipping practice when I heard the screen door of the clubhouse slam and animated voices coming down the slope. It was a foursome: three strapping young men, two of whom I knew, and a gaunt, white-haired, older gentleman in a madras porkpie hat—Buddy.

"Jesus Christ, Klemmer, sober up," I heard Buddy say. "We're trying to stage a competition here." Each had a can of beer in hand.

The young men pulled putters from their golf bags, which were leaning against a stone wall nearby, and carefully placed their beers down on the grass. It was fast getting dark.

"All right, the rules of this competition will be as follows," Buddy began. Then he noticed me. "I see we have an interloper." One of the young men was Buddy's son, Chris, who introduced me. "Oh, yes. The writer fellow," Buddy said, bowing slightly from the waist with mock formality. "Charmed, I'm sure." He appeared to be in his early sixties, with pale skin, ruddy cheeks, and ice-blue eyes.

After a few minutes of organization, the putting contest began. But before the first hole could be completed, Buddy grew distracted by my chipping.

"Jesus Christ, J. P., is that how an intellectual chips?" he said. "Klemmer, get over here and show J. P. how to chip. And for God's sake, don't embarrass me."

Joe Klemmer was one of the tour's top players, a strong, lanky, good-looking pro in his mid-twenties. Klemmer did as he was told. He asked for the seven-iron I was using and demonstrated his method of chipping to a particular spot on the green rather than to the hole itself—not unlike Joe Daley's technique, only less scientific. Then he returned my club and Buddy demanded that I show what I had learned, which I reluctantly did. My first two attempts came off well enough, but I bladed the third, the ball skittering to the far edge of the green.

"Too much thinking, J. P.," Buddy said, shaking his head. "You'll find that most of the guys who do well out here are morons. Not that I have anything against morons, mind you. Nice guys, a lot of them. But they don't have a thought in their heads."

Buddy invited me to join in the putting competition, but this required a resetting of the complicated wagering system, which resulted in ten minutes of silly bickering over such minutiae as "double-nickel presses" and "automatic stymies," none of which I understood. In the midst of this discussion Klemmer came over to me, planted himself unsteadily, grabbed both my biceps with his hands, and made a heartfelt little speech. "The North Atlantic

Tour is the best tour anywhere. I've played all over the world and these people are the nicest people I've ever met. They are the nicest and the best people you'll ever meet. I'd rather get a ruling from Mr. Young here than from anyone else in the world, period."

"They *do* seem very nice," I agreed, prying his fingers off my biceps.

By the time the bets could be worked out, the putting competition was abandoned on account of darkness. More haggling ensued, this of a logistical nature, and somehow I was elected to give Buddy a lift to his motel. Normally Buddy and Chris rode together, but Buddy explained to me en route that Chris was "trying to secure alternate lodging for the evening." Translation: Chris had the hots for a waitress at the clubhouse.

ON THE TWENTY-MINUTE drive to the Best Western motel in Mansfield, Buddy told me about the tour. He purchased the business in 1993. Previously it had been less a mini-tour than simply a series of indifferently managed summertime tournaments on Cape Cod. Buddy's vision was to transform the North Atlantic Tour into a relatively big-time mini-tour drawing professionals from across the country. His model was the Dakotas Tour, which with the backing of local banks, sporting goods stores, and chambers of commerce attracted scores of fine young players to the featureless Midwestern plains each July and August.

"No reason we couldn't do that here," Buddy said. "Because where would you rather spend the summer—Bismarck, North Dakota, or New England?"

Despite Buddy's efforts, the tour had not yet jelled. Mini-tours suffer from the same catch-22 that nightclubs and restaurants do: large numbers of paying customers don't show up unless the place is perceived as "hot," but the place will never be "hot" until large numbers of paying customers show up. To get the ball rolling, Buddy told me he had already sunk forty thousand dollars of his own money into the tour, mostly by guaranteeing a two-thousand or three-thousand-dollar check to the winner even when the size of the field didn't warrant it. Certainly this guarantee helped attract players, but Buddy was disappointed in their number. The pro field at that week's Willimantic tournament, for instance, was only twenty-one.

If anyone had the credentials to put New England on the national mini-tour map, it would be Buddy. His special expertise was the rules; immediately before buying the North Atlantic Tour he had been the head rules official for the New England PGA section. Before that he had been tournament director for the South African PGA Tour, where he got to know such future stars as Ernie Els. "I've run more than four thousand tournaments in my life," he said. "Have you ever met a guy that could say that?"

I asked Buddy if he played golf himself.

"I did in my day. I played my million rounds, won my share of tournaments—won over a hundred amateur tournaments—but I never could master it. Let me tell you: the game will drive you shithouse if you let it. Now I don't play at all."

Buddy said he didn't expect many of the North Atlantic players to reach the big time. The only one he was willing to vouch for was a guy named Rodney Butcher. "Rodney's not here this week, but you'll see him. He's a dead cinch for the PGA Tour. He won the Vermont Open a few weeks ago. Another possibility is Klemmer. Klemmer has the talent and the temperament to make it, but whether he also has the desire, that I can't predict. Most of the other kids got no chance. But how are they going to know that unless they try? All I'm trying to do is create a place where guys can get some experience without being chewed to pieces. We know our station, here on the North Atlantic Tour."

When we got to the Best Western, I carried Buddy's bag up to the room. Unfortunately, Chris had somehow given Buddy the wrong key and we barged in on a guy in his underwear flicking channels on the TV. It wasn't an easy life Buddy had laid out for himself.

· · ·

THE WILLIMANTIC TOURNAMENT would actually be my second North Atlantic event, but Buddy had not been at my debut tournament the week before, the so-called Narragansett Open at Exeter, Rhode Island. All of Buddy's tournaments had grand, classy-sounding monikers: the New Hampshire Classic, the Greater Rome Open (Rome, New York, that is), the Catskill Classic. Technically the tournament at Willimantic was the Eastern Connecticut Open, but no one ever called it anything but "Willimantic." Likewise, no one ever called the Narragansett Open anything but Exeter. As best as I could tell, the official names were basically fictions designed to look good on players' résumés.

Exeter was something of a mess, as far as tournament organization went. To spare myself the expense of staying in a motel the night before, I had arisen at 5 A.M. to catch the dawn ferry from Orient to New London, Connecticut, and then driven like a maniac up Interstate 95 to reach the Exeter course fifty minutes before my scheduled 9:55 A.M. tee time. During this entire commute I wondered whether I was crazy, since it was raining cats and dogs. Simply throwing my clubs into the trunk of Mr. Lucky had left me drenched. My assumption was that the tee times would be postponed until the storm passed through and the course had a chance to dry out, but in this I was dead wrong. When I arrived, Chris Young, running the tournament in Buddy's absence, informed me that due to multiple player withdrawals on account of the rain the schedule had been collapsed and my tee time had been moved up to 9:20 A.M.—fifteen minutes hence. By the time I registered and put on my spikes and rain suit, it was time to go. Not that I could have warmed up anyway. There was no range at Exeter, only a shaggy, waterlogged pasture where players could whack their own balls if they were so inclined, which no one was on this particular morning.

Under the circumstances I probably should have been content with my score of 80, but of course I wasn't. In light of Key Biscayne and the stretch of good play at Vermont, my expectations were now much higher than they had been. After the round I had lunch in the clubhouse with one of my playing companions for the day, a fellow amateur from New Hampshire named Kurt Kwader, and used the occasion to gripe nonstop about the many unfair forces at loose in the world that had kept me from achieving my rightful score of 72 or 73: the rain, the hustle, the leak in my Foot-Joys, the arthritis-inducing cold of the early morning ferry ride.

"It's a hell of a game," Kurt responded.

"You bet it is. How do they expect us to play without warming up?" I was outraged.

"It's a hell of a game," he repeated.

Kurt, of course, had played in precisely the same conditions and shot what was for him a disappointing 78, but he wasn't whining. He hadn't complained during the round, either. I remembered once, when a wet grip caused him to utterly mangle a shot, he had merely shrugged, hoisted his bag to his shoulder, and stoically muddled on. "If the rain hadn't stopped on the back nine, no telling what we would have shot," he said with a laugh. This was his only acknowledgment of the conditions. I felt ashamed.

Kurt had bright red hair and broad shoulders and was wearing a turtleneck beneath his golf shirt. As it turned out he had spent the winter competing on the mini-tours in Florida as I had, although in his case in Orlando, and like me was disappointed at the glacial rate of his progress. As we talked I learned that he had recently retired as a captain from the army, despite being only thirty-two, and was using the nest egg he had accumulated in the service to finance his run at professional golf. He had a girlfriend, Tracey, who joined us in the middle of lunch but who lived and worked in Florida and thus would not be around most of the summer.

The more I got to know Kurt the more I liked him. Though he grew up playing golf, he had not played competitively in college, opting instead for ROTC. Unlike the typical twentysomething

cadets who drifted into golf either directly out of a privileged background or because they lacked anything better to do, Kurt had
made an eyes-wide-open adult choice to pursue the sport. I
admired that.

Later that week, after the first round at Willimantic, we played
a practice round together. By this time I had learned that everyone on the tour called him Captain Kurt, a natural nickname but
one that also reflected the respect people had for him. He told me
during the round that for most of his army career he had served as
head of an ordnance unit in Germany and spent several months in
Saudi Arabia as part of Operation Desert Storm. The main reason
he had left was his inability to stomach Bill Clinton. "He dodged
the draft, he lied about having affairs, he smoked dope. How can
you ask guys to lay down their lives when someone like that is the
commander-in-chief?" he said. Now I happened to be a Clinton
fan, but the sincerity of Kurt's moral conviction made it impossible
to object to his opinions. I let him know my politics were main-
stream Democratic, if anything a bit left-leaning, but he didn't
hold it against me.

As far as golf went, however, there was no divide. Our games
were similar. Kurt was more accomplished—his scores over the
next two months averaged three or four strokes lower than mine—
but we drove the ball about the same distance, our swings and
rhythms were similar and, most important, our devotion to practice was the same. After our round that afternoon we spent nearly
an hour competing with one another around the practice green—
putting games, pitch-and-putt drills, chipping competitions. I felt
like I was twelve again. What could be more fun than playing outside with a good new friend until it's too dark to see?

THAT EVENING BUDDY gave a dinner speech on the rules of golf at
the Willimantic Country Club (which despite its name is simply the
local municipal course). I was surprised to find more than fifty people in attendance. Apparently over the years Buddy has earned a

reputation as a raconteur extraordinaire, the Mark Twain of rules officials.

When I wandered into the banquet room, Chris Young and Joe Klemmer waved me over to the large round table where they were sitting with Captain Kurt and a half dozen other players from the tour—no caste system here like on the South Florida Tour. During the course of the talk the ten of us polished off seven pitchers of beer, as well as dinner.

Buddy began the lecture with a brief, true-or-false quiz. Sample question: "If you move your ball on the green while trying to swipe a bug off it with your cap, there is no penalty." (Answer: true.) The quiz, however, seemed to be the extent of Buddy's prepared remarks. After that the speech was simply a potpourri of historical oddities and off-the-wall opinions.

"In my day we never had *distances*," Buddy said, spitting out the word "distances" in disgust. "Now everybody's running around looking for sprinkler heads as if knowing whether it's 137 yards or 139 yards to the center of the green is going to make a difference. Mark my words: in the not-too-distant future you'll see fairways chalked off every ten yards like football gridirons. Someone will come up with that brilliant idea to speed up play. Which happens to be another pet peeve. Fast play is overemphasized. Christ, let people enjoy themselves. Golf's a game."

After a while he opened the floor to questions.

"Last winter I had a problem down at Windemere in Naples, Florida . . ." one question began.

"I use Serenity pads, myself," Buddy interrupted. He was a regular comedian.

Another questioner complained that the two-stroke penalty for going out-of-bounds wasn't fair. Buddy gawked at the guy. "Who said golf was fair? If you want fair, go bowl. That's just my opinion, of course, though it is a rather insightful one."

The talk always returned to its announced subject, the rules, and it was clear that Buddy knew his stuff. More than that, he clearly *loved* golf rules and the history of the rules and made them seem more lively than I'd ever imagined. Back in 1846, for instance, the unplayable lie rule was completely different than it is now. Back then, if player A claimed that his ball was unplayable, player B had the option of taking two swings at it. If B succeeded in moving the ball, A had to play it where it came to rest (if B hit it into a lake, A incurred the standard penalty for a hazard). On the other hand, if B failed to move the ball in two attempts, A got free relief and B took a one-stroke penalty. Buddy thought this was a fun rule and threatened to invoke it the next day in the tournament.

Buddy explained that rules changes evolved out of long debates within the two principal rules-making bodies, the Royal and Ancient Society of Golfers in Scotland and the United States Golf Association. The two-stroke out-of-bounds penalty, for example, has been debated for decades. Buddy walked us through the various proposed alternatives and explained why they were inadequate: playing out-of-bounds as if it were a hazard is not severe enough; reducing the penalty to one stroke and distance would almost be like granting Mulligans. "It's not a perfect rule," he concluded. "But there's no better way to do it."

Apparently guys like Buddy studied not just the rules themselves—the Ur-text—but many supplementary volumes called "Decisions on the Rules of Golf." Just as medieval Christian theologians argued about how many angels could fit on the head of a pin, so golf's ancient tribunals lavished countless hours on such issues as the proper recourse should a rodent swallow a golf ball or a ball become lodged against manufactured ice as opposed to ice of the natural kind.

To every conceivable problem or situation, an unambiguous answer exists—and it occurred to me that this was part of golf's great appeal. How many other institutions in modern life enjoy such authority and respect? The Law is evolved but highly subjective in practice, the Church these days is a hodgepodge of conflicting belief, and who knows what the rules and roles of marriage are anymore? But golf offers an all-encompassing order. Within just one round there is scope for vast human drama—triumph and despair, courage and fear, betrayal and redemption, good luck and misfortune—but at the end of the day everything boils down neatly to a few inarguable numbers. You scribble those numbers on your scorecard with a stubby pencil, turn the scorecard in, and that is that. If only the rest of life could be so simple.

The inherent wisdom of the rules, I think, also helped explain Buddy's popularity with the players. He was like a kooky father— irascible, prone to detonation (he has unpredictably suspended players from the tour for minor offenses like slow play), but *ours* nonetheless. His authority was unchallengeable because, well, he embodied and invoked the ancient rules of the game.

After my second round at Willimantic (I shot a piddling 82), I hung out for a bit in the clubhouse bar where the cardboard scoreboard had been erected. Finishing players drifted in and out, most of them pulling up a chair for at least a while to listen to Buddy spout opinions and to tell him, if they could get a word in edgewise, about their rounds. "I'm gonna be playing for Buddy through July," one young pro told me about his schedule, "and I'd like to get back in September to play for him some more." That phrase—"playing for Buddy"—was telling. In South Florida, I'd never heard anyone talk about "playing for Tom."

IN WILLIMANTIC, I had been stung by having to pay sixty-nine dollars for my motel room. You'd think a washed-up mill town would have at least one place you could flop for twenty-five bucks a night—I mean, where do the seasonal farmworkers stay?—but if so, I couldn't locate it. I did find an isolated motel about fifteen miles from town on a darkened stretch of highway. The sign was broken and unlit and the manager appeared only after my persistent banging on the desk bell. He looked like a creature from the World Wrestling Federation: six-foot-eight or so with a weight lifter's build, greasy hair in a ponytail, and a Fu

Manchu mustache. He demanded fifty-two dollars a night for a room and, fatigued and intimidated, I briefly agreed. But when I pulled out my Visa card he told me the rate for credit cards was sixty-two bucks, and I snapped to my senses. Imagine the Bates Motel managed by Charlie Manson. In the parking lot there had been only one other car, a 1974 Impala. I figured I'd pay seven bucks more and feel safer returning to the Best Western.

Lodging is a problem for Buddy's tour. New England is an expensive part of the country and the tournaments are so widely dispersed that players can't save money by tripling up in some centrally located apartment, as they can in Florida.

In Norwich, Connecticut, the site of the next tournament, I spent nearly two hours trying to find a cheap motel, but finally had to admit defeat and check into the AAA-approved Norwich Inn for fifty-eight dollars a night. As it turned out, most of the other players were staying there, too. Walking down the breezeway to get ice, I glanced in the open door of a room and spotted two telltale golf bags leaning against the far wall.

"Hello golfers!" I hailed, poking my head inside.

On the bed, switching the TV among sports channels, was Eric Coultoff, the guy who had recommended the North Atlantic Tour to me back in Florida. He invited me in and showed me some of the letters he had written seeking sponsorship. One was to Hertz, offering ad space on his bag in exchange for a year's use of a rental car, which he did not get. Another was to Oakley, asking for free sunglasses, which he got.

"He told the amazing story of how he parlayed a good round in a Nike qualifier into free clothes and a new set of woods. The 73 he shot that day got him into the Nike Tour's Buffalo event (one of his two Nike Tour appearances.) On the practice tee there, he spoke with the Callaway tour representative and convinced him to exchange the Callaway driver Coultoff had bought a few months earlier for a model with a slightly lower trajectory. The following week (after missing the cut) Coultoff followed up with a call to Callaway headquarters in California requesting a three-wood matched to the driver the tour rep had given him in Buffalo. Callaway sent one. A few weeks later, the tour rep gave him a new four-wood. These transactions enabled Eric to telephone the Sun Mountain company, tell them he had competed in the Nike Buffalo event, and request a clothing deal. A bundle of Sun Mountain shirts soon arrived by mail. Later someone stole Coultoff's clubs from the trunk of his car in Manhattan. Callaway refused to replace them, due to policy, but resourceful Coultoff contacted Goldwin, an upstart club manufacturer, and asked if they had some clubs for him to try. Goldwin rushed him three new woods, the clubs he used now.

The only dent in the armor of Coultoff's professionalism was that he wasn't such a great golfer. He had his flashes, such as the 71 he shot later that summer to lead the North Atlantic Tour Championship after the first round. But around the clubhouse the other pros rolled their eyes. They thought the 71 had been a fluke. Coultoff eagled a par four on the front nine by holing out from the woods with a shot that sailed unscathed through the limbs of two trees, and he was saved on another hole when the ball he airmailed over the green rolled back fifty feet on a cart path to a choice spot on the apron in front of the green. Bets were made on whether he would break 80 in the final round. He did, shooting a more typical 78 to finish fourth, his highest showing of the year.

But I liked Coultoff. He kept plugging away. He refused to let little things like consistent mediocrity undermine his self-confidence, which was just what Dr. Deborah Graham and Chuck Hogan might have ordered. Rather than dwell on his shortcomings, Coultoff nurtured a vision of himself as a successful pro, a champion, and who was I to say that this strategy wouldn't eventually work? Plus, he was fun to talk to, always brimming with energy, plans, and dish. He planned someday to write a book about his experiences entitled *If It's a Gimme, Make It*. This was a quote of Eric's to his golf coach at Binghamton University as his coach was putting out the gimme and sure enough he missed. Eric felt the quote nicely captured the ironic impossibility of golf.

Compared to Coultoff, many of the other regulars on the North Atlantic Tour seemed to be taking things pretty easy. After my practice round that afternoon I had a beer in the grill room with two guys watching motocross on TV. One was a big, lumbering galoot from upstate New York who could hit his pitching wedge 170 yards and probably three times higher than that into the air. I had never seen anything like it.

He had played golf at Ohio Wesleyan but gave it up for three years until—as he tells the story—he wowed some golfing friends of his parents on the course and they insisted on sponsoring him. "I thought, 'What the hell? Why not give it a whirl?' " he said. "They asked me to write out a budget, I came up with fifteen thousand for a year, living at home most of the time, and so here I am today." The week before he had won his first money as a pro (a fifty-dollar split of the last-place check) and pranced around the scoreboard crowing, "Career earnings! Look, Mom, I've got career earnings!"

The other guy at the bar, chubby-cheeked and blond, had played golf at an elite private boarding school in Massachusetts but never went to college. "I got into Georgetown, but I was so fed up with all the bullshit, I got a job as a runner on Wall Street instead," he told me, pulling on a Camel. Over the next seven years, while taking a few business classes at New York University, he worked his way into a good-paying commodities trading job at A. G. Edwards. From time to time he played golf with some of his former high school acquaintances. "The guys I beat back then were now beating me, because they'd played college golf and I hadn't, and that pissed me off. So I quit the Wall Street bullshit and spent a year and a half getting my game back in shape." He had turned pro just a few months before in Florida but did not yet have career earnings.

"The biggest difference now is I'm about two or three strokes worse than I was as an amateur," he said. "Also, I play a lot slower because there's more on the line." It was hard to tell, with many of the pros, precisely what was on the line. A lot were just biding their time, living out their twenties with a vague dream and a pleasant lifestyle. And I can't say I blamed them. I'd spent a good chunk of my twenties doing something similar, supporting myself minimally as a housepainter and substitute teacher while trying to write the great American novel. And I'd learned something useful from the experience, namely that I wasn't cut out to write the great American novel. This let me get on with the rest of my life.

That evening I went with a group of players to the double-A baseball game between the local Norwich Navigators and the Hardware City Rockcats—Hardware City being New Britain, Connecticut, home of Stanley Tools. Among those in the pack was Ivan Lendl. Lendl's frequent presence was a highlight of the tour. He was a world champion—albeit at another sport—which lent the lowly North Atlantic some much-needed glamour. Furthermore he was well liked: no special treatment asked for, none given. From time to time he invited selected players out to his northwestern Connecticut estate for the weekend.

As the only player who knew where the stadium was—I had driven past it several times during my earlier, futile search for a cheap motel—I was elected to lead the caravan of cars from the golf course, and Lendl fell in behind me. To put it another way, I in Mr. Lucky, which cost $500, was leading Ivan Lendl in his custom-made, race-track Porsche, which cost $80,000. I smugly calculated during the drive that for the price of Lendl's Porsche I could have purchased 160 Mr. Luckys! But naturally such a thought cannot go unrewarded. As we approached the stadium, steam started billowing from Mr. Lucky's hood. In the rearview mirror I could see Lendl laughing to someone on his cellphone. He later told me it was his four-year-old daughter. "There's a funny man up in front of me," he was explaining, "who's got a funny car."

But I didn't begrudge Lendl his little chuckle. He and Captain Kurt stopped to render assistance (we concluded I could refill the radiator after the game and make it home safely) and then joined the others in the stands. The main topic of conversation was how, compared to minor-league golfers, minor-league baseball players had it easy. They got monthly paychecks (however modest), team transportation, free food, free lodging and—if one could believe the movie, *Bull Durham*—groupies. Minor-league golfers got none of the above.

I sat next to Lendl and we talked about his tennis career. One of the reasons Lendl was so well-regarded on tour was that he didn't balk at talking about what made him famous, unlike some celebrities who defer such questions out of supposed modesty and so actually come across as patronizing. Lendl said he thought his tennis background helped *some* in golf, but not in the way most people supposed, such as with hand-eye coordination. He saw a connection in rhythm. "After age eighteen," he told me, "my coaches didn't give me any more instruction about hitting the tennis ball. All we worked on was timing and fitness. They would hit the ball two feet in front of me, then five feet, then three feet, so I'd get the rhythm. I would like to get to that point with golf, where all I have to work on is timing and rhythm."

He had a good ways to go yet—his left-handed swing was imprecise and still a bit loopy at the top. But Lendl worked as hard on his game as anyone. At home he had created a few practice holes and worked regularly with a swing coach, who also sometimes caddied for him in celebrity events. Regarding the other players on the North Atlantic Tour, Lendl was fond but forthright. "Coultoff plumb-bobs putts twice from both directions in his effort to break 80," he dryly joked. "And some of the ones with the most talent, you never see them on the range. They also drink too much."

As a teetotaling tennis champion, Lendl's work ethic had been legendary, so perhaps his opinions should not have been surprising. We all bring our peculiar perspective to the game.

THE PRACTICE RANGE serving the Norwich Golf Course is a quarter mile up the highway from the clubhouse, just far enough away so that most players use their cars to shuttle back and forth. One downside of this arrangement—which happens probably, oh, once every century—is that some poor schmuck will lock his keys and his golf clubs in the trunk of his car a few minutes before he is scheduled to tee off in a tournament.

For this particular century, the schmuck was Captain Kurt.

When I came off the range, there was Kurt in stockinged feet (his shoes were held hostage, too) picking at the lock with a piece of wire he had found in the gravel. He was in flop sweat, but *controlled* flop sweat, as befits a former army captain.

In similar circumstances I would have been running around in circles with the whites of my eyeballs showing, shouting, "I'm screwed! It's hopeless!" But not Kurt. "This is a *problem* that can be *dealt with*," he said between clenched teeth. He asked to inspect the locking mechanism of Mr. Lucky's trunk for comparison and borrowed my tire tool and a screwdriver. He jiggled and pried. Sweat rolled down his nose. I was impressed—he remained in control of the situation. But to make my own tee time, I had to leave before he could get the trunk open.

My round started out sloppily. I three-putted the first hole from twelve feet, bogeyed the third, and freaked out on the par-five fifth. After a good drive and an even better two-iron second shot, I had only twenty-five feet left for eagle. Feeling the pressure to make a good attempt, I cravenly dribbled the downhill putt only about ten feet. Disgusted, I knocked the next putt seven feet past and pushed the comebacker wide.

Four putts from twenty-five feet! It was unbearable. Hyperventilating, I stalked to the sixth tee box ahead of the rest of my group and looked in vain for some handy implement with which to hurt myself. The hopelessness one feels after such stupidity is overwhelming. You cannot believe there isn't some loophole, some high legal principle on which to appeal, some cosmic undo button to press. But there isn't. All you can do is stew.

It was odd, though: somehow that four-putt got me going. From the tee box I happened to scan back up the fifth fairway and saw Captain Kurt, with his distinctive red hair, teeing off. I couldn't believe he had made his tee time. Somehow he had popped the trunk (later I learned he had done so without damaging it). Spotting him made me ashamed of my uncontrolled frustration. If he could deal with his problem, I could deal with mine. Nothing could change the four-putt, but at least I could put it behind me with a jag of good play.

And that is what happened. For the rest of the round I seethed—I refused even to look at the faces of my playing companions—but the seething fed my concentration. I cannot recall ever being so ferociously riveted on making shots. Nothing miraculous happened. It was six holes before I got a birdie. But even in those six holes I was giving myself chances, hitting roughly half of my approach shots to within makable birdie distances. My swing and my whole attitude felt different: unselfconscious, determined. Over the final thirteen holes, I scored two birdies and no bogeys and posted a 73.

It's a funny game, golf. Here I had gone from cosmic despair to my best score of the year in the course of two hours. One shot at a time. Sometimes the clichés turn out to be true.

My 73 actually beat all but four of the pros, and this put me into the next to last threesome for the final round. I was elated. On the practice green before the round I got a kick out of watching my betters—Joe Klemmer, Ivan Lendl, Captain Kurt (whose 76 was a triumph, considering the circumstances)—pick up their bags and head off to the first tee before me. "Good luck!" I called. "I'll just stay here on the green and putt a little longer. I won't be going out for a while, you know."

By the time my turn came around I had grown a bit giddy, which Buddy must have sensed. "Come over here, J. P.," he said at the tee box. "If you want to win this thing, you'll need a last-minute putting tip." He pulled a dime from his pocket and told me to grip my putter. As I did so he pressed the dime into the fleshy palm pad of my right hand that faced the target. "Think of the dime as the head of the putter. It goes toward the hole. It doesn't go up, it doesn't go down, it doesn't go left, and it doesn't go right. It goes toward the hole."

The tip was a good one and I focused on it during the round. But Buddy gave it to me, I think, primarily to distract me. I was jittery—not as outright nervous as I had been before the final round at Key Biscayne, because here I knew my presence among the leaders was basically freaky, but I certainly felt dazed and out of place. Buddy's intercession was a blessing.

I didn't play badly. Midway through the round my concentration lagged for a while and my short game grew tentative. On three consecutive holes I failed at getting up-and-down, which was normally a strength, and I three-putted twice. Still, I coaxed a birdie out of number five, the hole I had four-putted the day before, and finished with a respectable 77. Had I been a professional and scored one stroke better, I would have tied for the last paying place and split a three-hundred-dollar check with two other guys. I would have had career earnings.

What I remember most about the round, however, was the lethargic calm of the two pros in my group, Josh Cupp, a lanky, towheaded twenty-two-year-old from upstate New York, and Todd Benware, a journeyman from North Carolina. With four holes left they were tied for the lead, but this news—delivered by Buddy after checking with all the groups still on the course—had absolutely zero impact on their games or comportment. This kind of down-to-the-wire, head-to-head battle would have made great drama on a TV tournament, but observing it from within the threesome, I wondered if either pro had a pulse. Benware curled in a thirty-five-foot birdie putt on sixteen, which Cupp matched, from forty feet, on seventeen.

"Nice putt," said Benware, with all the emotion of a depressed housewife.

"Thanks," shrugged Cupp.

ON THE FINAL hole, a long par three into a hard wind, both players missed the green but both got up-and-down to force a playoff.

I hung around to watch and found myself once again pondering the Fine Green Line. What was the difference between me as a player and these guys? Off the tee I consistently matched them, and I myself had rolled in a twenty-five-foot birdie putt on number twelve. My score in round one had been only one shot worse than theirs. The analogy that popped to mind was automotive, probably because I'd spent two hours the previous afternoon waiting for Mr. Lucky's cooling system to be repaired. Those guys were driving overpowered luxury cars, like Lendl's Porsche, whereas I was in a jalopy. When everything was going well, cruising down the highway under normal circumstances, there wasn't all that much difference. Mr. Lucky could cruise at seventy mph, except uphill. But they had power to spare whereas I was at my limit. When they needed to pass or suddenly swerve to avoid an accident or score a birdie or two down the stretch, they had resources to call upon that I didn't. Not to mention, of course, that Mr. Lucky fell apart in one way or another every couple of hundred miles and their fancy cars didn't. And all this gave them confidence, which probably counted for as much as the actual horsepower under the hood.

The most impressive shot of the playoff was Josh Cupp's drive on the second hole. It carried almost three hundred yards in the air, across a dogleg, and stopped on the fringe of a tiny, elevated green. The guy had no fear.

After smiting this monster, Josh hopped onto the fender of Buddy's cart with his bag and asked, "Would this disqualify me if I hitched a ride?"

"No, no, not at all," Buddy responded and they puttered off

down the hill. After they had gone about fifty yards, Buddy added, "You'll be penalized two strokes, of course, but you won't be disqualified."

Even no-pulse Josh had to laugh at that one. Three shots later he won the playoff and the two-thousand-dollar champion's check.

I WAS FEELING BETTER ABOUT MY GOLF GAME, and therefore about myself, as the July Fourth weekend approached. No tournaments were on the schedule, just some practice to keep my skills in shape and some writing work at my desk.

To Polly I was unusually cheerful, which made her nervous. "All this means is you'll crash that much harder when the bottom falls out next week or whenever," she said. I had to admit that sometimes in the past that had been the case, especially when my good moods stemmed from writing; I would be chipper as hell until one morning I woke up and realized that the premise of whatever it was I was working on was *entirely wrong*. Then I became suicidal.

"But this is different, Pol," I protested one evening as I washed the dinner dishes. "I've really and truly broken through to another level in my golf game. I'm playing with a precision that I never dreamed possible. You should see me hit my short irons!"

"Hmmm," she said eloquently.

That weekend we had two houseguests, Chuck and Billy, a gay couple who were great friends of Polly back from her louche downtown artist days. On Friday night Chuck prepared a masterful seafood pasta. Sitting around the table after dinner, wine flowing, the three of them hilariously deconstructed their lives back in SoHo, updating the stories of mutual friends and generally reveling in their memories. I listened attentively, alert for an opening to change the subject to golf. The moment finally came when Billy casually remarked that religion had become newly important to several of his old cronies.

"You know, golf is a lot like religion," I mentioned.

A pall of silence descended over the dinner table. Polly laughed apologetically. "To John Paul, everything is like golf."

More silence.

Finally Billy sighed and said, "Oh?"

"Sure, to hit a great shot you have to empty yourself of ego and bring down a kind of peace upon yourself. The routine you go through before each shot is a lot like prayer."

For some reason Chuck found this amusing. "To think, all those old guys riding around in plaid pants are actually having profound spiritual experiences. I had no idea."

He was being sarcastic, I think. But then he knew nothing about golf. He had told people at his office that he would be spending the weekend with a player on the PGA Tour.

"I'm not saying most golfers think about golf as religion *consciously*," I said. "But underneath, unstated, golf can fill a spiritual vacuum. Even the rankest duffer understands at some level that to improve you have to get in contact with something deeper or quieter or higher. You'd be surprised how golfers talk among themselves."

"You mean like getting 'in the zone,'" Billy said. "That's just standard sports psychology, not religion."

I rolled my eyes, thinking "Non-golfers just don't get it," and then launched into my golf-course-as-cathedral rap: tall trees pointing gothically to heaven, fairways as emerald aisles, the elevated green as altar. This was my best stuff, but they were unimpressed. "Maybe it's not religion exactly but at least it's not TV," I concluded desperately. "Golf's one of the few things you can do anymore in America where there's no advertising. On the golf course you can get away from commercials, commercialism, consumerism. It's pure, it's a refuge. It has spiritual overtones. I could go on and on!"

Polly suggested that, instead, I help her get dessert. In the kitchen she informed me that I was already going on and on.

A FEW DAYS later I had my first lesson with Michael Hebron since March. I hadn't sought Hebron's help in recent months because I had been focusing on the mental game and didn't want to confuse things with still more swing thoughts. Plus, there was that $125-a-pop charge. But the off-week in my schedule seemed like a good time to check in and get Hebron's blessing (I hoped) for the way my swing had evolved. In the last few tournaments my backswing had definitely changed, especially on my short-iron shots. I had discovered that when I absolutely had to put the ball on the green, as in a tournament, I felt most confident using a short, truncated backswing. This swing seemed to work—it allowed me an unusual sense of control—but I was concerned that perhaps I was unwise to resort to it. Was this a cowardly swing, a gnarled, impure parody of a proper swing that was doomed to disintegrate between now and Q School?

"Perfect!" Hebron said after watching me hit a few shots.

I didn't take the compliment literally. Golf teachers tend to exaggerate the positive. In golf instructor-ese, "perfect" means, "Hey, you might finally be getting the hang of it after all." But even so, my chest bloomed with pride.

Hebron said the main difference between my new, reduced-backswing swing and my older version was "a little less IDC." "What's that?" I said, mildly alarmed. "I Don't Care. You were looser with the other swing. You swung with more abandon, and that's generally a good thing. But still, the new one is appropriate." He told me that what I'd done without realizing it was find my "go-to" swing. "All good players have one, a swing they can absolutely count on under pressure," he said.

We went inside to watch the swing on video. I was pleased. The backswing stopped just a touch short of horizontal, even though my perception when actually swinging was that I barely took the club back halfway. Then Hebron popped in a cassette of Sam Snead. His swing—classic, silky, as simple as 1-2-3—made my swing look like a Keystone Kops routine. "That's ridiculous," I complained. "He's not even trying." I was instantly depressed.

"Not much happening in Sam's swing, is there?" Hebron smiled.

Back on the range he gave me three points to take home. The first was to take my club back a little more to the inside on the first three inches of my takeaway. The second had to do with my swing plane (my tendency on bad shots was to swing too flat). And the third was to keep my weight (the "entire system," as he put it) a tad more to the right, behind the ball.

Three koans from the Zen master. Those ought to last me for several months, I thought.

I enjoyed the lesson more than I had any other, primarily because I felt less dim-witted than I had before—more like a peer than a novice. As Hebron and I shook hands in parting, he said, "You know, I never felt this was a typical teacher-client relationship. If you don't have enough money for a lesson sometime, give us a call anyway. We can work something out, maybe you can pay later when you're better set."

I was immensely grateful for this remark, even though I knew I wouldn't want to take his time without paying. "Golf cannot be taught, it can only be learned," he had told me at the start of our relationship. In his own indirect way, I felt, Hebron was telling me I was a good student.

SINCE RETURNING TO Orient from Florida, I had befriended the twenty-eight-year-old head pro at the North Fork Country Club, David Bakyta. He let me use the club's range whenever I wanted (so long as I was semi-sneaky about it and didn't offend the members) and also the short-game practice facility, which was a mini-tour golfer's wet dream. It featured a fast, undulating putting green, a chipping green surrounded by thrilling swales and hummocks, and yet another green for practicing shots out of the sand. Often when I practiced David swung by for a chat.

"Hello, Pro," he typically greeted me. I liked that he called me Pro.

David was a slender, clean-cut, good-looking fellow with a quick smile and calm disposition—perfect traits for a club pro. The trouble was, he would have much preferred to be doing what I was doing, testing his mettle on the mini-tours with an eye to the Big Time. Each winter when North Fork closed for the season he was able to get a taste of the action. He retreated to the West Palm Beach area and played on a special mini-tour there for PGA club pros. This past year he won one of the events, and a three-thousand-dollar check, and finished in the money at most of the others. Impressively—or frustratingly, depending on the point of view—he had dropped his stroke average by two full strokes compared to the winter before, which was significant, and his jones to compete full-time was almost unbearable. But he had a wife and his wife was pregnant and the pay at North Fork was good and an adventure like mine didn't seem in the cards.

David asked about my lesson with Hebron, whom he knew and admired, and I told him how I had felt a little more equal in my relationship with Hebron this time—*almost* fellow-pro to fellow-pro," I said. Then I told him about my 73 at Norwich and how I'd played in the final round with the two tournament leaders. "I'll probably never get that kind of close-up view again," I said.

"Want some free advice?" he replied.

"Sure." I felt comfortable around David because I knew he wasn't trying to sell me anything. He simply wanted me to do well, and our chats were invariably invigorating.

"Stop being this guy experiencing things. Get out there and *live* the life. The only way you're going to make real progress is to start thinking like a pro. You've got to wake up every morning and tell yourself, 'I am a professional golfer. I play golf like a professional golfer. If I don't make any money today as a professional golfer, my baby will starve.' That's the way to look at it: with every stroke, everything's on the line. Grind it out. Grind, grind, grind."

This was basically a recast version of Chuck Hogan's advice: "Champions *are* their vision, and it's concrete. Wanna-bes merely *have* a vision, and it's abstract." It's funny how, when you start hearing the same bits of wisdom over and over, coming from different quarters, they start to sink in.

That night I broke the news to Polly that henceforth she should think of me as a professional golfer. "Polly," I said, "I have now become your worst nightmare."

"Clothes and all?" she said. She couldn't get beyond her image of golfers as guys who hung out with Jackie Gleason at the Moose Lodge.

"Maybe not the clothes," I replied. Though no one actually wore plaid pants on the mini-tours, some of the young cadets I'd played with in Florida did look pretty silly, all grim and tricked out in their Pro Golfer fashions. They were desperately trying to imitate the Tour pros, but the Tour pros were *paid* to dress that way. I was willing to go only so far.

THE NEXT DAY, by chance, the reporter from the local weekly newspaper who had written about my upcoming Year in January called to do a follow-up. One thing led to another and the lead of the story appeared a few days later and read, "Orient golfer-writer John Paul

Newport has announced his intention to turn pro at the New Hampshire Open at the end of this month."

It scared me to read this in print. Yes, I may have mentioned something along that line to the reporter, but it wasn't like I exactly wanted to *announce* it to the world. What if I changed my mind? Economically it still made no sense to turn pro. My entry fees on the North Atlantic Tour would rocket from $75 per event to $325 per event, and the likelihood of winning even some of that difference back was negligible. On the other hand, I would have to turn pro at some point before Q School (amateurs are not allowed), so why not now? At Norwich I had come within one stroke of winning some money. Turning pro might push me to the next level. That was my logic. As Bakyta advised, I wanted to stop *pretending* to be a pro and actually become one.

The day the newspaper article came out, the antiquated wiring in our basement blew. The electrician who came to fix the problem recognized me from the accompanying photo, which depicted me practicing at the Island's End range.

"Yeah, I was just remarking to my wife this morning," he chuckled, "I've never seen a golf pro wearing short pants before."

AT THE NEXT two tournaments, in the sterling lead-up to my pro debut, my scores were 80, 80, 80, and 86.

"Nice playing," Chris Young said dryly after my 86. I had just signed my card at the scorer's table in North Kingston, Rhode Island (at the so-called Washington County Classic), and was too heartsick even to utter the clever retort that came to mind: "Screw you."

My reaction to this round—the lowlight of which was a nine on a single par four—was confusion more than despair. How could such a studly near-pro as myself play golf so shamefully? My positive self-image was at risk. Chris carefully inked my numbers up on the scoreboard for all to see, the awful 8 and the awful 6, and for the next fifteen minutes or so I lingered nearby hoping Chris would leave so I could scrape the numbers off the poster board with my fingernails. I didn't have the nerve to do this, but my *desire* to do so was profound. In any case, Chris never left. After a while I plodded zombie-like to the parking lot, loaded my clubs into Mr. Lucky without speaking to anyone, and headed home.

It was a bleak and lonely drive, the main theme of which was self-hatred. To pass the time, speaking into my tape recorder, I compiled a list of plausible excuses:

1. Lyme disease.
2. Crippling arthritis in left knee.
3. Too high expectations after recent successes.
4. Not enough practice time over holiday weekend—sapped confidence in my new, truncated swing.
5. Failure to make ferry reservation for trip to Connecticut resulted in a five-hour waiting-list ordeal at dock, destroying tranquility for entire week.
6. The arrogant college kid in my threesome at first tournament was annoying as hell. After each shot he flicked his clubs to his caddie (who was also his college golf coach) like some pampered superstar. His mom and dad tagged along and applauded when he did things like tee up his ball correctly. Then the asshole had the nerve to shoot a 69.
7. The tournament course was Mickey Mouse.
8. Overnight stay with parents-in-law Monday night disrupted my routine.
9. I had to pay $64 for nine hours in a threadbare motel room Tuesday night.
10. Queasy stomach after that odd-tasting ham on Wednesday: food poisoning?
11. Lousy greens at North Kingston.
12. Money anxiety. July rent past due. $3,000 fee from magazine apparently "lost in the mail."
13. Profound moral weakness.
14. Life not worth living.

Not all of these excuses were without merit. My left knee, the victim of three football-related surgeries, truly was aching worse and worse with each tournament. Also, I truly did have some telltale symptoms of Lyme disease (fatigue, low-grade headache), which I had confirmed on Monday night in my father-in-law's Merck Manual. And truly, the money issue was troubling.

Money is a funny thing. All my life I hadn't cared a fig about money. As a challenge for life, making money never appealed to me—what white male in America, especially one with an Ivy League education, couldn't make buckets of money if he just set his mind to it? My goals (I told myself) were loftier: to plumb-bob the human spirit, to open my soul to life's cosmic epiphanies, to reduce my handicap to scratch. The irony, of course, was that two adult decades of such high-mindedness had left me in a position where money was now practically all I could think about. We were almost broke. How could I possibly make what little money we had left last until the end of the Year? Shooting an 86 only made the panic worse. What was I doing out here anyway? Why didn't I just get a job?

By the time I boarded the ferry at New London for Orient, I had lost interest in my list of excuses. Excuses are too easy. Don't get me wrong: the ability to concoct convincing excuses is an important skill in golf. In those critical first few minutes after an unpardonably bad shot or round, plausible excuses protect against lasting psychological damage. But sooner or later the magic of excuses wears off and the healthy individual wants to know, for better or worse, what *really* caused the collapse.

I took a seat on the upper deck of the ferry for the ninety-minute crossing. The sunset sky was a spectacular blaze over Long Island Sound and soon the light and fresh sea air restored my equilibrium. Polly and Anna were waiting at home on the other shore and I yearned to see them. Though I had only been gone five days, golf had beaten me up good and I yearned for some simple domestic comfort.

It occurred to me for the first time ever that maybe the reason I had played so poorly was that I didn't care enough—not way down deep where it mattered. Certainly I cared *some*. I had made a well-intentioned effort. Before each round I had stretched thoroughly, listened to waltz tapes, warmed up on the range with concentration, rehearsed key holes in my imagination—in short, I had gone through the usual routines. But somehow the tournaments had lacked intensity. I couldn't make myself believe that what I scored really mattered. The week before I had played well, proving to myself that I was *capable* of progress, and I had decided to turn pro a few weeks hence. *That* would be important, a tournament to psyche up for. For now, however, it felt like I was just marking time. And as a result I had played the kind of golf that came easiest for me: fair-to-middling golf, golf in the eighties, bogey-par-par-bogey-par-par-bogey kind of golf, with an eccentric nine thrown into the mix when I zoned out.

From out of the blue, a phrase from my college biology class popped to mind: regression to the mean.

In evolutionary science, regression to the mean describes how any extreme characteristic of an organism, such as being tall or stupid, tends to moderate in succeeding generations. Unless the extreme characteristic is suddenly necessary for survival, the normal traits of the species will soon drown it out. Thus, for example, if an uppity paramecium grows a bigger than usual dendrite, regression to the mean in succeeding generations will whittle it back down to regulation size. Or, to apply the concept to golf, if an uppity golfer goes out and shoots a 69 or a 73 one day, regression to the mean will assure that he or she quickly returns to shooting more typical scores—in my case, 80s and 81s.

Was this dynamic inevitable? Was regression to the mean an inviolate *law* of golf?

As I thought about this on the upper deck of the ferry, I recalled the practice round I had played on Wednesday that week with Captain Kurt and a few other North Atlantic Tour regulars. It seemed a pretty convincing case study of regression to the mean.

Originally Captain Kurt and I had planned to play alone, but before we could get off the first tee a couple of pros, Doug Borck (the one who could hit his pitching wedge 170 yards) and Bruce Miller, asked to join us. We wasted five minutes arranging a suitable wager for the match—pros vs. amateurs—by which time another foursome of pros arrived on the tee and before I knew it an extremely complicated, high-stakes, multitiered bet had been arranged between the two foursomes. Given that some members of the other foursome, which included Joe Klemmer and Chris Young, appeared to have already drunk half a large cooler of beer, we felt reasonably confident.

It was, I have to say, a fun round of golf. Klemmer and his gang pounded us on the front, but on the back our hopes began to rise. Captain Kurt got hot with his putter and birdied three of the first four holes. Behind us the effects of alcohol were becoming more and more apparent. Klemmer began yodeling on every hole. We took this as a positive sign. On the fifteenth, as all four of us were walking to our balls in the middle of the fairway (a pretty sight), we heard a truly bloodcurdling yell from the tee box behind us and turned just in time to see Klemmer sprinting full-out toward the adjoining pond and jumping in head first, fully clothed. It seemed that a non-drinking member of the foursome, Coultoff, had bet Klemmer a hundred dollars he wouldn't dare.

None of this seemed to affect their game, however. On that very hole, a sopping-wet Klemmer drove his ball 320 yards down the middle and scored a birdie. On the next hole Coultoff snaked home a curling, downhill thirty-five-foot putt. "Coultoff, you're too dumb to have any nerves," our man Borck called out when we witnessed this, but the putt was just like Coultoff, the tour's most streaky player.

In the end we halved the back nine but lost the match, twenty-four dollars a man. Klemmer, the best golfer, had managed to dominate the scoring despite all his shenanigans. Bruce Miller on our team had been consistent as he usually was, short but sweet, and Borck had been erratic, putting for eagle on one hole and punching from the woods the next. I had played cautiously, acceptably, but had not helped the team very often. Kurt had been unshakable under pressure and made a half-dozen clutch putts.

In short, each of us, in our way, had regressed to mean.

I suppose regression to the mean is simply another way of saying we are what we shoot on average, but I had never before thought of it that way. The week earlier Klemmer had told me that the key to success as a pro was "finding a way to cash a check with your 'B' game." This is an old saw among golf pros; someone at Q School had told me the same thing, using exactly the same words. But back then I had thought of one's "B" game as the way one played on "off" days, those "unusual" days when balls tended to go sideways and your rhythm was shaky. Now I was beginning to see that one's "B" game was, in fact, the norm and one's "A" game was the way one played when one was "off." The "A" game was gravy, a treat, an experience to be savored. The "B" game was what you had to work with.

And frankly, working on the "B" game is not very glamorous.

I thought of the arrogant college kid I had played with on Monday of that week, the guy who shot 69. The main reason he'd got on my nerves, I decided, was because he hadn't really seemed that much better than I was. For instance, during a stretch on the back nine he rolled in three or four putts in the ten- to fifteen-foot range—the putts Bert Yancey called "things." Big deal, I thought at the time. Who can't luck out and roll in an occasional fifteen-footer. But in retrospect I'm sure this kid had spent months of time practicing "things" (I imagined the bored family butler tossing the ball back to him after each putt) and the result was, in our little tournament, he banged home a series of them.

This is not trivial. Take a hypothetical pro in his early twenties. The day he graduates from college he might be able to sink, on average, three "things" out of ten. Three years later, having devoted himself to practicing "things" in the interim, he has improved his odds to four out of ten. To anyone casually watching this pro compete in a tournament, whether he misses or makes any particular "thing" would seem pretty arbitrary. In golf some putts go in, some don't, that's the nature of the game. But statistically, the pro's three years of diligent practice on ten- to fifteen-foot putts translates into one or two fewer strokes per tournament. That's hardly a dramatic payoff, but in some weeks, even on the North Atlantic Tour, it could mean the difference between a $2,000 first-place check and a $500 third-place check, and on the PGA Tour it could potentially make hundreds of thousands of dollars' worth of difference.

Sprawled across a bench seat on the upper ferry deck, watching the sun dip behind Connecticut, I pondered the implications. The problem for me was that getting better required improvement on so many different fronts.

All year I had been working especially hard on my driving. My goal by Q School was to increase the average number of fairways I hit per round from eight out of fourteen to nine out of fourteen (Tour pros tend to hit about ten per round). If I accomplished this, I would be ecstatic. It would represent a major step forward. But putting one more drive per round into the fairway would not drop my stroke average by one stroke, not nearly. It would only give me one more chance per round to go for the green from a sweet fairway lie. I would still probably miss the green half the time from those fairway lies, on difficult courses, just as I would sometimes still hit the green from lies in the rough, which aren't always that bad. So maybe the result of all my work with the driver would be to increase the number of greens I hit in regulation by one every two rounds or so. Which, of course, does not in turn translate into one fewer strokes per round, because I still have to putt. So maybe, factoring everything together, the net result of hitting one more fairway per round would be one stroke off my score every four rounds or so. Which would lower my scoring average from, say, 80 to 79.75.

Now, at the same time that I'm working on my driving, I'm working on other skills, too, so hopefully a year of devoted effort would push my scoring average down by more than that. But there are so many skills to work on and keep tuned up! Even driving, to stick with that example, is not a single skill, but many skills: driving into the wind, driving with the wind, driving with out-of-bounds looming left, driving with out-of-bounds looming right, driving on holes that dogleg right and left, driving to a wide-open fairway where you can really bust loose, driving to a narrow fairway where control is essential, driving under various psychological conditions such as having just gagged on a three-foot putt, and so forth. And other types of shots involve even more variations. From the fairway one must, in addition to the above, master hitting from all manner of uneven lies (the ball above one's feet and below one's feet, off of downhill slopes and uphill slopes, out of divots) and with various types of spin, fade, and draw. From the rough one must learn the tricks of hitting from different types of grass (thick, thin, grain with, grain against) and to protect against fliers. One must learn to hit knockdowns and flops and bump-and-runs, to stop the ball quickly out of the sand, to hit low runners and high runners, and on and on and on.

Always before I had loosely imagined there to be no more than, say, a dozen necessary skills in golf: the drive, a few distinct types of iron shots, the pitch, the chip, the sand shot, the putt, and a few cute variations thereof. Master those, more or less, and you were off to the races. But now I was beginning to see that in reality golf encompassed a vast matrix of skills—four or five hundred of them, including various psychological skills, if one really sat down and analyzed the situation. And each skill clamored for attention.

In my mind's eye I pictured a giant "Skill-O-Meter," like one of those whirring, constantly updating arrival-and-departure boards at airports. Each skill has its own window displaying your current proficiency level at that task, graded on a scale of one to ten. Assuming, for simplicity's sake, there are five hundred skills, that would make five thousand total "points" available, which puts things in about the right perspective. If you work extremely hard for a couple of months on skill #289—maybe skill #289 is flop shots from ten to thirty feet—you could conceivably improve your rating for that shot dramatically, from five to maybe even nine. Terrific. As a result, your total rating as a golfer skyrockets from, say, 2,670 to 2,674. But unfortunately, having lavished so much time on flop shots during those two months, you neglected to practice left-to-right breaking medium-length lag putts (skill #316), so that skill rating dropped a couple of points. So you're back down to 2,672. But you did learn for the first time how to extricate your ball from a deep fried-egg lie in the bunker, so your rating there (skill #121) zoomed from zero to five overnight, pushing you to 2,677. You're making progress, slow but sure. When you get to 4,000, you might be ready for a shot at the PGA Tour.

The problem with golf, I decided as the ferry pulled into the slip at Orient, is that it's calibrated wrong. Baseball has the good sense to compile its statistics out to three digits. Thus fans can easily recognize the difference between a .344 superstar and the grub who bats .256, even though the difference between the two is golf-like: less than one hit every ten times at bat. If the PGA Tour were keeping score, both players would be batting 3.

The Fine Green Line only *seemed* fine to someone as naïve as I had been at the start of the Year. It was actually a gulf. And the only way to cross that gulf was to patiently tilt away at the Skill-O-Meter, pushing, pushing, pushing at all five hundred skills, and hope that over time the mean to which you regress gradually improves.

THE NEXT NORTH Atlantic Tour event was an unusual two-man affair on the hardest golf course I have ever played: The Shattuck.

With a slope rating of 145, The Shattuck winds through a pristine wilderness of forests, gorges, and beaver ponds near Mount Monadnock in southern New Hampshire. To obtain the environmental permits needed to build the course, the developers had to agree to disturb the natural setting as little as possible. So the fairways tilt madly with the natural contours of the land and impenetrable woods come right up to their edge. Many holes require long carries across marshes and chasms, which players cross via boardwalks. Basically, there is no room for error at The Shattuck.

To enhance the drama of competing on this monster (and perhaps attract a larger field), Buddy Young dreamed up a special two-man format. For me it was a nightmare, especially the first round when each team played only one ball, alternating shots. This altered the entire psychological dynamic of the game. My partner was Captain Kurt, as supportive and even-keeled a partner as you could ask for. But still, I was unnerved. Whatever mess I might make of things, Kurt would have to clean up. It's one thing to shoot yourself in the foot, but to let down a friend. . . . Before the round I was almost sick with anxiety. In a flash I understood why the biannual Ryder Cup team matches are so emotionally fraught.

On the first tee Buddy patiently summarized the rules. "In particular," he said, holding up a rhetorical finger, "I want to point out that when you miss a short putt, don't reach out and tap it in. Your partner has to come over and do that. This is pretty obvious, of course, but I guarantee you some dumbass out there today will forget."

The dumbass turned out to be me.

From the start things went badly for Kurt and me. I hit the opening drive into the woods and Kurt followed suit on number two. After four holes we were already five over par. On five Kurt made our first good shot of the day, a chip from a nasty lie in the rough to two feet below the hole. A turnaround seemed imminent. But I missed the putt—I pushed it grossly three inches wide of the hole, and disgustedly reached out for the ball with my putter.

"Wait! Don't!" Kurt cried.

Too late. I had tapped the ball into the hole. As a penalty we had to respot the ball for Kurt to tap in and add two strokes to our score. Our score for the hole was seven whereas it would have been a four if I'd made the two-footer.

It would be impossible to exaggerate how distraught I was after this mishap. For the rest of the front nine I could hardly drive the cart. Time after time when I intended to accelerate I applied the brake instead. And vice versa. I once nearly ran us off a bridge. We finished with an 87.

After the round we had lunch. Long periods of staring into space. Then we went outside and sat on a bench. Long periods of staring into space.

Then we went back on the course for a practice round (not normally allowed during tournaments, but Buddy had made an exception) and both played like champions. Cumulatively after the first five holes we were three under par.

"What's the difference?" Kurt asked as we puttered down the sixth fairway in our cart. "Same two guys, same day, same course, worse conditions [it was raining intermittently]. Why did we play like such dog-asses this morning and such studs this afternoon?"

"The pressure of a tournament," I offered.

"Yeah, but where does the pressure come from? What is it exactly?"

"When something is at stake, you tense up. It becomes too important."

Kurt wasn't satisfied. He wanted to go deeper. "If what you really, really want is to score well," he said, "you and I both know you're more likely to do that when you're relaxed and having fun. Like now. This is great. We're the only ones on the course. It's beautiful—look at the mountains! Why can't we just *will* ourselves to feel like this tomorrow, go out and have some fun and score like bandits?"

I couldn't frame a response.

Before we could finish the front nine the rain picked up and we waited out a heavy shower in our cart. It was pleasant, sitting there on comfortable foam seats in the middle of the wilderness, watching the weather do its worst. We talked about our fears and ambitions. I remember reading once that boys typically bond with their fathers and other boys side-by-side—that is, physically facing the same direction, engaged in a common task—whereas girls tend to bond with their mothers face-to-face, so they can monitor the subtle little body-language clues men tend to ignore. If so, this might be one of the secret reasons golf appeals to men so much: you have a lot of time to bond side-by-side, sitting in a cart or walking down the fairway.

Kurt said that when he took up golf seriously after the army the summer before, he had been so nervous in tournaments his hands shook visibly when he putted. It was particularly bad the one time his father caddied for him. He was trembling so badly he had to back off nearly half his shots just to reattach his hands to the club. In the last few months he had improved, but he still got the heebie-jeebies and couldn't understand why.

This surprised me, since I thought of Captain Kurt as Mr. Clutch, but I told him some of the things I had learned from Chuck Hogan about relaxation and self-hypnosis. "Hogan's deal is to create such vivid images in your brain that there's no room left for nervousness," I explained. "You just let go. You trust the images and your intuitions to do the work. Sometimes it seems to work."

"I don't get letting go," he said. "I hear people talk about it, but I don't know what it means. I like to be in control."

Kurt had been gracious enough to invite me for the night to his parents' house, about forty-five minutes away. Given that Kurt often spent nights in the backseat of his Oldsmobile and showered in tournament clubhouses, I had assumed he came from modest circumstances. But in fact the Kwader house, overlooking the White River valley from a high ridge near Keene, was spectacular. It even had a name, Cedar Crest, discreetly displayed on a plaque at the head of the long gravel road leading up to the house.

Kurt's dad, Jack, met us at the door. A rough-hewn redhead like his son, he was the chief executive of a specialty paper company with twenty-two mills across the eastern United States.

"Let's see the scorecard," he said.

For twenty minutes Kurt and his dad dissected the day's round, blessedly leaving aside my own contributions to the disaster. They dwelled on each of Kurt's mistakes in detail, Jack Kwader offering neither sympathy nor reproach, only analysis. When a pattern emerged that Kurt was leaving his long uphill putts short, Jack offered a solution. "Figure out the degree the green is slanting, approximately, and dial in two feet for every one degree of slope. So if there's five degrees of slope, you pick a spot five times two feet, or ten feet beyond the hole and hit to that spot. It's a good way of quantifying the problem," he said.

Kurt wrote down this bit of advice in a little notebook he kept in his bag. It turned out he was a meticulous note keeper. After dinner he showed me a large manila envelope containing a record of every tournament he had played in. In most cases he used the pin location sheet given to players before each round and penciled in his annotations near the diagram of each hole. He recorded such details as the iron he had used for each approach shot, where his errant shots went (left or right, short or long), his success at getting up-and-down from near the green, the number of putts he took on each hole, the direction of the green's grain, and summary information about the round at the bottom of the page: fairways in regulation, greens in regulation, and so forth.

Was all this attention to detail a good idea? My instinct was no, it divorced a player from his intuitive self. But what did I know? I was the one that day who had screwed up so royally. Maybe I needed to disconnect from my intuitive self, since my intuition under pressure seemed to be to freak out.

IN THE SECOND round at The Shattuck, Kurt and I played better. The format was best ball, which meant my miscues didn't affect Kurt as directly. On the front nine, in fact, Kurt drove miserably and it was I who held the team together. Then on the back Kurt caught fire, playing his own ball in one over par. "Way to ding-dong, partner," he said when we shook hands afterward. We posted a credible 76 on the Shattuck monster—the best round of the tournament among amateurs.

Having been among the first groups to finish, I grabbed a hot dog and went back on the course to watch the leaders play the final holes. The team of Joe Klemmer and Rodney Butcher had started the day with a two-stroke lead and were paired in the final foursome against a former Temple University golfer who three weeks earlier had won the ten-thousand-dollar top prize at the Portland (Maine) Open, and a white-haired fifty-six-year-old head pro at a ritzy country club in Massachusetts.

"Tony [the fifty-six-year-old] will never shoot a 65, he doesn't have the length," Buddy observed when I caught up with him and the group at the fifteenth tee. "But he'll never shoot worse than 75, either."

The fifteenth at The Shattuck is a tricky 544-yard par five. Everyone else off the tee used a driver, but Klemmer hit a one-iron. When his ball was still in the air—way, way up in the air—someone remarked, "It must be nice to wake up every morning knowing you can hit a one-iron 280 yards." The ball landed in the fairway but bounded through the dogleg into a dense patch of rough.

"Make that 290 yards," Butcher said, a little annoyed.

Klemmer does not look like an aggressive player standing over the ball, his hands held unusually close to his groin. With his glasses on, eyeing the target, he appears studious and unassuming. And his swing is unassuming, too: no big, John Daly-esque windup, merely a cock and flick of the wrists. But the ball whistles. His length comes from his hands, which he whips through the ball with such a relaxed grip he almost seems to be throwing the club.

On this day, however, Klemmer was off his game. His wayward tee shot forced Butcher to hole a fifteen-foot putt to halve the hole. Then the other team birdied the sixteenth to close the gap to one stroke.

As we all trudged up to the elevated seventeenth tee box, I noticed a wicked grin on Buddy's face. "I thought I'd make things a little interesting here," he whispered gleefully into my ear.

So that was it. When Kurt and I had played the hole earlier, we had wondered why the tees were moved so far forward. Normally the hole, a short but perilous par four across a gulch to a narrow, tilted fairway, plays at 339 yards. But for this round Buddy had put the men's tees where the ladies' tees normally are, transforming it—for long hitters like Klemmer, Butcher, and Quinn—into a 290-yard temptation. The green was perched way up on top of a hill, with a rocky chasm falling off immediately to the left and forbidding woods to the right and behind. I had not even *thought* about going for the green off the tee. It had taken all the nerve I could muster to lay up with a five-iron and *pitch* into the treacherous green.

But sure enough, three of the four players in the final foursome—all but the old guy—pulled out big lumber. None of them happened to make it, but all hit decent shots and, besides, that's not the point. The point is they each had the confidence to *try,* under down-the-stretch tournament pressure. I stood in awe. Any lingering doubts I might have had about the gulf between me and golfers at the top of the mini-tour world (much less the PGA Tour!) vanished in that moment.

Klemmer and Butcher ended up losing the tournament on the fourth hole of a playoff. Afterward I ran into Klemmer in the men's room. "Commence drinking," he was saying to himself in the mirror. I asked if he'd been nervous in the playoff; if he had not missed a three-foot putt on the final hole, the playoff would have continued.

"Nope," he said. "I was completely focused on seeing the ball drop into the hole. It didn't work this time but, hey, if you don't win you gotta lose."

"What does that mean?" I asked.

"If you lose, you lose," he shrugged.

This clarified nothing, but my interpretation was that Klemmer accepted his place along the Fine Green Line's continuum. At that point in his career, he was as good as he happened to be—no better, no worse—and whether one particular putt fell into the hole or not didn't change a thing.

TWO WEEKS LATER, at the New Hampshire Open, I chickened out about turning pro, despite what I had told the reporter from the *Suffolk Times.*

It wouldn't have been hard to turn pro. All that is required is to declare yourself eligible to win money in a tournament, even if you never do win any money in a tournament. But the act, once taken, is irrevocable. The only way to regain your amateur status is by making a complicated application to the United States Golf Association and waiting sometimes for years. In other words, once I turned pro there was no going back—from that point forward I would have to pony up two hundred to four hundred dollars extra per tournament in entry fees. Why not save trouble, I asked myself, and flush the money directly down the toilet?

Did this reveal a fatal lack of confidence? Of course it did. What about David Bakyta's advice to live the life, to wake up every morning thinking like a pro or else my baby would starve?

Well, I just wasn't there yet. I *was* thinking about my baby, only realistically. I remembered a story a college roommate of mine told about his high school football team in Atlanta. He went to a small, private school and at halftime in a game against a much bigger public school they were getting trounced. The score was 40 to 0 or something and in the locker room the coach was furious. He thought he detected a lack of gumption. "Is there anyone in this room," he screamed at his charges, clearly hoping for a Knute Rockne–like miracle, "who thinks we don't still have a chance to go out in the second half and win this goddamn football game?" My friend thought about it for a second and cautiously raised his hand. One by one, all his teammates raised theirs, too.

That's the way I felt about turning pro.

Sure, it was pretty to imagine that I could go out and win a bunch of money, but based on everything I now knew about the Fine Green Line and the Skill-O-Meter and how progress is really made in golf, I knew it wouldn't happen anytime soon. I might possibly get lucky in a tournament or two, put together a few good rounds in a row and win seventy-five dollars, but that was the best I could hope for, and it wouldn't put any food in Anna's mouth.

On my drive to the New Hampshire Open, I had actually done a lot of thinking about confidence. It was the Sunday of the British Open and around noon I had stopped to eat lunch at a bar so I could watch the broadcast. My hero, Tom Lehman, had started the round with a four-stroke lead and from the moment the bartender clicked the TV on for me (I was the only customer), I knew he would win. I could tell from the way he was stalking down the fairway with that absolute focus and absolute confidence champions have. And he did win, by two over Ernie Els and Mark McCumber.

"Playing the mini-tours just a few years ago," he told the television interviewer after the round, "I would never in a thousand years have imagined myself winning the British Open."

But I didn't believe that comment. I recalled what Lehman had told me in an interview over lunch in Augusta, Georgia, at a now-defunct restaurant called The Green Jacket. "Your career advances through stepping-stones in confidence," he said. "I remember many times being more nervous on the mini-tours, literally, than I ever have been here at the Masters. When you're at someplace like the Waterloo Open (in Iowa) and you're down to your last few hundred dollars and you know you have to *win* because not even second place pays enough, that's real pressure. And you learn from it. You learn how your body reacts, learn how to use your nervousness to help you focus, learn what it feels like to come through. So that's a stepping-stone. And the next time you find yourself in a similar situation, you've got this reservoir of confidence to draw on. You see yourself as at a higher level than before, as a peer of the guys you're competing against instead of as inferior, and that's what it takes. That's how you make progress."

When Lehman came out of the blue at his first Masters to lead the tournament after round one, he wasn't surprised. "The guys in the press tent were, but not me," he said. "By that point I knew what I could do." I think Lehman imagined many years in advance that one day he would win the British Open.

I had climbed a few stepping-stones in confidence myself since the start of the Year. Compared to the apoplectic anxiety I had experienced at my first tournament back in Miami, I was now reasonably calm. Some of my specific golf skills had improved impressively: my trajectories were lower and more consistent than they had been before, I was better out of the sand, I could hit low pitches that stopped on a dime. Twice I had been at or near tournament leads— at Key Biscayne and Norwich—and had learned a little something about how pressure clouds perception and tightens the swing. In short, though it was surely frustrating to still be shooting 80s and 86s, I was on an upward track. I felt as if any week I might pull myself up to the next stepping-stone.

But I had not improved so much that I saw any point in forking over two hundred extra dollars for the privilege of competing head-to-head against guys like Joe Klemmer and Rodney Butcher. Based on Lehman's experience that would not be brave, it would be foolish. His first three years on the Tour, right out of college, were destructive. He was in over his head and he knew it, and the psychological damage of butting heads week after week against guys who were clearly better broke his confidence and sent him back to the mini-tours.

So that's why I didn't turn pro for the New Hampshire Open, and my play in the qualifying round bore out the wisdom of the decision. For the first seven holes I played as well as I ever had. Not only was I striking the ball crisply, but the rhythm of my swing felt connected to a separate, larger-scale rhythm I had never experienced before, a rhythm connecting shot to shot and hole to hole. The round itself flowed with a rhythm. Through seven holes I was two under par.

That was the good part, the confidence-building part I could take with me and build on for the future.

But then, sure enough, things started to fall apart. With my ball safely in the eighth fairway, our group had to wait for the green ahead to clear and this gave me time to think about how well I was playing. It scared the bejesus out of me. I was playing *too* well. I was out of my comfort zone. As a result, I hit the next shot self-consciously and faded it feebly into a bunker. Bogey. On the next two holes I scored double-bogeys. My rhythm, my focus, my confidence—poof! The round was all over but the gnashing of teeth.

In retrospect, I suppose, my sudden collapse was something useful to build on. The next time I started playing with the rhythm and precision I had possessed on the first seven holes, maybe I wouldn't be so spooked. My comfort zone would expand a bit further up the curve. And once I grew confident playing at that level—mid to upper seventies, say, instead of in the low eighties—I could progress to the next.

The only hitch was time.

If I were twenty-five with a lifetime of golf yawning ahead, this would be the way to proceed. Fumble forward and persevere. But I didn't have years, I had only three months now until Q School, and after that my pro golfing career would be over.

Was there some way to speed up the process? Was there some way to make an end run around the Fine Green Line?

15 . *The Dakotas*

IN EARLY AUGUST, TWO-AND-A-HALF MONTHS
before Q School, I headed west, like many an
adventurous American male before me.

Back in the nineteenth century, the lure of
the West proved irresistible to tens of thousands of guys like me. Out West you had your
big sky and your purple mountains and your
fruited plains, plus lots of thrilling danger
(bears, Indians, unreliable maps, the perpet-
ual threat of starvation) and—with so many
other guys heading West, too—camaraderie.
Best of all, the West offered you a chance to
make a fresh start. Instead of telling your wife
you were bopping over to the 7-Eleven for a
pack of cigarettes and then never coming
back, in those days all you had to do was mut-

ter a few words about helping America fulfill its Manifest Destiny, throw a saddlebag across the back of your horse, and ride off into the sunset. "I'll be back to get you soon, honey," you might have promised, but this wasn't absolutely required.

A hundred years later, heading West is not the same. But for me it was still a chance to make a fresh start. During the long drive from Orient to my first stop in Omaha, Nebraska—three interminable days, nights spent in a tent thrown up beside Mr. Lucky—I had plenty of time to draw connections. Back East, I figured, I was oppressed. I was stuck in a golf slump, "fenced in" by having to scurry home every few days to wife and daughter, unfairly burdened by the high price of motel rooms. Yes, it was intolerable. Out West things would be different. Out West I could let loose, become somebody else, play golf at the level I knew I was capable. The role I envisioned playing was that of the mysterious stranger. I would ride into town, rent a room at the Motel 6 for only twenty bucks, and let my golf game speak for itself. If someone asked where I came from, I would fix them with a withering stare and say, "Who wants to know?" The Gunslinger—that would be my version of Ken Harrelson's "The Hawk" alter ego.

If people perceived me fearfully, as a *player*, maybe I'd start to play that way. This was my Westward Ho! strategy.

MY FIRST COMPETITION out West was the Nike Tour's Monday qualifier for the Omaha tournament. These qualifiers raise a lot of money for the Tour. Any pro or amateur with a two-handicap or better and two hundred dollars to waste is invited to participate. At Omaha, 224 of us took the bait, competing for fourteen open spots in the tournament proper. By my calculations that transferred $44,800 into the Nike Tour coffers, less whatever it cost to stage the eighteen-hole event on a windswept municipal course west of town.

Until the early 1980s qualifiers such as this were a fact of life on the PGA Tour. Only the top sixty money-winners from the previous year's Tour were automatically eligible for each tournament. Another ninety or so spots went to those who played well on

Monday. Given that the odds of making it into the tournament each week were roughly one in two, this system created an entire class of PGA Tour "rabbits" who hopped from city to city hoping to get in, and an entire alternative universe of mini-events and gambling games to occupy those who did not. Since the introduction of the first modern Q School in 1982, however, the Big Tour has been "all-exempt" and reserves only four spots in its tournament fields for Monday qualifiers. Since it often takes a 63 or 64 to be one of those four—scores which no one can shoot except by accident—virtually no rabbits follow the PGA Tour around anymore.

On the Nike Tour, however, with fourteen spots available and sometimes more, the situation is more forgiving. Occasionally a score as high as even par makes the grade. A few dozen pros, many of them near-miss refugees from the previous year's Q School, actually try to eke out a living on the Nike Tour through Monday qualifying. If they finish in the top twenty one week, they are automatically exempt for the following week's event, and if over time they get into enough tournaments and win enough money, the Tour will get around to making them a full-fledged member.

In any event, it was at the Nike Omaha qualifier, on August 5 at 10:14 A.M., that I made my pro debut.

I could have competed as an amateur, but in this case the entry fee was the same, and besides, I figured, what the hell? The time had come. This was the West, land of fresh starts. I was tired of playing the dorky amateur. I was now The Gunslinger.

Naturally I told no one of my virgin status. Instead, with a cold glint in my eye, I sauntered to the tee box with contemptuous aplomb, waggled my titanium Big Boy with malice aforethought, and rifled a powerful drive down the middle of the fairway. I wasn't nervous, I was calm. I actually half-believed the image I was projecting.

"Golf shot," said one of my playing companions, pro-to-pro. I acknowledged the remark with a dismissive snort.

A few minutes later I spun my approach shot to a stop ten feet from the hole and made a credible run at a birdie. The ball just missed on the high side of the cup—the "pro" side, they call it. Without a stumble, with no apparent sign of weakness, I parred the next three holes. The last of those was the most impressive. From a greenside bunker I blasted out to seven feet and canned the putt for par, center cup, never a doubt.

"Golf shot," my fellow pro had said again after the bunker shot. I acknowledged him this time with a nod. Otherwise we still had not exchanged a word.

From the tee of the next hole, a 560-yard par five, I lashed a drive nearly three hundred yards. A strong tailwind was helping, but still, it was awesome. At least I thought so. And by the time I reached my ball, perched pristincly on fluffy grass in the middle of the fairway, I had no doubt I would try for the green in two. By normal standards this was a silly decision. A creek ran in front of the green. The ball would need to carry 240 yards in the air and stop on a dime. But I didn't care. These were not normal times. This was the new me.

Confidently I drew my driver from the bag and squinted into the sun, surveying the landscape like a scout. Was anyone besides me thinking Gary Cooper in *High Noon*? This was a showdown: the old me vs. the new me. Every ounce of my being was aware of the moment's drama. Silence closed in around me. The sun was hot overhead.

I swung, and swung hard.

The ball dribbled maybe fifty feet.

I had cold-topped it. I had probably come within a millimeter or two of missing the ball altogether, a total whiff. I was dismayed. In shock, without returning to my bag, I marched after the ball and swung at it again with my driver. This time I caught the ball square and sent it scorching over the green into a bush, for an unplayable lie. With the penalty, a chip, and two putts, I saved seven.

"I sure goofed up there," I chitter-chattered like a schoolboy as our group walked to the next tee. "I was really nervous. This is my first tournament as a pro, you know. I'm writing a book. I'm really just a three-handicap amateur."

Thus did my Westward Ho! strategy collapse the first time.

· · ·

HAD I BEEN a regular Nike Tour rabbit, I would have spent a large part of the next week in a motel room watching movies. Unsuccessful Monday qualifiers, I had been told, are generally not welcome around the tournament site. The whiff of failure clings to them too redolently. They bring bad karma. So they go home or drive on to the next week's site (in this instance, Utah) for some early practice at the qualifier course.

My case was different. I could legitimately pose as a journalist. At the Q School's final stage in December, I had interrogated quite a few players about what it took to make it on the mini-tours. But back then my curiosity was theoretical; I had not yet played in any tournaments myself. Now my curiosity was desperate. Most of the guys on the Nike Tour had struggled at one time or another on the North Atlantic and South Florida tours of the world. They were the mini-tour sweepstakes winners. I felt sure they could tell me what I needed to know.

The first player I latched onto was Steve Pleis, a tall, broad-shouldered Floridian with a jittery demeanor. Pleis was one of the few to have some success qualifying for the Nike Tour on Mondays. So far this year he had squeezed through seven of the nine qualifiers he had entered and made the cut in five Nike tournaments to win a total of $1,565. This Monday he had shot 70 in the qualifier and as a result was now on the range at the Champions Club, where the Omaha tournament would be held, hitting all the shiny new balata range balls he wanted.

"You have to pay your dues," he told me. "There's no substitute for experience."

I had met Pleis a few years before when I did my story on the Space Coast Tour. Back then he was known as a serious long-ball hitter who sometimes lost interest in the competition. At one tournament I attended, he and a guy named Brad both posted first-round scores in the eighties. For the second round they played in a twosome as the first group of the day and raced around the course in two hours and fifteen minutes. "It was like they were in a hurry to take a shit," one of the marshals told me. After the round they took their cart back onto the course and tormented a rookie friend of theirs who had started the day in the lead but was rapidly falling apart. They said things like, "There's a lot of chicken left on that bone" after the nervous rookie left a forty-foot putt fifteen feet short. They couldn't stop giggling.

But now Pleis's attitude toward golf was entirely serious. For six months that winter and spring he had caddied for Paul Azinger on the PGA Tour. The experience had toughened him up, he said. "The main thing I learned was patience. It used to be I'd let a bad shot get to me, which compounded the error for the next three holes. Now I just leave it behind."

"Yeah, yeah, yeah," I said. "That's what everybody says. But how do you actually do that? Yesterday I hit one bad shot on six and it cost me three straight double-bogeys."

"Experience, man, like I said. Mentally I'm so far ahead of where I was last year at this time—I can't explain it."

"Can't you try?"

"It's experience but also, like, knowing you can make up for mistakes. I picked up a lot of tricks from Zinger. For instance, he says there are six different ways to hit a ball out of the rough, and you gotta know which technique to use in which circumstance."

I recalled reading once that Azinger hit his chip shots off the toe of the club. That way he avoided having some of his shots jump off the clubface when he caught them on the sweet spot and others come off dead—he hit them all dead. "Is that one of the tricks you learned?" I asked Pleis.

"Yeah, that's one of them."

"And what were some of the others?"

Pleis thought about this. Finally he said, "I'm not telling the guys out here all the things I learned. It's a competitive business."

I spent the better part of two days harassing the Nike Tour players for tips. Most were reasonably cooperative, but their answers were hardly encouraging. "The first thing you've got to do is figure out how to play at the best of your ability," said Eric Johnson. "Out here, everybody's pretty much done that. On the mini-tours, not even half the guys have."

"It's a matter of being confident and comfortable at whatever level you're at," a Texan named Brad Ott assured me. "Once you can beat all the guys at one level, you're ready for the next step up!"

"There aren't any shortcuts," echoed Jack O'Keefe, who had been the Hooters Tour's top money-winner the year before. "You've got to put yourself into contention as much as possible, learn how your game behaves under pressure, and then get comfortable with it." For example, he said, he had been paired with Tom Lehman in the third round of the 1995 U.S. Open at Shinnecock. (I was impressed that he had progressed through the two Open qualifying stages and then made the thirty-six-hole cut.) "Tom shot a 65 that day and showed me a lot about staying calm and focused under pressure. That's the kind of experience you have to have to push things along."

Great, I thought. It's really very simple. First, you get really, really good. Then, you get comfortable being good. Then, if you persevere and you're lucky, you'll get the chance to spend year after year on the Nike Tour going broke.

THE DAKOTAS PROFESSIONAL Golf Tour began in the 1970s as an attempt by local golf clubs to import a little late-summer excitement for the benefit of their members. All the events are pro-ams. Local businesses chip in extra prize money to help attract bigger fields and hopefully beef up the tourist trade (a dubious benefit, given the beggarly budgets of most mini-tour pros). But somehow it worked. They built a tour in the cornfields and people actually came.

Most Dakotas Tour events take place in the eastern part of the states, far from Mount Rushmore and the Badlands where legitimate tourists congregate. For the players, this has its pros and cons. On the downside, after-hours kicks are hard to find, pretty much limited to gambling at Indian-run casinos scattered out in the bush and drinking beer at strip joints on the outskirts of Sioux Falls and Fargo. The upside is that the locals are fabulously hospitable. Many players stay for free in private homes. Almost every day during the tour's nine-week schedule, players can participate in some organized activity or prize-offering competition.

My first event was the Sioux Falls Open, for which I had preregistered and prepaid despite the inconvenient fact that it took place on the same days as the Nike tournament (with all that implies about my confidence at qualifying in Omaha). The course, a 7,200-yard-long municipal affair on the outskirts of town, was indeed surrounded by cornfields. (Who eats all this corn, anyway? For five hundred miles of my drive from New York, corn was the only attraction on both sides of the interstate, stretching as far as the eye could see.)

The pros who make their way to the Dakotas Tour are about as diverse a lot as can be imagined. The three I hooked up with for my practice round are representative.

First was The Proselytizer, a bespectacled recent graduate of Texas Lutheran College who didn't wait long to make his first pitch. "You know," he said, apropos of nothing as we strolled down the first fairway, "golf and Christianity are just the opposite."

"How's that?" I said, fearing the worst.

"In golf, one guy wins and everyone else loses. In Christianity, one guy dies . . . and everyone else wins!"

"An interesting thought," I said. "So, have you ever played the Dakotas Tour before?"

I managed to avoid The Proselytizer for several holes, but on three he caught me standing near the hole when he missed a short putt. "Golf is a terrible servant and an unfair master," he complained.

"Yeah, I know what you mean," I said, replacing the pin and attempting an escape.

"You do?" he replied, peering deep into my soul.

"Sure. You can't win for losing, that sort of thing."

"That's part of it, yes. But what I was driving at is that the real Master is both a wonderful servant *and* a fair master."

"Oh."

"Are you a Christian, John Paul?"

The Proselytizer wasn't a bad guy, I suppose. Once or twice he essayed some humor, such as when he winked at me while standing over an eight-foot putt and said, "I'm going to make this—unless as a Calvinist I'm predestined not to!" I finally managed to deflect his assault by mentioning that my dad was a Baptist seminary professor. This didn't grant me full immunity, but it elevated the discussion into an abstract theological sphere where it was easier to be evasive.

I also sought protection by sticking close to the second pro in our group, The Chief Executive. He was fifty-seven, from California, and had an intriguing story to tell.

Three years before, The Chief Executive—then head of a multimillion-dollar aerospace company—had suffered a stroke. His life flashed before his eyes. As he recovered he took stock of what was truly important to him and what was not, and came away with a completely rearranged slate of priorities. He quit his job and devoted himself to his new number one commitment: getting better at golf.

Being a former chief executive, he set about this task by crafting a systematic business plan. He set quarterly objectives, scheduled periodic evaluations, and established quantitative criteria for judging his progress. He retained the services of several independent golf consultants (better known as teaching pros) but eventually dismissed them when he found that none contributed to the bottom line as effectively as the book *Five Lessons* by Ben Hogan. This he studied backward and forward for over a year.

From his corporate experience the concept he found most valuable was "failing forward," which he explained to me in some detail. "The basic idea is to view each failure as a positive opportunity for analysis rather than as a disappointment. If you have a problem and can understand why it developed, you can learn from it and make progress."

The Chief Executive started this experiment as a fine golfer already, a club champion, but said he improved dramatically. A few weeks earlier, for example, he had reached the finals of the U.S.

Senior Open, which he called the greatest "spiritual accomplishment" of his life.

"Spiritual?" I said, impressed but surprised. "How was it spiritual?"

"You don't imagine you can make the sort of progress I've made by just going out and trying hard, do you? The whole thing hinges around your whole life. You can't play golf one way and live your life another. You've got to get your whole life in order, and that's what I did."

In addition to his post-stroke work on golf, The Chief Executive said he had also worked with a psychologist—a regular psychologist, not a golf psychologist—to resolve his most important "life issues." These he did not detail, but he implied that they were substantial. In addition he became enamored of Zen, particularly a book published in 1953 called *Zen in the Art of Archery* by the German philosopher Eugen Herrigel. "That book taught me the value of emotional detachment in golf," he declared solemnly. "Without emotional detachment, success is impossible."

This talk was right up my alley, particularly the part about emotional detachment. I was unable to detach. When I struck a bad shot or anticipated an important round, my emotions dragged me off like a team of rabid sled dogs. Emotional detachment, or lack thereof, was my undoing—yet here was a guy who knew the answer!

I told The Chief Executive about my difficulty detaching and explained that I was writing a book about getting better in a way not that much different than he had done.

"You're writing a book?" he asked suspiciously.

"Yes."

"I'm planning on writing a book, too."

"You are? That's great," I said, thinking fast. "Maybe I can use some of your stuff in my book and it will be good publicity for yours."

"I don't think so."

"Well, I don't have to use your stuff in my book, but you could still tell me how you emotionally detach."

"I don't think so," The Chief Executive said again, and after that he mummed up. I couldn't get another word out of him. In an instant I had become a business rival, and that put things in a completely different light. The rest of the round I noticed he and The Proselytizer talking a lot, though I couldn't tell from a distance who won.

Which left me alone with the third pro in our group, a journeyman from Springfield, Missouri, named Chris Fredenburg. He was far more entertaining, anyway.

Chris, who sported a smart goatee and cropped his black hair close to the head, played golf at a maniac pace and possessed, I am certain, the quickest, most unorthodox windup I have ever seen. His swing looked more like a brief epileptic fit than anything deliberate, though the ball came off the clubface with amazing consistency. Stalking the course, he muttered constantly, only brief snippets of which were intelligible. He seemed to be obsessed with monkeys. "Fucking monkeys" and "retardo monkeys" were phrases I detected. Also, "monkey see, monkey do" and "whipped cream on shit," though this last had nothing to do with monkeys.

I had no trouble striking up a conversation with Chris. He was funny and friendly. He said he had played college golf at Southwest Baptist College in Missouri and after that spent some time on the Hooters Tour. "It was just like college," he said. "Every night you'd go out drinking. The only guys who ever won were the monkeys who didn't drink. How do you beat that?"

I agreed that it sounded terribly unfair.

"Don't get me wrong. There was some real talent out there. Sometimes it took 24-under-par to win a four-day event. I'm sorry, but I just don't know how to shoot 24-under-par. I don't know how to think like that."

Another problem Chris had was practice. He said he didn't know how. "Everybody out there is a teacher. They don't mean any harm. They're just trying to help. They say keep your wrist here and keep your wrist there, but I don't give a shit about that stuff. I've never had a swing thought in my life, much less a lesson. I just go out and hit the ball. You'd see guys beating balls every day on the range and they were good players so I tried it, too. But all that happened to me was I goofed up my swing. I got worse and worse. Finally it just wore me out."

For a while he sold golf equipment and earned some decent wages, but then he quit. "My wife makes good money working for the mobile phone company and I've got a low nickel, so that's why I'm able to play." He explained his family finances, even though I hadn't asked him to. His truck was paid for (though it had 150,000 miles on it), his house payments were low, and his wife's car payments were even lower. At this point we had known each other for about five holes.

"So it works out pretty well. She gets health insurance at work. Plus I make a little money on the side." On his drive up to the Dakotas he had won a thousand dollars playing Texas Hold-em on a riverboat in St. Louis. "Guy betting against me had the two kings on the flop plus three sevens and thought he was unbeatable. But I had the two kings and two more in my pocket. 'Thank you very much,' I told him. Retardo monkey."

Earlier that summer Chris had won some money on a mini-tour called the Prairie Tour. "I was doing okay. Several of us were. Then Steve Gotsche from the Nike Tour decides to pay us a visit for a few weeks. For guys like that, the Prairie Tour is basically the Free Money Tour. He comes out, looks around, and thinks, 'There's not one of you guys who is capable of beating me, even if you get hot.' And probably he's right. Well, okay. Thanks a lot for dropping by, guy. You got your card, why don't you stay up on the Nike Tour where you belong?"

"What makes Gotsche so much better?" I asked.

"Dunno. Guys like that just got it. Confidence, I guess. Experience."

The old refrain.

I TRIED REALLY, really hard at the Sioux Falls Open. I really did. I readopted my Westward Ho! strategy and kept the cold glint in my eye with very few lapses. I examined my putts from every conceivable angle, paced off precise distances on the fairways, threw lots of grass in the air to test wind speed and direction, and kept my ball assiduously clean. I visualized extensively. I breathed deeply between shots to relax. I played one shot at a time. I tried my best to detach emotionally.

But in the end I shot an 81—exactly as if I hadn't been trying at all.

In the second round I tried really hard again. I refused to be discouraged. I took deep breaths. My concentration never wavered. Once again I shot an 81.

Honestly, it was hard to understand. Here I was in my first full-scale tournament as a pro, making use of all the fine advice and experience I had accumulated in nine months of unceasing effort, using custom-made clubs with a retail value four times that of my car, and still I shot twin 81s. And the worst of it was, I hadn't actually played that poorly. I had lost a couple of drives left—one went out-of-bounds barely, the other landed in a ditch—and that was it for bonehead plays. I missed a couple of five- to six-foot putts, the type that are makable and missable in equal measure. I failed to get up-and-down a few times when I easily could have. And before I knew it I was nine over par: 81.

Only after the round did I give in to disappointment. It was growing increasingly difficult to accept 81s gracefully, as part of the learning experience. An edge of helplessness was creeping into my psychology. What did it take? I *knew* I could play better than this, even if—in the wisdom of all I had learned—I knew I could expect to play only a handful of strokes better. Even flukishly, I had not shot an even par or subpar round all Year, whereas a year earlier, before all the practice and devotion, I had shot a half dozen such rounds. What was holding me back? Why couldn't I get just a *little* better?

I finished the second round before noon on Saturday. The final round for those who made the cut would be the next day. That meant that for most of two days I had nothing to do but stare forlornly at the South Dakota prairies and hit range balls, which at this point I didn't think would do me much good. Unable to muster the energy even to walk out to Mr. Lucky in the parking lot, I spent half an hour on a white plastic chair near the clubhouse studying my scorecard. I calculated that the square of my score, 81, was 1,377 strokes more than the square of 72, which was the score I would have needed to shoot both days to qualify for the final round. That seemed about right. The gap between me and winners: 1,377 strokes.

FROM SIOUX FALLS the Dakotas Tour traveled a hundred miles north to Watertown, with a quirky drive-by tournament scheduled for Monday in the small farming community of Madison. Tournaments like the one in Madison were why mini-tour players loved the Dakotas Tour. On any regular tour, Monday would be an off-day, but the Dakotas Tour seldom passed up an opportunity to squeeze in some more hospitality. The good farmers and farmers' wives of Madison treated the visiting pros like kin from the city come to visit: hearty welcomes, coffee and doughnuts before the round, marshals on every hole, a barbecue-and-white-bread feast afterwards. All that plus twelve hundred dollars to the winner.

By Monday morning I was feeling bluesy but optimistic. I spent a long time in the bed of my room at the Rushmore Motel in Sioux Falls ($17.45 a night) visualizing success. On my drive up Interstate 29, I swayed rhythmically to waltz tapes. I grew so mesmerized by the rhythm, in fact, that I drove right past the clearly marked exit for Madison and nearly reached the turnoff for Volga before realizing my mistake. Two minutes before my tee time Mr. Lucky screeched into the gravel parking lot of the Madison Country Club and I hopped to the starter's table on one bare foot while trying to slip my other foot into a golf shoe. This task was made more difficult by the clattering golf bag slung across my back.

"You look like one hurtin' unit, son," observed Chris Fredenburg, who just happened to be my pro partner for the day. We were paired with a local feedlot honcho and a retired casket maker.

"No, no. I'm calm," I said. "I'm very, very calm."

The Madison course was short and easy. I shot an 81.

.   .   .

WATERTOWN, IN EAST-CENTRAL South Dakota, is a fine, old-fashioned American town, population seventeen thousand. The main drag is lined by three-story brick storefronts filled with banks, farm-supply stores, and blue-plate diners. Regrettably the Dakotas Tour event in Watertown did not coincide with the fiftieth Annual Corn Fest and associated Tour de Corn bicycle race just two weeks earlier, but the organizers made up for it by presenting at least one organized event for the golfers each day: the Pro-Gal on Tuesday, the Pro-Am on Wednesday, the four-day tournament itself starting on Thursday, and a Calcutta dinner on Friday night. The golf course, called Prairie Winds Country Club despite being a municipal, was five miles from town out by the reservoir.

It was nice to spend a whole week in one spot. Without the pressure to pack up and move on after only a day or two, I got to know more of the players.

Fredenburg was my favorite. "We got pained yesterday, partner," he told me when I first saw him in Watertown, lounging under a shade tree near the clubhouse after the Pro-Gal.

"How do you mean?"

"We almost won us some money back in Madison."

I had not stuck around after my round long enough to see the results. Apparently, due to the handicap spread of our amateur partners, Chris and I came within one stroke of winning seventy dollars each.

"You mean if I'd shot 80 instead of 81, I might now have career earnings as a pro?"

"That's about the size of it."

I was distraught—as much for Chris's sake as my own. But he made me feel better by relating how he'd gotten lucky at poker the night before and won $160. "So don't feel bad on my account," he said. "Now I'm gonna go win me some more." A friend on the putting green was motioning for him to come over and I watched from afar as they played "21" (five points for an ace, three points for closest to the hole, winner is the first to reach twenty-one).

Five minutes later Chris was back with me under the tree. "There goes another fifty," he said. "Shoulda known better, trying to putt with these stone hands."

Another character I fell in with at Watertown was one of the few outright womanizers I met on the mini-tours, and you had to admire his energy and skill. On his drive up from Florida he claimed to have met a girl in Indianapolis who accompanied him to Sioux Falls. But at Sioux Falls he'd met another girl on the golf course he liked better—this one came from a rich family thereabouts—and so he had sent the Indianapolis girl packing. The Sioux Falls girl was driving up to Watertown to meet him the next day, but this put him on the horns of a dilemma because meanwhile he'd fallen in love with the girl who sold soft drinks there at Prairie Winds.

The beverage girl was cute: red hair, short-shorts. The womanizer introduced me. Then he bought her a hamburger and coyly gained permission to park his RV (I'm thinking: Lovemobile) in the parking lot of her apartment building.

"Now don't come waking me up at eleven o'clock tonight," he warned her. "I've got a tournament to play." Pure subliminal suggestion. I felt I was in the presence of genius.

For most guys, however, when the subject of women came up, the issue was of the one left back home, not the one or ones they hoped to meet on the road. One of the older guys on the tour— Steve Hay, forty-nine, with white hair and ice-blue eyes—told me his longtime girlfriend back in Florida had been calling him every night, wanting him to come home immediately or end the relationship. There was another man involved, but Hay refused to return.

"It may sound brutal, but I cannot be distracted from golf right now," he told me. After three years of preparation, his first shot at Senior Tour Q School was less than three months away and he felt he was finally on a roll.

Bill Wheeler, a twentysomething cadet from Alabama, was in a roughly similar pickle. He was in love with a girl back in Mobile. They were engaged, but she came from a fine, educated family and wasn't totally sure she wanted to marry a professional golfer.

"Can't say I blame her," said Wheeler, a burly fellow with close-cropped hair and a goatee. "I'm gone five weeks at a time. There's constant money stress. I've been ready to quit a dozen times, but then I always go out and shoot something like a 63 and I say, 'Whoa, slow down there, fella.' My fiancée says it may come down to me choosing between golf and her."

He paused for a moment, during which I thought he might cry.

"Let me tell you something: that would be one very, very tough choice."

This conversation took place at a bar, a bar with dozens of actual women in it, the closest thing Watertown had to nightlife. Standing nearby was a pro named Ed Halsell, the one and only black golfer I encountered in a year on the mini-tours.

Halsell was being hassled, presumably in good fun, by a pro from Alabama, Todd Bailey. "Don't think just because we're white we couldn't slap you upside the head as well as black people," Bailey was telling Halsell. "You'd be on the floor crying by the time I got through."

"Hey, you come play the Harlem Tour," Halsell retorted. "You won't even break 90."

Bailey and Halsell were friends. But Halsell later told me that "it" was almost always the subject of their friendship, "it" being race. "I have a hard time out here socially, despite how friendly folks seem," he said.

Halsell grew up in the Detroit inner city, the son of a single mom. He got started in golf through an outreach program at a downtown driving range. A bus would drop kids off at the range for as long as five hours a day.

"Were there any courses you could play?" I asked.

"Yeah, they had a course right there. Three holes. We played 'em over and over and over."

Halsell displayed a knack for the game, and after playing well on his high school team earned an athletic scholarship to the University of California at Santa Barbara. There, not surprisingly, he was the only black player on the team. He had struggled on the mini-tours for three years since graduation, mostly with the help of a few white sponsors.

"I've tried to get some black sponsors," he said. "I had an in with Bill Russell and some other black basketball guys in California, but I don't think they understood how long it takes to bring a pro golfer along. They wanted a quicker payback, so they weren't interested.

"Then someone put me in touch with Michael Jordan. Jordan said he was interested but wanted to see how good I was. So we arranged a match, for five hundred dollars, on his home course. That was a lot of money for me, but I figured it was worth the gamble if it helped me get a sponsor, so I accepted. Jordan asked for three strokes a side. Obviously, I couldn't argue because I was there to show him how good I was, so I gave it to him. And I played pretty good. I shot a 68. But Jordan shot a 73 and beat me on the last hole by a stroke.

"I wasn't sure he'd take my money, but he did. I'll never forget what he said. He said, 'I was gonna have hamburger for dinner tonight, but now I think I'm gonna have steak.' Can you beat that? Like the guy can't have steak any night of the week he chooses."

"Did he give you some sponsor money?" I asked.

"Nope. I never heard from him again. He told me to call him and he gave me his special office number and I left a bunch of messages, but I never heard back. It still pisses me off when I think about it."

The next day I made a point to watch Halsell play, and with my own eyes witnessed him drive to the fringe of the 345-yard eighteenth hole. His backswing was nicely compact, yet his coil still somehow produced awesome clubhead speed. Another player told me he had played with Halsell several times and used the word "dysfunctional" to describe his game. "When Ed is on, he can go deep. He'll shoot 67 or 68 as easily as you or I can shoot par. But when he's off or gets in a sulk, he'll shoot 85. And you don't win any money out here playing like that."

MY OWN PLAY in Watertown continued to disappoint. In the Pro-Gal (my score was 77), I pulled almost every drive into the rough, for no apparent reason. In the Pro-Am (81), I dumped two balls into the water hazard on a par three, carding a seven. During the first round of the tournament proper (80), I got the yips and missed three putts of less than three feet. In the second round (also 80), I bladed two wedge shots over the green and stubbed another chip.

In other words, it was always something. But rather than being mildly exasperated by these bonehead plays as I had been earlier in the Year, when I felt sure that with experience I would stop making them, now I began to panic. I had learned enough by now to know that these "always somethings" were not just trivial annoyances. It reminded me of the old joke: "Apart from that, Mrs. Lincoln, how did you enjoy the play?" Well, there was no "apart from that." Eliminating or reducing dumb mistakes is the essence of golf's challenge. But somehow, try as I might, I could not, and I was running out of time and ideas.

On Friday night, before the third round of the tournament, the host club held a Calcutta in an upstairs dining room. Calcuttas used to be popular before most states started cracking down on them, but in the Dakotas, where gambling laws are loose, they still thrive. From a dais at the head of the room an auctioneer sold off stakes in each team, usually two pros and three amateurs. Most teams fetched between $150 to $700, although some teams (such as my group of no-name pros and no amateurs) didn't sell at all. Betting strategies seemed to focus primarily on the perceived validity of various amateurs' handicaps, which were raucously discussed. Much hilarity ensued. Altogether the Calcutta raised $11,095, a fourth of which would go the pros on the top eight teams. This in addition to the $65,000 in other prize money available that week.

Observing this hoopla from the back of the dining room (I attended primarily for the free meal), I couldn't help but wonder why a small community like Watertown would choose to bestow nearly $70,000 of its hard-won resources on a group of itinerant mini-tour players. Oddly, the best analogy I could think of involved a temple of young Buddhist monks I once visited in Ulan Bator, Mongolia.

I happened to be in Ulan Bator on assignment. In this dismal, impoverished city plunked down in the middle of the vast, treeless steppes, the temple provided one of the only splashes of color in town. Inside, row after row of saffron-robed monks—most of about mini-tour age—sat in the lotus position, rocking back and forth, bumbling beads, and chanting. It was lovely. The chants made the whole vaulted room vibrate and the monks were all in states of tranquil bliss. A steady stream of Ulan Batorians filed through the temple, spinning the prayer wheels and depositing currency in the collection boxes. Why did they give? Not because they were religious—few Mongolians were, I was told—but because it was important to them, as a society, to enable this small band of fanatics to pursue their transcendent chanting for its own sake. Maybe the monks in their bliss gave people hope that something better was possible for them, too.

Watertown's generosity, I decided, was similar, as is the reverence golfers everywhere hold for anyone who plays the game well. It is important for golfers, as a community, to enable a small number of devotees to do nothing but play golf all the time and get really, really good. Without tangible proof that somebody somewhere has mastered the game, flailing away yourself would be too depressing.

Which was maybe my problem. Maybe I'd lost hope.

One of my chief pleasures in golf, from the moment I rediscovered the game as an adult, was getting better. The rest of my life might be crumbling like the Acropolis, but if I was making progress in golf, I had something positive to hang on to. And I always had made progress. My scores over the first five or six years I played the game came down, down, down. It was exhilarating. Adding to the pleasure, I have to admit, was the knowledge that I was making faster progress than those around me. I didn't progress to scratch in eighteen months as Greg Norman did when he took up the game as a teenager, but I did well. I was shooting rounds in the seventies when some of my pals still couldn't break one hundred, and it was good for my ego. What can I say? I am not the Dalai Lama.

But now the tables had turned. Not only was I no longer making progress, I was usually the worst player around—often by a great margin. Frankly, it was getting to me.

Yes, I could rationalize the situation: I had no intention of making a career as a pro golfer, I was a writer conducting an experiment. But no matter what words I used, the day-to-day reality was that I teed it up in straightforward competition against other players and day after day they beat the pulp out of me. If I had been an objective observer, I might have taken pleasure in their crisply struck drives and brilliant short-game play. But playing head-to-head against them, I took it personally. "Oh, yeah?" I thought to myself, watching a fellow pro bang a drive cleanly 280 yards down the fairway. "I can do that, too." And I could, too—just not as often. And each time I failed, my sense of self-worth took another hit.

The only thing that stood between me and the abject humiliation of being, certifiably, the worst pro on the Dakotas Tour was the name of Aaron Farkas. I never met Aaron Farkas in person. I didn't want to—I was afraid he might have only one arm or something. But after every round his name was the first I looked for on the scoreboard. Sometimes Farkas's score would be better than mine but usually it was worse, and when it was I felt a surge of relief. His scores were a fig leaf for my ego. On most days a few other pros joined Farkas and me in the high-seventies, low-eighties ghetto. I presumed they were hung-over, because the next day those pros always seemed to shoot 68. Only Farkas and I were at or near the bottom of the list every single day. Emotionally, he was my Rock of Gibraltar.

ON MY LAST day in Watertown—my last day in the Dakotas—I put together a decent round. Partly this was because I finally stopped trying to impress my fellow competitors. It was way too late for that. The Westward Ho! strategy was a flop: the cold glint in my eye had long since turned fuzzy, like the doleful gaze of a wounded dog. Equally important, however, was the play of one of the pros in my group. I allowed myself to be inspired.

The player was Mark Wood, a self-effacing, rawboned galoot

from a tiny town in West Texas. Mark had been a walk-on member of the Texas A&M golf team and since graduating a year before had logged more than forty thousand miles on his Chevy Blazer playing the mini-tours. Drawn to each other as fellow Texans, we'd actually become pals that week in Watertown. One night we drove out to an Indian casino in the bush and lost a few bucks playing blackjack; the next night we traded stories over Tex-Mex enchiladas. He told me he often thought about quitting, his short game was in the tank, most of the irons he hit went sideways, and so forth.

The next morning he went out and shot 65.

I had never played with anyone who shot 65. It was more than just good shots. He eagled the first by holing an approach shot from 125 yards, but the eeriness began on number five when he rolled in an essentially unmakable forty-foot putt. The putt, from just off the green, had at least twenty feet of break to it.

Mark walked off the green shaking his head. "It was weird," he said. "I *knew* it was going in the hole. I had no doubt."

From that point we didn't speak. I was afraid almost to look upon his face, so strange and unsettling was the power he exuded. I remembered in my long-ago round of 69 feeling a harmony with both my swing and the golf course, and Mark seemed to have this, too. But there was nothing meek about his round. He manhandled the course. Standing on the tee, he had the air of Zeus hurling thunderbolts from Olympus. On the par-five fourteenth, for instance, he powered his drive over a crest in the fairway and the ball didn't stop rolling, by my calculation, until 410 yards from the tee. (From there he knocked a wedge shot to eighteen inches and tapped in for eagle.)

Hitting from the tee box after Mark was like slipstreaming behind a massive tractor-trailer rig. Maybe it was just a matter of internalizing some of his leftover confidence, but it seemed like all I had to do was swing the club and watch my ball be sucked along by his. It was *fun*. For the first time in many months I felt *free* to rare back and swing, to knock the ball around the course like this was just a game, to play golf rather than work at it. I came away with a

75. It could have been better, of course—I missed a couple of makable putts, I plunked another ball into the pond on six, yadda yadda yadda—but who cares? The round wasn't much in the grand scheme of things, but it cheered me up on the long drive home. I decided it was premature to worry that I had reached my limit as a golfer. From what everyone said, it took at least two or three years of constant competition to get a fix on one's potential. It took Tom Lehman seven years of marching up those "stepping-stones in confidence" to discover how good he could be, and a few more years after that to actually get there.

I was in a slump, that was all—a predictable, just-turned-pro, everything-has-to-be-perfect-this-instant kind of slump. To escape the slump I only had to relax, have a little more fun, shake out the tension in my arms and my head, and let whatever talent I might have find its own good way out. If I could just manage that, I felt sure, I could attain the next level.

What that next level might be, precisely, I did not know. Nor did I know precisely *how* I might suddenly convince myself to stop thinking so much and let loose. Thinking too much was, essentially, what I as a writer had been trained to do for a living. But one advantage I had was a deadline. The first stage of Q School was now just two months away. Deadlines, like the prospect of being hanged, have a way of concentrating the mind. Faced with a genuine deadline, I liked to think I could come through.

End Game

✤

One makes love with The Joy of Sex *hanging
over one's head.* . . . *Unmediated experience is
hard to come by, is probably reserved, in our
time, to as yet undiscovered tribes sweltering
in the jungles of Bahuvrihi.*

—DONALD BARTHELME

DO YOU BELIEVE IN COSMIC COINCIDENCE?
I don't. On the other hand, what else could I
make of the message from a golf magazine editor that was waiting on my answering machine
when I returned from the Dakotas? He was
offering to send me, all expenses paid, to the
Monterey Peninsula of California, where I
would play Pebble Beach, Spyglass Hill, the
Links at Spanish Bay, Poppy Hills, and several
other fine courses and stay at the most expensive resort hotels I could find and eat costly
meals at four-star restaurants and get mas-
sages. As a theme for the article, the editor
wanted me to focus on how golf and the New
Age movement were merging.

"The Monterey Peninsula has become an

almost religious kind of spiritual golfing retreat," he explained.
Those were his exact words. It was as if Someone Up There had
sensed my discouragement in the Dakotas and decreed, "Let's send
this Newport guy on an almost religious kind of spiritual golfing
retreat."

I thought about it for maybe half a second and accepted.

And so it was that less than two weeks after driving cross-country
in my overheating five-hundred-dollar car, I found myself checking
into a $425-a-night room at the Lodge at Pebble Beach.

THE UR-SOURCE of my adult fascination with golf had been Michael
Murphy's novel, *Golf in the Kingdom.* I read this strange book
shortly after taking up the game and it convinced me that golf was
nothing to be ashamed of. The book describes Murphy's supposed
encounter at an ancient course in Scotland with a metaphysical caddie named Shivas Irons. For Irons, golf is merely a convenient step-
ping-off place for exploring the infinite. In the course of the book,
he and Murphy commune with the dead, detect blue auras around
successful competitors, score a hole-in-one at midnight using a
featherie ball and an old wood shillelagh, and get drunk with friends
discussing golf's cosmic power. The possibilities the book hinted at
were all I needed to embrace the game.

Once I'd read *Golf in the Kingdom,* I began noticing signs of its
influence everywhere. During my first visit to a Q School, I over-
heard two journeymen pros—one wearing obscene pink pants—
chattering about "true gravity," one of Shivas Irons's more obscure
concepts. A *Simpsons* episode about miniature golf made reference
to Zen. The Chevy Chase character in *Caddyshack* babbled about
"being the ball." I even stumbled across a passage by John Updike,
which described golf as "of games the most mysterious, the least
earthbound, the one wherein the wall between us and the supernatural is rubbed thinnest."

Cumulatively these mystical conjectures were a great comfort to
me. They opened up an alternative myth about golf which I could
use to refute charges of bourgeoisie Republicanism. "Golf is the

Yoga of the supermind, don't you think?" I could plausibly mention at liberal cocktail parties. When some mindless antagonist challenged me ("What could you *possibly* see in *golf?*"), I could usually shut them up with a stray line or two from Murphy, such as "the sight of the golf ball hanging in space anticipates our desire for transcendence."

All this was well and good, but on the flight west to California I had to admit I didn't know what most of these notions meant. Not really. They were evocative but bewildering, like Bob Dylan's early lyrics. Dylan was brilliant at creating atmosphere, at linking words and mood with music for poetic effect. But who was Quinn the Eskimo and why, "when Quinn the Eskimo gets here," is "everybody gonna wanna doze?" Dylan himself admitted in an interview he had no idea. Was *Golf in the Kingdom* merely atmospheric poetry, too?

One of my fondest hopes for the Year was to get to the bottom of golf's metaphysical, true gravity side. A year of Zen-like discipline and profound reflection ought to be sufficient, I imagined, to unify my mind, body, and spirit into a cosmic whole, or if not, at least to get a good start in that direction. But as things turned out, I had hardly thought about golf's cosmic side. I had been too busy learning about how to keep the right knee bent during takeaway and whether the rules allow one or two club-lengths' relief from an immovable obstruction.

Now would be the time to plunge in. At this point, frankly, I was less worried about the state of my soul than the state of my game, but I was open to anything that might help the latter. At the end of the week I would have a chance to interview the Great Man himself. Murphy, who grew up on the Monterey Peninsula, still lived nearby and I had arranged to drop by his house for a visit.

DR. BEE EPSTEIN-SHEPERD, golf hypnotist, was walking her Yorkie when I arrived at her condo. She (Dr. Bee) was five feet tall, in her mid-fifties, with close-cropped hair, brown eyes, and a much higher voice than you'd expect of a hypnotist.

"Tiger Woods has a hypnotist," she informed me as the dog peed. "I can't prove it, but I have no doubt. No one could play the way he does without outside help." She also claimed that in 1956 the Russian Olympic team traveled with eleven hypnotists. Dr. Bee was wearing an aquamarine running suit and dazzling gold-spangled sneakers. It occurred to me she might use the shoes to put me in a trance, but this proved groundless.

Inside on the couch, she debriefed me. Dr. Bee knew golf. She had worked with several LPGA players and written a book called *Mental Management for Great Golf: How to Control Your Thoughts and Play Out of Your Mind*. We agreed that my primary goal should be to achieve a relaxed, effortless swing. "An anxious mind and relaxed body cannot coexist. They are mutually exclusive," she said. Then we repaired to a recliner chair in the corner of the living room and began hypnosis. I was willing and eager.

"You will go deeper and deeper," she intoned, "for your own benefit and your own good."

And I did. I never stopped being aware of where I was or what Dr. Bee was saying (at least I don't think I did), but I did grow profoundly relaxed and tingly around the extremities. When she felt I was "under," she tested my paralysis by asking me to lift my arms. I suppose I could have if, say, Dr. Bee's Yorkie had taken that moment to drive his paws into my groin, but my arms felt comfortably heavy right where they were and I chose not to. My will was to be paralyzed in hypnosis, not to resist hypnosis.

"You have a beautiful, easy, fluid, harmonious swing," Dr. Bee said. Her voice was calming yet surprisingly energetic and insistent. I know this because Dr. Bee recorded the session on a tape for me to use later.

"The swing is within you. From now on you trust your swing. From now on you relax your body by taking a deep, eeeee-asy breath, and as you exhale all tension and stress leaves your body. Your mind focuses on the target, so that your relaxed, fluid, harmonious swing comes to you without thought, letting go of all thought, other than total focus and concentration on your target."

She droned on like this for another ten minutes or so, the same concepts over and over, then snapped her fingers. And that was that. A few minutes later we did it again, this time with a different emphasis: leaving poor shots behind. Her goal was that I learn to hypnotize myself, not only before each tournament round using the tapes she had made, but during it. Ideally, I would become so attuned to hypnosis that a deep relaxing breath before each shot would trigger the desired hypnotic state. "It's nothing more than a state in which your mind is so focused on something, like the target, that you're unaware of what your body is doing," she explained. It was a way of consciously putting yourself into "the zone" before each shot. "You *will* notice a difference," she promised as I left. Her fee was $150.

Surely it was unfair to test Dr. Bee's work that afternoon at Poppy Hills. This course, with a slope rating of 143 from the back tees I was foolish enough to use, is simply too hard for mortals, hypnotized or not. The first hole I played was number ten, a severe dogleg requiring a blind uphill tee shot and a downhill approach shot to a multilevel green fronted by a ball-eating pond and a vast system of bunkers. With each succeeding hole, no matter how melodious I tried to make myself feel, tension and stress *entered* my body, they did not leave it.

But Dr. Bee had warned me that it takes time and many repetitions for her trancelike state to work optimally, and from what I knew of how the mind works, that sounded right. At the same time, I was disappointed—not that I had played poorly, but that hypnosis wasn't somehow spookier. I had half hoped I might trudge out of Dr. Bee's office with outstretched zombie arms and play Poppy Hills in a daze. But that wasn't the case. Hypnosis was just another plausible mental-game technique—maybe better, maybe worse than pre-shot routines and guided visualizations—but in the same ballpark. I would give hypnosis a chance; I would listen to Dr. Bee's tapes again. But it would still be nice to experience true gravity.

When I called Dr. Bee to tell her about the round, she sympathized and mentioned again that the Russians had taken eleven hypnotists to the 1956 Olympics.

THE NEXT MORNING was my round at Pebble Beach. On the first tee I genuflected while holding a club suspended in front of me: the holy sign of the plumb bob. For golfers, this is sacred ground.

I had never played Pebble Beach, never even seen the course before, and thus was prepared to be disappointed. But I wasn't. A few holes on the back nine perhaps bordered on the ordinary, but even those you play in anticipation of the famous finishing holes and some of the early holes—particularly six, seven, and eight, which jut into the bay—are almost too much to bear. For me the most unexpected pleasure was the vastness and infinite visual complexity of the land- and seascapes. From almost anywhere on the course, you could pull up a lawn chair and spend a week enumerating the discrete objects and colors your eyes take in: the pebbles, wildflowers, sea grasses, dunes, gorse, boulders, gnarled cypresses, exploding plumes of surf, shifting shafts of sunlight, rolling clouds, patches of fog, patterns of blue in the sea. Even for those who play it often, I'm sure Pebble Beach never looks the same twice.

For my round, on a perfect, sunny, nearly windless day, I hired a caddie named Dawg. Dawg, a Vietnam vet, wore beige dickie jumpers, two diamond studs in his left ear, and a Fu Manchu beard. Like caddies everywhere his skin was incredibly leathery. During most of the round he kept one fist wrapped around a cold Budweiser.

Dawg had opinions. Sauntering down the seventh fairway, the surf crashing at our feet with hypnotic suggestion, I asked if he saw much evidence of the New Agey side of golf here at Pebble Beach.

"Nah," he replied. "Golf is a simple game. It's just you, the ball, your club, and conditions. Do you think Nicklaus and Watson and the best players in the world pay any attention to that crap?"

"I don't know."

"Of course they don't, because that's just what it is: it's crap!"

"But some players on Tour are into thought control and meditation, things like that," I countered. "Guys like Peter Jacobsen."

"It's crap."

"What about Nicklaus? He said he never hit a shot without visualizing it first. That's New Agey."

"Pure dee crap."

The only superstitious thing Dawg believed in was talking to the golf ball. This he did incessantly: "Kick right, kick left, hit a barn." Caddying for Tour pro Roger Maltbie, Dawg once failed to chatter at the ball and it flew into a hazard. "Never take your mouth off the ball again!" Maltbie chastised him. He has learned his lesson.

I loved playing with Dawg. Once he got to know my game, which took about three minutes, he made all my clubbing and strategy decisions. This was liberating; it cut out ninety percent of the things I usually fret about during a round and allowed me to concentrate solely on executing the shot. As a result, I played well. Putting aside the mulligan on number one, which Dawg said I could have because I appeared so pathetically nervous, I scored 79—and from the pro tees, no less. On eighteen I hit a drive I will never forget, almost reaching the famous tree in the middle of the fairway.

Afterward, over a burger in the grill room with the two guys from Mississippi I'd been paired with, I was exhilarated. To play that well during the one round of my life at Pebble Beach was a thrill beyond compare!

But later that night, over a fancy fish dinner all by my lonesome, it occurred to me: what's so great about shooting 79? Especially since, with the mulligan, it was really an 81? In tournaments when I shot 81 I stormed off the course in disgust.

The difference, of course, was expectations. In tournaments my hopes were infinite: no score was good enough, yet everything depended on score. At Pebble Beach my hopes were modest: to enjoy the round and relish the experience, nothing depended on score.

STEPHEN COHEN, a jolly, white-bearded, Bronx-born Gestalt therapist, sat on the couch in the living room of his chic house in Carmel, stroking the satin-black fur of his cat. "Our primary purpose here is to promote the pleasures and beauty of golf," he said.

Cohen is president of the Shivas Irons Society, a group dedicated to the spirit of golf as promulgated by the mythical protagonist of *Golf in the Kingdom.* Among things the Society promotes are the use of featherie balls and playing rounds in the company of strolling musicians. My magazine editor had suggested I call on Cohen and his sidekick, Andy Nusbaum, another Shivas Irons Society director.

"The main problem most golfers have is an obsessive focus on score," Cohen said, as if he had been reading my mind. "In Scotland, golf isn't mainly about score. Golf is just an activity that allows people to get outdoors and enjoy themselves with others. That's the way it ought to be everywhere."

Cohen and Nusbaum co-teach an annual five-day seminar called "Golf in the Kingdom: An Exploration of the Deeper Game" at the Esalen Institute, an influential, freethinking academy of the far-out which Murphy founded in the mid-sixties on his family's land on the Big Sur coastline forty-five miles south. According to the Esalen catalog, the seminar "explores the inner self and how one interferes with its emergence."

"Most workshops are about improving score," Nusbaum said. "Our workshop is more about people's relationship to score and building awareness of what they really want out of the game. Stephen and I use golf as a hook to get people to look at the rest of their lives."

I told Cohen and Nusbaum that exploring my Inner Whatever was one of my motivations for embarking on the Year, but that thus far I'd been too perplexed by the nuances of my new swing and tournament rituals to make much progress in that area.

Nusbaum, who once competed as a pro himself, said he knew what I meant. "I finally realized that being free, open, and creative on the course was much more fulfilling to me than shooting for score." The paradox, he said, was that some society members saw their scores drop dramatically once they started playing for the glory of golf and the glory of golf alone.

"I believe it," I said. "But the deal is, I've got Q School in six weeks. I can't just wait around for magic to happen."

Cohen stroked his white beard and black cat simultaneously. "Well, then, perhaps you could set some other goal for Q School, such as trying to play each round with equanimity."

"Or go ahead and play for score, but try not to get emotionally *attached* to your score," threw in Nusbaum.

"The important thing," Cohen said, "is to be clear about your goal and why you're trying to reach it. Try to think about what your performance means to you as a person, as a family man, a writer, and so forth—not just as a golfer. When people get to high levels of play, a lot of them have trouble disassociating their self-worth from their scores."

"If you can go to Q School with the attitude that discovering who you are as a person is more important than what you shoot, so much the better," Nusbaum concluded.

Dawg, I am sure, would have called all this crap, but I refused to think so. I had come to California looking for a new paradigm, some way to leapfrog the glacial progress golfers usually make. Who knew? Maybe changing my attitude so as to liberate my Inner Golfer was just the ticket.

THAT AFTERNOON I took the paradigm out for a test drive on the Links at Spanish Bay, paired with a honeymooning couple from upstate New York. The groom possessed an elegant swing but unfortunately sliced his opening drive into the dunes. After a grim ten-minute search, he declared his ball lost. On the third hole he lost two more balls in the dunes, began cursing, and by the turn was a dark funnel-cloud of rage. It didn't help his mood any that meanwhile his pretty wife was carding all pars and bogeys, with a birdie thrown in for good measure. By the fifteenth hole the lovebirds weren't speaking to each other and the groom was playing only random shots—pitching wedges from the par-five tees, for instance.

It was a pathetic spectacle, especially since Spanish Bay, one of America's few true links, is a masterpiece of course design. Also, the weather was lovely—sunny, sweet zephyrs rolling in off the Pacific. But I was sympathetic. Watching the groom ruin his honeymoon was like watching myself play in tournaments. He did everything wrong the same way I did: tightening up, trying too hard, treating each mistake as a sign of personal failure, spiraling quickly into a funk.

I would have consoled the poor guy but I was afraid if I did he might shove his wedge up my rectum—especially since I myself was flitting from hole to hole with the lightness of a butterfly and having the time of my life. I did not keep score, consult yardages, or fret when I hit bad shots. Instead, I played by instinct. On each tee I asked myself, "What would be the coolest way to play this hole?" Sometimes I hit driver where normal caution would have advised three-wood and other times I hit irons where normally I would have hit driver, just because I felt like it. Most of my approaches into the greens were low, bump-and-run shots, because the links design encouraged such shots and because they're fun as hell to pull off. The breeze, the sun, the singing birds, the scudding clouds—they were all part of the experience, too. Re-creating the round later, out of curiosity, I figured I probably shot 77 or 78, but it didn't matter in the least. Mostly I just had fun. "Golf's a game, for chrissakes," Buddy Young's voice rang in my head, and that was the way I played it.

The next day I played two more rounds in this vein. The starter at Robert Trent Jones Sr.'s wonderful Spyglass course allowed me out as a singleton ahead of the first group of the day. Striding the dew-wet fairways, the sound of the surf and barking seals in my ears, I birdied three of the first five holes. It was magical, those first few holes: the setting, the course, my elevated mood. How could I possibly hit a poor shot? If only I could live my whole life like this, I thought: happy, fascinated, unbounded by fear.

Immediately after the round at Spyglass, unwilling to quit, I trucked over to the Pacific Grove municipal course near Monterey for an unscheduled round. The back nine there, beautifully situated right on the shore, is every bit as much a links course as Spanish Bay, and by the time I teed off the wind was howling off the sea, thirty miles per hour at least. Like most golfers, I am normally loath to play in gales—doing so is tiring and your usual skills don't apply. But on this day I couldn't have been happier. The wind made the game of golf seem even more like a game. Yardages and score in relation to par are irrelevant; your only option is to play inventively by the seat of your pants. One shot in particular I remember: a knock-down five-iron into the teeth of the wind which ricocheted off the side of a dune—precisely as I envisioned!—and trickled onto the green. I laughed and laughed out loud, the shot was such a marvel.

"Nae wind, nae rain, nae gowlf," the Scots supposedly say, and for the first time it hit me that maybe they weren't just being gloomy.

That night, riding the crest of my elation, I lavished some of the magazine's money on a fine meal at a white-tablecloth restaurant in Carmel and afterward wandered the streets. Carmel (whose mayor for most of the eighties was Clint Eastwood) is a pricey, pristine, picture-postcard village devoted to high-end shopping and the general advancement of New Age culture. Sleek designer boutiques stand cheek-by-jowl with emporiums selling healing crystals and books about transformative Yoga. Bulletin boards in virtually every shop are covered with flyers touting life-enhancing therapies such as chakra integration, in-depth astrology, tantric sex instruction, shaministic encounter therapies, and transcendental meditation.

I had arrived on the Monterey Peninsula more or less agnostic about the New Age movement, but Carmel made me think that much of what passes for "spiritual nurture" is really just a new form of elite pampering—Yoga as the postmodern equivalent of taking the waters at Baden-Baden, transcendental meditation as the moral equivalent of mud baths at a fancy desert spa. Yet even if this was so, did that invalidate the concepts? Who says the rich can't be on to something just because they're rich? After all, they have more money than the rest of us and therefore more time to investigate life's options.

The Shivas Irons Society guys thought golf should be fun. Since they seemed to play regularly on courses like Pebble Beach, Spyglass, and Cypress Point, I should think so. They also saw golf as food for the soul, and I will admit that my rounds on the Monterey Peninsula had been invigorating. They were a throwback to my earliest golf experiences when I was filled with wonder and excitement—only now, if anything, the satisfaction was greater because so were my skills. That bounding five-iron at Pacific Grove was not a shot I would have known how to *attempt* a year before; pulling it off had been a high level thrill.

It occurred to me that executing shots like this, at the extreme limit of one's ability, is what the Tour pros did regularly. But how did they manage it under pressure? This was the question that haunted me. Maybe later, after the year was over, I might think about pursuing golf as a New Age therapeutic modality, but for now, my urgent concern was Q School. Was there any way to make the Shivas Irons paradigm work when gut-wrenching panic had you by the balls?

Maybe Michael Murphy could help. I had my audience with him on my final day in California.

"I ONLY PLAY golf about five times a year," said the author of *Golf in the Kingdom,* perched on the edge of a couch in the spacious living room of his grand old Queen Anne house in San Rafael, just north of the Golden Gate Bridge. "My golf career, if you want to call it that, only lasted about six years, from age fourteen until age twenty, when I quit golf at Stanford to give myself more time to study Indian philosophy with Frederick Speigelberg."

Murphy, now sixty-six, was a ruddy, cherub-faced man with thinning gray hair split across the dome of his skull. He looked far younger and cheerier than any man his age has a right to. Most remarkable was the fluid way he moved, brimming with energy, like someone in his twenties.

"What I bring to the party now, regarding golf, is what I hear," he said. "I get letters practically every day from people still responding to *Golf in the Kingdom.* It's extraordinary. Mostly they want to tell me about experiences they have had they can't explain, like seeing a ball marker on a green four hundred yards away or seeing auras or sensing things with absolute certainty they shouldn't be able to sense."

Murphy shrugged.

"And these are Republicans, mind you. Stolid, rational citizens who wouldn't be caught dead at a séance. They don't know what to make of their experiences, and I'm not sure I do either. But I collect their stories and I share them. It does seem that golfers, when they are in the zone or whatever you want to call it, sometimes kick into some kind of clairvoyance—that is, they have extrasensory feelings or perceptions that go beyond the realm of the senses as we usually understand them."

Murphy had just finished writing a sequel to *Golf in the Kingdom* called *The Kingdom of Shivas Irons,* and it is *way* out there. In it, the fictional Murphy character returns to Scotland to track down Shivas Irons. Some of the action takes place in an occult, window-less chamber called a necromanteion. We learn much about Sufi and Islamic meditative traditions and encounter various "life-giving effervescences" and "luminous phenomena." But one senses, from the general good humor of the book, that Murphy doesn't take most of the far-out stuff seriously, or at least literally.

This is certainly the impression one gets from Murphy in person. His little-known magnum opus was a much soberer book published in 1992 called *The Future of the Body: Explorations into the Further Evolution of Human Nature.* This was an encyclopedic, rig-orously researched study of saints, artists, scientists, psychics, and other geniuses who apparently "extended the usual reach of human possibility." Murphy marshaled eyewitness accounts, scientific studies, biographies, and other historical documents to support his contention that we as a species have much more potential on the "mind-body" front than is normally assumed. So when Murphy gets a letter from someone claiming to have seen a ball marker at four hundred yards, he doesn't automatically dismiss the possibility, even if he doesn't automatically say, "Of course."

"Golf is a wonderful laboratory, created willy-nilly over the centuries, to see how all this works," he said. "The game has a peculiar genius for framing these problems." Primarily, he said, that's because the mind and body are so tightly bound together during play.

At this point I jumped in to tell Murphy about my Year and my struggles with golf and the looming deadline of Q School. "Is there some way I can use all these insights of yours to get better by Q School?" I asked.

"I'm afraid there's no magic bullet," Murphy said, shaking his head and laughing merrily. "Long-term practice leading to incremental improvement is really the only thing that works."

It was the same refrain I'd heard since day one of my Year, but I hadn't expected it from Murphy. I was crestfallen.

"I realize that saying so is out of fashion in American society these days," he said.

I nodded.

"But that's one of the beauties of high-level athleticism," he said. "Here are people who really *do* practice hard and accomplish extraordinary things."

Murphy must have sensed my disappointment.

"If I were you," he added kindly, "I'd focus on the mental game. How do you handle your inner demons? How do you handle all the perverse, negative thoughts that come up and interfere with optimal performance? If you can identify your negative patterns and practice cutting back on them, maybe you can make a little progress by Q School, and that would be good."

We talked a bit more, mostly about the history of golf on the Monterey Peninsula. As a teenager he had played Pebble Beach as much as he wanted, for five dollars a round. "It was paradise," he said. The greens fees now were shamefully high, he said, but he was grateful at least that so much of the peninsula's extraordinary land had been preserved for golf.

"I like to think of all the world's golf courses as one enormous garden," he said as he walked me to the door. "Altogether there are about twenty-five thousand to thirty thousand courses, usually one hundred fifty to two hundred acres each. Think of that. Never in human history has so much land been put into use as gardens around one activity."

This was indeed a happy thought.

"What a wonderful game golf is," he said. "I hope you can still enjoy it after your Q School is over."

DRIVING AWAY FROM Murphy's house, it hit me that he was the Wizard of Oz and I had just had a peek behind the curtain. Here was an impish, preoccupied man—he even looked a bit like the actor who played Oz in the movie—who was more than happy for people to believe in the fanciful images he projected, but who, behind the scrim, was a good bit more down to earth.

I can't say I was disappointed by the visit. Secretly, I suppose, I had hoped that Murphy would reveal some extra-dimensional secret that would transform my golf game, but in my heart I knew he wouldn't. In a way I was relieved to scratch "true gravity" off the list of possible solutions. It meant I could focus with less cosmic confusion on the straightforward task of playing better golf.

That night on the phone I told Polly about my meeting with Murphy, and how it left me feeling as if I'd shed a delusion.

"To tell you the truth," she said carefully, "I always thought you were a bit over the top on the golf and the spiritual stuff."

"That's because you think golf's stupid."

"No, I don't," she said. "I take your word that it's not. But the spiritual stuff, it seems to me, ought to come up naturally. It's not something you go looking for. Cézanne was a very spiritual painter"—she had just returned from seeing a major Cézanne exhibit at a museum in Philadelphia—"but he didn't *set out* to be a spiritual painter. He set out to paint apples and pears as purely and honestly as he could."

The more I thought about what Polly said, the more I understood she was right. Maybe *I* was the one who patronized golf, not Polly. I often defended the sport against charges of plaid-pants Republicanism on the basis that, properly pursued, it could lead to other, higher things—spiritual things, Zen, inner peace, cosmic humility, or whatever. But the unwitting assumption behind such defensiveness was that golf itself was inferior, useful only as a vehicle to reach these loftier, more "legitimate" ends. What if golf itself were the higher thing? Zen, to use Zen as a rough stand-in for the many presumed New Age potentials of golf, is no doubt a wonderful discipline for those willing to devote themselves to austere meditation—but why did I automatically assume Zen's superiority? Because it was Eastern, oracular, and practically unattainable?

Golf was here and now, accessible, part of my real-life social fabric. Better partial enlightenment (or whatever you want to call it) through golf than the mere smoky promise of enlightenment through Zen. Maybe if I stalked birdies and pars with the attitude Cézanne painted apples and pears, for no other reason than to get at their true nature, the game would open itself in a richer way. If I understood Murphy correctly, it was the quality of devotion and the constancy of effort that led to enlightenment, much more than the object of devotion itself.

I called Polly back, waking her up, to say she was a genius. "Golf is a lot like painting," I said.

"Cézanne would be rolling in his grave," she mumbled.

17 . *The End Game*

"AM I THE MAN OR WHAT!?"

The words slipped from my lips unbidden while my tee shot on the thirteenth hole was still in the air. The ball was vectoring toward the hole like a laser-guided missile. I had just executed a nearly perfect swing, the type that generates effortless, Rolls-Royce power.

Three groups of pros were backed up on the tee, watching. The ball landed a few feet past the flagstick, hopped a couple of times, and then spun backward. With eerie slowness, as if it couldn't decide what to do, the ball trickled downhill toward the hole. I was thinking ace, and held my breath. Gradually the ball neared the hole, closer and closer. Time stood still. For a moment I felt certain the ball would drop. But then, alas, it just slipped past, missing the hole by no more than an inch, and stopped two feet below the hole.

"Golf shot," approved one of the pros in my group.

"No big deal," I shrugged. "I hit shots like that all the time." Nonchalantly I snatched my broken tee from the turf and flipped it toward a trash can. Bingo! It rattled home. "You get used to it, when you have a talent as awesome as mine."

Obviously I was trying to be funny, but the irony was lost on the assembled pros. Stone silence. The only visible reaction was a raised eyebrow from the guy who had said "Golf shot." It was an eyebrow that suggested "You Da Jerk," not "You Da Man."

But I couldn't blame them for not laughing. In the first place, what I had said wasn't that funny. In the second place, the atmosphere was tense. We were playing in the Monday qualifier for the BC Open, a bona fide PGA Tour event. To these guys the competition was serious business, a chance to break into the big time, whereas to me, realistically, it was a lark. What chance did I have of getting into a PGA Tour event?

In the third place, I was beating the socks off all of them. Maybe that was the reason for their lack of humor. Freakishly, through twelve holes, I was two under par and looking at a tap-in birdie to go three under. The previous year a score of two-under-par 68 had been good enough to make it into a playoff for one of the four open spots in the tournament, and three-under-par 67 had made it outright. For all these guys knew (and I'd never met any of them until the first tee), this *was* the way I normally played. Thus to be crowing, however ironically, about my "awesome talent"—well, I could see why they thought I was an asshole.

I vowed to restrain my enthusiasm down the stretch, but it wouldn't be easy. I was giddy, and had been from the start of the round. On the first hole, a par five, I had nailed my second shot, a driver off the deck, to twelve feet from the hole; my eagle putt had stopped a half-revolution short, hanging on the lip, so I had to "settle" for birdie. On the second hole I had rammed home a birdie putt from six feet, and after that my scorecard read all pars.

I don't know what got into me. Part of it was the free-swinging psychology of an eighteen-hole qualifier, which is completely different from that at a normal, stroke-play tournament. At a qualifier, the only scores that count are the four best. There is no prize money, only the reward of inclusion in the BC Open field for four lucky finishers. With 127 pros gunning for those precious spots, there was basically no reason to hold back on any shot. All the usual risk-reward calculations went out the window. And when you happened to be playing well, as I was, the experience was exhilarating. The question was how long I could keep my balance on the tightrope.

Before the round I had spent a solid hour in the parking lot reclining on the backseat of Mr. Lucky, listening to Dr. Bee praise my swing. "Your beautiful, fluid, harmonious swing will make the ball go exactly where you want it to go," her raspy voice rang in my ears, via the Walkman, and I believed it. Also, the day before, during my drive to the qualifier —which was in Endicott, New York, about 160 miles north of New York City—I had specially devised two mantras for the round: "easy swing" and "ball in the hole." These mantras I repeated ceaselessly during my warm-ups and as I walked the fairways between shots. It all seemed to be working. Everything I tried succeeded. The only trouble I faced all day came on the fourth hole, when I had to hit a high flop shot over a bunker to a close pin—off a steep downhill lie. This was the type of shot I never would have attempted in a regular tournament, or even in a recreational round; I would have pitched safely to the fat part of the green and been satisfied with a bogey. But miraculously in the qualifier I stopped the ball dead in the twelve-foot gap between the bunker and the pin and salvaged my par. Even Phil Mickelson would have been impressed.

After my most excellent tee shot on thirteen, as I waited for the others in my group to hit, I began to think how fabulous it would be actually to claim one of the four open spots. The BC Open is not one of the best known PGA Tour events, mostly because it doesn't get network TV coverage, but the one-million-dollar purse (the

biggest tournament I'd played in so far, the Watertown Open,
offered a forty-six-thousand-dollar total payout) counts as official
money and among those participating this year would be John Daly,
Tom Watson, Jim Furyk, and . . . Tiger Woods. Tiger was the big
story. This would be his fourth start as a pro and already by Monday,
the day of the qualifier, Tigermania had transformed Endicott. TV
trucks were crowding the parking lots and Tiger decals sheathed the
windows of local businesses.

Imagine, me playing in a tournament with Tiger Woods! It was
not inconceivable, I reflected as I marched to the thirteenth green,
that I could wind up in a twosome with Tiger for the third round. In
the first two rounds I would surely be paired with other unknowns,
but if I made the cut after two rounds and my scores matched
Tiger's exactly—admittedly a long shot, but theoretically possible—
there I would be on Saturday, swapping chitchat with Tiger as we
strolled down the manicured lanes of En-Joie Golf Course attended
by caddies, Tour officials, media, and some lucky local kid hoisting
a sign with the names "Woods" and "Newport" side-by-side. It
occurred to me that I would have to develop an autograph policy.
My number one rule would be: accessibility. I wouldn't leave the
course until the last fan had my name on his or her visor.

But this was putting the cart before the horse

Reaching the green, I discovered that my ball, which had
appeared from the highly elevated tee to be two feet from the hole,
was actually six feet from the hole. It would not be a particularly difficult putt—straight uphill, no break—and I had been successfully
holing out everything all day, but when I marked the ball and waited
for the other two guys in my group to chip on, I noticed with alarm
that my knees were shaking—literally. Looking down, I could
detect a faint, actual tremor in the fabric of my khaki trousers. And I
began to think about the consequences of missing the putt; if I did,
I would then have to birdie at least one and possibly two of the
remaining five holes to have a chance of playing with Tiger. True,
one of those holes, the short, downhill par-five sixteenth, was the
easiest birdie hole on the course. But still—I needed this putt.

I tried to bring my mind back to the present, but it was spinning like a dervish. I was simultaneously conscious of a dozen things: my shaking knees; Tiger Woods's giant smile; the peril of missing the putt long and facing a tricky downhill comeback putt; Dr. Bee's praise for my fluid, harmonious, full swing but, now that I thought about it, nary a word about my putting stroke; the futility of repeating the words "ball in the hole" when, in actual fact, I couldn't conjure an image of the ball going into the hole; and my shaking knees again.

As I stood making my practice strokes, a new image surfaced into my consciousness like a breaching white whale. It was the vivid memory of myself as a high school quarterback. Fourth quarter in the Big Game. We were driving, we had fourth-and-one on the opponent's fifteen-yard line and our big fullback had been gaining ten and fifteen yards at a pop. On the simplest possible play, I turned the wrong way and was instantly buried under a herd of jubilant defensive linemen. Of all my sports memories, this was the most traumatic, and as I relived it while standing over the putt, an enormous blue-green neon sign appeared in my mind's eye, flashing: "CHOKER, CHOKER, CHOKER."

I backed away once, twice, trying to shake this evil from my head. But it was no use. I was helpless. Accepting the inevitable, I finally stepped up and jammed the putt wildly to the right. The recovery putt was impossible, at least for me at that point; downhill, side hill, I missed by a mile. And for good measure I missed the putt after that, as well.

Four putts from six feet for a double-bogey five.

That weekend I played no golf with Tiger Woods.

Q SCHOOL NOW loomed only a month away. My schedule called for two final tournaments on the North Atlantic Tour, a Hooters Tour event in Atlanta, perhaps a last-minute tournament in South Florida, and then the big test itself, in Naples, on Florida's west coast.

I had become obsessed with devising an End Game Strategy. The only consistency in my approach to golf during the Year had been a willingness to experiment. There is a world of fine golf advice out there, and unfortunately I seemed to have taken most of it. The time had come to narrow my focus—in short, to figure out who I was as a golfer.

On the flight home from California a few weeks earlier, I had taken out a yellow pad of paper to compile a definitive list of the tactics and techniques that had worked best for me during the Year. I scribbled like mad for thirty minutes and came up with a list that was more than fifty items long. Each one of these tricks had indeed been a winner at some point or another, though in some cases only for about ten minutes.

"Keep the right knee bent to avoid reverse pivot," was item number one on the list. This had been effective in curing a bad habit early in the Year, and occasionally I still caught myself straight-legged, but it hardly seemed like a core piece of advice around which to build a working End Game Strategy. "Use a stronger grip" had been similarly useful, once upon a time, but now was simply the way I held the club. "Paint beautiful patterns with the golf ball across the sky." Yes, there had been a day last spring when that strategy worked for about three holes. "Strut down fairway like I own the joint." Same. "Hit ball on center of clubface." For a week or two, this had been my primary swing thought. But now, looking at it written down, I thought to myself, "Like, duh."

Reviewing the list was discouraging. It reminded me of all the hard work and enthusiasm I had devoted to golf, with so little tangible progress. Perversely, I flipped to a new page on the yellow pad and tried to calculate the number of times I had hit a golf ball since the previous October. The figure I came up with was 58,000—18,000 full-swing practice strokes; 30,000 practice putts, chips, and pitches; and nearly 10,000 strokes during actual rounds, either practice or tournament. Ten thousand strokes! The number seemed incredible, but it was accurate. Ten thousand times I had stood behind the ball, mustered will and concentration, lined up the shot, taken a few practice swings, breathed deeply, advanced, waggled, and swung. Simply thinking of all that energy expended made me want to nap. And of those ten thousand shots, how many had ended badly? I calculated again, and came up with another discouraging answer: one thousand. *One thousand times* during the Year, or roughly eight shots per eighteen holes, I had screwed up so royally as to inspire intense self-loathing and disgust. Teeth gnashing. Vile cursing. Humiliation and dismay. Furthermore, it seemed like I could recall every one of those shots. The duffel pitch shot in round two, hole six of the South Florida Cobblestone tournament? Sure, I remember. Hole eight? A pull-hook off the tee. As for the nine thousand or so shots during the Year which did *not* end badly, thinking hard, I could recall about a dozen.

No wonder I freaked out under pressure. When the time came to dig deep, all I could drag up were nightmares. Maybe this was the secret source of my love for golf—the sport helped me experience pain? But I didn't want to go there. So instead I lolled my head back on the airline seat and fell fast asleep.

Over the next few days, back home in Orient, I continued working on my End Game Strategy and eventually boiled it down to six injunctions:

1. Work on beliefs and confidence more than skills.
2. Go with what you've got, mechanically.
3. Sink putts to score well.
4. On full shots, think only about making the golf ball go "over there."
5. Use every bad shot as a "trigger" to make the next shot superb.
6. Use every good shot as a "trigger" to make the next shot even better; don't be afraid of birdies.

In my practice leading up to the BC Open, these principles had worked well, as they did during the first twelve holes of the qualifier. I played easily, confidently and my putting was excellent. But then on thirteen it all fell apart, and in retrospect I figured this was because I had made a fatal error in compiling my list: it contained only six items! Good lists have seven items: The Seven Habits of Highly Effective People, The Seven Spiritual Laws of Success, and so forth. So I had to dream up a clincher.

The first concept that popped to mind was, "Don't screw up so much." This had the advantage of being pithy, direct, and unequivocal, but the disadvantage of being stated in the negative. My attempt to come up with a positively worded alternative failed: "Succeed wildly!" sounded too much like a Chinese fortune cookie, and "Play really, really well!" lacked punch. Another promising concept I toyed with was "Keep your mind in the present," which seemed to address my biggest problem directly. But ultimately I rejected this as excessively distracting. It treaded into the territory of Tolstoy's impossible Don't-Think-About-a-White-Polar-Bear Club. The moment you have to remind yourself to keep your mind in the present, your mind, ipso facto, is not in the present.

What I needed, I decided, was a way to approach golf with the same consuming avidity that characterized my attitude toward sex. During sex, my mind never seemed to wander. During sex, I never had to tell myself to keep my mind in the present—it stayed there of its own accord. Polly, of course, would scoff at the words "sex" and "golf" appearing in the same sentence, but I had heard golfers rhapsodize about the shuddering thrill that comes after catching a drive pure on the screws. And about the sensual rise and fall of a golf shot in parabolic approximation of the female breast. And, after several drinks, about how golf holes are deliberately tucked in provocative places, surrounded by shaggy rough and undulating mounds, and the duty of each golfer, wagging a long, rigid stick between his legs, is to seduce the course. I had also observed during the Year how some pros played with a kind of sexual aggression. They talked passionately about their desire to put their ball in the hole and hissed, "Bitch!" when a putt failed to drop.

Maybe my problem was a low golf libido. My desire before tournament rounds was mild compared to some of the guys I had encountered. I mostly just wanted to avoid humiliation. They wanted to *win.* And so, in my motel room on the night after my collapse at the BC Open qualifier, I amended my list to include a seventh item: "Score!"

If I could get passionate about score, I figured, everything else would fall into place. "Score!" would be my shorthand for Cézanne's apples and pears.

FROM ENDICOTT I drove thirty miles north the next day for the North Atlantic Tour's second-to-last event of the season, the "Colgate Classic" in Hamilton.

"The Author returns," Buddy Young announced upon seeing me in the pro shop. "And we're a pro now, I see from the size of your entry fee." As always with Buddy, it was hard to know how to interpret this remark: Was there a note of derision in his remark about my new pro status? Or was he simply making conversation?

"Yeah, I thought I'd dump a little more money into the pot for the other guys to divvy up," I replied.

"That's very thoughtful, J. P. Perhaps I could interest you in a little poker game tonight, as well."

I had half-hoped for a Prodigal Son reception upon returning— warm slaps on the back, heartfelt inquiries about my adventures in the Dakotas, the killing of a fatted calf, random cries of "Hosanna!"— but this was not forthcoming. Buddy inquired about the Dakotas, but primarily from the perspective of a competing tour owner (How many pros showed up? How big were the purses?). As for the other players—they hardly seemed to notice, all except Captain Kurt, who rushed over to shake my hand and catch up.

This general air of negligence made me more eager than I should have been to say something impressive. "Shot 74 at the BC qualifier yesterday," I told Buddy nonchalantly, apropos of nothing. "Had it to two-under after twelve."

"A 74, did we?" Buddy responded with mock surprise. "That's good, J. P. I'd like to see you shoot 74 out there today, that would be the mark of a true pro."

The Seven Oaks course, where we were scheduled to tee off in less than an hour, was completely underwater. It had been raining bullfrogs and heifers all night and continued to rain.

"We aren't going to play in this mess, are we?" I said.

"We are," Buddy replied. "Whether *you* are or not, that's up to you. Unless it starts to lightning, the game is on."

There was a lot of grumbling about this decision among some of the regulars. They muttered that Buddy didn't want to postpone play because he had captured a half dozen more paying pros than usual by scheduling the event so close to the BC qualifier, and feared losing their entry fees. But play we did, for five hours in ceaseless rain, and it wasn't much fun. Ninety percent of one's attention under such conditions is devoted to staying dry—to rotating gloves, wringing out towels, zipping and unzipping garments and bag covers, prying muck out of cleats while balancing an umbrella in the crook of your neck, wiping mud off balls.

The weather rendered my brilliantly conceived new End Game Strategy moot. Slog! would have been more to the point than Score! I shot 82 and felt lucky to do so. The next day, under slightly better conditions (it rained only half the round), I improved to 81. Only Captain Kurt, among the golfers I knew, was able to transcend the conditions. In the first round he shot 73 to share the tournament lead.

"Army training," Kurt explained. That same stoic, imperturbable attitude which enabled Kurt to pick the lock of his trunk at Norwich and still make his tee time enabled him to treat the rain as a minor annoyance.

The more I hung around Kurt, the more I liked him. As one of the few young players who had pursued a real-world career before coming to golf, he had a perspective that was tonic. That night after the first round we had pizza together, and Kurt nodded toward the depressed-looking twentysomething dude behind the counter. "You think that guy wouldn't trade places with any of us? Even playing in the rain?" Like me, Kurt was appalled at the handful of club-throwing, country club brats on the tour who seemed to think the world owed them the right to make a living in tournament golf.

In the six weeks since I'd last seen Kurt, he had purchased an old van and rigged it up with a mattress, tiny lights along the ceiling, and a mini-stereo system.

"It's a chick-mobile," I suggested.

"Now, now." He had a girlfriend in Florida and was loyal. Usually Kurt spent the night in the parking lot of the club where we were playing and showered in the locker room. The setup suited him perfectly; he was organized, meticulous, and self-reliant.

Unable to Score! at Colgate, I worked myself into a metaphoric frenzy of scoring passion before the next (and final) event of the North Atlantic season, the Tour Championship in Rome, New York. I wanted desperately to make a good showing. The North Atlantic Tour was the place I felt most at home, the only tour where I had some sense of connection to the other players. For my own ego as much as anything, I yearned to depart with a bang, not a whimper.

On the night before the first round of the Tour Championship, Kurt and I had dinner with Buddy at a semi-fancy Italian restaurant. For the first time, with extreme sheepishness, I revealed to Buddy my plans to compete at Q School, and he was kind enough not to laugh in my face.

"An old Tour player named Paul Harney once told me that no one should think about trying to make money as a pro until he shoots under par on his home course every single time out for an entire year," Buddy said.

"That counts me out," said Kurt.

"I used to think his assessment sounded right," Buddy continued, "until I heard Trevino say that to have a chance on Tour a man had to be able to shoot *five under par* on his home course at least every other time out."

"So what you're saying, Buddy," I interpreted, "is that you think the pros on Tour are better than I am."

"Oh, Jesus, no, J. P. I'm sure you'll make it right to the top."

Buddy was a font of golf tidbits, most of which had the effect of making your own efforts to master the game seem puny by comparison. But you couldn't resent the guy because you knew he was just being honest. Plus, he was funny. Playing for Buddy made you feel connected to golf's big picture.

The next day—inspired, determined—I went out and shot an 80. I had two birdies, ten pars, and two bogeys (even par on those fourteen holes), but also four round-killing "others." It was, I had to admit, pretty typical, and thus left me feeling defeated. I had prepared for this tournament as hard as I could. I was focused and determined But with a moment of doubt here, an instant of fear there—poof!—I was back in Mediocreville.

The following day, in much the same fashion, I shot 80 again. My End Game Strategy had made no difference whatsoever.

In the parking lot after the final round, the tour regulars milled around nostalgically, unwilling to depart. Joe Klemmer held court in the open well of his van and distributed beers. Harmless insults were swapped, schedules for the winter season down South compared. For six months most of these guys had traveled in a pack, and now the leaves on the trees were turning red and yellow.

As I was loading up Mr. Lucky, Captain Kurt came over and said, "Good luck at Q School, man."

"You, too," I replied inanely, though he wasn't going to Q School. "We'll have to play some golf next year."

"For sure. But you know, I was wondering . . ." He fumbled for words. "You see, I'm headed down to Florida myself for the winter and, I mean, if you needed a caddie at Q School, I'd be happy to do it."

"Really?" I was flabbergasted.

"Yes, I'd like to. I need to see what Q School's all about, anyway."

My first thought was that I'd play so badly Kurt would be embarrassed. "It might get ugly," I warned.

"I know your game. We won't let it get ugly."

I hadn't thought about needing a caddie at Q School. Carts were

allowed and most players used them. But thinking back on my visit
to Q School at Bear Lakes the previous December, I remembered
that most players also had someone they knew and trusted at their
side.

"I'd love it if you came."

"Well then, you're on," the Captain replied, and we shook hands
on the deal.

Kurt's generous offer, an act of grace, made me think that maybe
my days on the North Atlantic Tour had not been such a waste after
all.

FROM NEW YORK I drove to Atlanta to compete in the season-
ending Hooters Tour event.

The Hooters Tour began life as the T. C. Jordan Tour, which itself
had been cobbled together in the late eighties from the remains of
two other short-lived tours, the United States Golf Tour and the
National Golf Association Tour. (The difficulty of survival in bush
league golf is not limited to players.) Drawing on the analogy to
minor league baseball, if the North Atlantic Tour was single-A ball,
the Hooters Tour was double-A, and the Nike Tour was triple-A.
Like the Nike Tour, the Hooters Tour traveled around the country
and its events comprised four full rounds, with cuts after the second. As on the single-A tours, however, eking out a profit was
almost impossible. Part of the problem was the high cost of living on
the road ("I'm getting beat by the knife and fork," one player told
me), but an even bigger problem was the disturbingly high level of
talent. At one tournament a few months earlier, the *cut* had been
eight under par. The average winning score was *sixteen* under. In
one event a guy named Rob McKelvey shot twenty under par and
took home just $2,400. That's because his score was only good
enough for sixth place, six shots behind the winner.

My qualification for playing in the final Hooters Tour event was
simple: I had submitted, on time, a $450 entry-fee check that did
not bounce.

And yes, Hooters girls were present, abundantly (though in most regular tournaments they are not). During the pro-am event on Wednesday they swarmed the course, all wearing the titular restaurant chain's trademark uniform of sexy orange short-shorts and a tightly tied, navel-baring T-shirt. Each fivesome in the event was issued one Hooters girl, who held the pin, fished beers out of the cooler when the amateurs (but not the pros) got thirsty, and generally made herself useful, if not available in the sense you are probably wondering about. As an unknown player, I was understandably not invited to participate in the pro-am, but I did spend a considerable amount of time on the practice putting green watching the groups file past. The whole exhibition was shameful. Afterward I allowed myself to be photographed with a half dozen Hooters girls hugging my neck. Two were named Tiffany.

In the first round of the tournament proper I played in the next to last group of the day with a fifteen-year-old amateur from a nearby high school and a nonpaying assistant pro from the host course, Whitewater Country Club. We were not the premier threesome, nor did my round start well. On the second hole I lost my ball in a tree. This had never happened to me before. The ball drifted into the branches of a pretty skimpy-looking willow and never came down. I waited and waited but finally had to traipse back to the tee to rehit. As I did so, the high school kid went ahead and hit his second shot. He holed it for an eagle. I ended up with an eight on the hole. And so it went all day. I finished with an embarrassing 85. The kid, meanwhile, kept dropping putts from neighboring counties and carded a 67, which tied him for second place.

All in all it was a disappointing day, but then I had been sour and discouraged to begin with. The night before, to save money, I had shared a Holiday Inn room with a roly-poly guy I barely knew from the North Atlantic Tour and two other guys I didn't know at all: two beds, two cots. My acquaintance looked exactly like the *Mad* magazine cover boy, Alfred E. Newman. He hailed from the Bronx and claimed to have been dating a Hooters waitress until his father forced him to choose between the girl and his heavily subsidized golf career. Reluctantly, he chose the latter but was heartbroken—

surely a tragedy worthy of Shakespeare. In the room with us that night were everybody's golf bags but mine, plus all their muddy golf towels from the day spread about on the sinks and closet racks to dry. Making one's way to the bathroom in the middle of the night was like threading one's way through the Civil War wounded in *Gone With the Wind.* After one such excursion I lay in bed thinking: How has my life come to this point? Why am I here in this room with these numskulls instead of at home with my wife and child? Especially when I'm shooting 85?

No compelling answers were immediately forthcoming.

I did redeem myself, somewhat, in the second round. At the nine-hole turn I stood at one under—I was playing simple, solid, put-the-ball-over-there golf—and might have finished that way but for two unlucky breaks on the back: a well-played ball on eleven that hit a sprinkler head and bounced over the green out-of-bounds, and an aggressive, purely struck fairway wood on the next hole that just trickled into a creek and got me into further trouble.

For the round I finished with a 76 and tried to view my situation in the most positive light. Twice in eleven days—here and at the BC qualifier—I had played stretches of golf at the level I felt I "should" be playing at. By turning a blind eye to the intermediate rounds, I might almost have conned myself that things were coming together nicely for Q School—might have, I say, except for an unfortunate last-minute meal with a guy named Fritz Gambetta.

Gambetta was one of the few fortysomething regulars on the Hooters Tour: a Hooters coot. During the Year I found myself gravitating to the older players, as they were usually more entertaining than the twentysomething crowd. For instance, earlier that week I'd chatted with a drawling Mississippian about the difficulties he had encountered in "cranking up the old golf dream" after a decade away from competition selling peat moss. "There really ain't much crossover in the two professions," he allowed.

Gambetta, I figured, would be interesting, too. At our table in the grill room, he was certainly intense. At forty-nine, lean, tan, and curly-haired, Gambetta had one purpose in life: to qualify for the

Senior Tour. And that had been his one purpose for the last five years. "The bottom line is you've got to make a flat-out commitment," he told me. "You've got to have long-term goals, midterm goals, and short-term goals, and write them all down—I use a little book in my golf bag, and review it every week. Then you've got to compete constantly: the mini-tours, state opens, Monday qualifiers, overseas, wherever. It takes a lot of money. I have no interest anymore in playing golf for fun."

Gambetta won his first golf tournament at age nine. After playing college golf at Cal State, he plied the U.S. mini-tours and Asian tours for a decade, with marginal success. In 1986 he quit "for good" after shooting 66 in a four-spot qualifier for the Phoenix Open but losing out to Tommy Armour III, who shot 62, and three other guys with 65s. "Enough was enough," he explained. But in the early nineties, after watching pros he had played against and beaten make a bundle on TV, he couldn't take it anymore. He retired from the ad agency and jewelry distribution businesses he and his second wife had started and charted his five-year plan.

A hallmark of the plan is fitness. Gambetta runs, does daily stretches and calisthenics, works out with weights, and eats scientifically. "I carried my bag seventy-two holes in the heat in Miami a few weeks ago and it didn't phase me. Nobody else my age is doing that, I guarantee." In addition, he employs a sports psychologist and a physical therapist and went through dozens of swing teachers until he found one he trusted, Ronnie Stockton (son of Dave) in Redding, California.

As Gambetta fired off a list of the further measures he had recently taken to assure success at his first Senior Tour Q School in five weeks' time—a systematic rebuilding of his swing, extensive mental game drills, a new wrinkle to his putting stroke, managing the relationship with his wife—the fragile sense of optimism I had concocted that afternoon crumbled like Roquefort cheese.

"But the key thing is," he continued, "you've got to work this stuff out in advance. Years in advance, really, and then settle into it, so that when the time comes to hit that first ball at Q School, there's not a doubt in your head."

He took a sip of bottled water and shook his head. "If you wait to the last minute, you're dead."

Gee, thanks for the advice, I thought. Now I'll just step outside and shoot myself.

NATIVE AMERICAN HUNTERS, I recall dimly from history class, timed their wanderings by the cycles of nature. "I will return before the second full moon shines upon our wigwam" was the kind of promise a hunter might have made to his wife. In the same spirit but also as a way of limiting my time away from home, I had promised Polly never to stay gone so long that I couldn't keep the grass mowed.

With only two weeks remaining until Q School, I might have begrudged having to fly home from Atlanta just to mow the lawn, but in fact I was relieved. At home my life made sense. I had a role to play. My presence was needed and even desired. On the road, I was out of place, merely pretending to be a professional golfer. The thought of Q School made me panic. I was overmatched and under-prepared. Home would be a haven from worry, I thought.

"How did you do in the Hooters tournament?" Polly asked. She tried to pronounce the word "Hooters" with a straight face.

"Seventy-six yesterday," I replied.

"That's pretty good, isn't it?"

"I guess so. Who cares."

Polly looked at me seriously. "It doesn't sound like you're having much fun out there."

"Of course I'm not having fun. Q School's the week after next and I'm doomed."

This made Polly angry. She turned her back, started to walk away, and then wheeled back around. "Well, you'd better be having fun out there because I'm sure the hell not having fun here, stuck all by myself with Anna."

My guilt during the Year had passed through three stages. At first there was none at all; I was brimming with too much hope and excitement to feel guilty. Then gradually, as the reality of the price Polly was paying so I could play golf sank in (she had stopped painting almost altogether and cut spending to the bone), I felt guilty for being away so much and not earning any money. And in the last few weeks, with Q School hanging over me, my guilt had primarily to do with my poor performance. Polly, of course, didn't care what I shot, but lower scores would have helped *me* feel better, as if her sacrifices weren't in vain.

Now, it seemed, my guilt was about to enter a fourth stage: guilt that I wasn't having more fun. It wasn't just Polly's understandable resentment that made me feel this way. Even on my own terms, viewed strictly from the perspective of doing well at Q School, not having more fun was counterproductive. Making myself uptight and miserable with fear was the surest possible way to fail my end-of-the-Year exam.

Every day during my home stand, I hit balls at Island's End, the site of my once-upon-a-time 69. What an Eden that round had been. In those days I truly did play golf for the fun of it. I was relaxed and un-self-critical and produced a score that still stood out as my best ever. But then I had taken a bite from the apple of the Tree of Knowledge and began asking how and why. How could someone like me, out of the blue, shoot a 69? Why couldn't I shoot 69 every time? Pride and ego got caught up in the quest, which introduced fear. And that was the end of Eden.

On my final night in Orient, I played blocks on the floor with Anna. As usual, she was fearless and enchanted—Anna on the Beach, part two. She laughed as gleefully when the tower went down as when the tower went up. If only I could play golf like that.

FROM ATLANTA I drove to Fort Lauderdale and played in two quick, final tournaments on the South Florida Golf Tour. In the first round of the first tournament I accomplished something I had never managed before: I hit fourteen of fourteen fairways. If I had any doubts that my skills had improved during the Year, that statistic put them to rest. Off the tee I was swinging with a rhythm and consistency far removed from my style at the beginning of the Year. Yet somehow—by tensing up around the greens, by giving in to my anxiety about scoring at Q School—my score for the round was 82. The parts of my game did not add up to a whole. For golfers who push to the next level, the sum of the parts is far greater than the whole.

In the second tournament I was paired, at my request, with two of the best pros on the South Florida Tour, Briny Baird and Jimmy Stobbs. Both were standard-issue, Q School–bound, twentysomething cadets, nondescript in every way except that Briny Baird's father, Butch, had won some tournaments on the PGA Tour. During the round they said hardly a word. Neither hit the ball noticeably longer than I did, nor even that much straighter (most of the time), but they possessed a subtle command of the game which, for the first time in my life as a golfer, I was knowledgeable enough to recognize.

The difference between their talents and mine struck me most powerfully on the thirteenth hole, a long par three. All of us hit the green. In fact, I was quite proud of my shot. It carried directly over the top of the pin and came to rest twenty feet from the hole twenty feet *above* the hole. Baird and Stobbs hit their balls only marginally closer, perhaps eighteen and fifteen feet from the cup, but as we got to the green it was apparent that they would have far easier putts, as both their balls were *below* the hole. Now, I had known, standing on the tee box, that the green was cantilevered and that ending up below the hole was preferable. That specific thought had passed through my mind. On the other hand, two yawning bunkers fronted the hole and I had made the risk-reward decision to go for the middle back of the green. In short, I was chicken. Baird and Stobbs, on the other hand, were not chicken. They were both clearly determined to park their tee shots in the dangerous twenty-five-foot slot between the cup and the bunkers, and they both had enough precise control over their distances to pull it off. A casual observer at the tee box, 184 yards from the pin, might have congratulated all three of us on our shots, but in fact there was a world of difference.

On the green, the gulf opened wider. As the farthest away I putted first and my sole objective was to stop the ball close, so that my third putt would not induce a bout of vertigo. I had no conscious thoughts of actually *making* the slippery downhill putt. My heart pounded, and I slapped the ball to three feet past the hole. This left me a larger comeback putt than I wanted, but, practically hyperventilating, I made it. The ball just caught the right edge and made one complete revolution around the cup before plopping in.

Baird putted next. I watched. He was calm, balanced, in control, intense. As he stood over the ball eyeing the line, I realized he was having no conscious thoughts except that he *would* make the putt, and probably no contrary subconscious thoughts, either. And of course he did, right in the heart, for a birdie. When Stobbs prepared to putt a few moments later, I had the same sense he was going to make the putt. He didn't, as things turned out—the putt skimmed past the hole, it may have hit a spike mark—but he had put a stroke on the ball that was in every way superior to my lame effort earlier.

On the scorecard our group had one birdie and two pars. Not bad. But walking off the green I had to laugh at how misleading those numbers were.

"You guys are just too good," I said admiringly on the next tee.

They looked at me and then at each other and shrugged, but said nothing. What *could* they say? They *were* too good, for me, at least, and they knew it. But they also knew they still weren't nearly good enough.

AFTER THE TOURNAMENT I loaded my clubs in Mr. Lucky for the final trek across Florida to Naples, where Q School awaited. The drive, due west across the peninsula via Alligator Alley, was an austerely beautiful one: swamps stretching in every direction, late afternoon clouds, the sun tumbling toward the horizon. The scenery fit my mood.

Something had gone out of me during the round with Baird and

Stobbs, though this wasn't necessarily bad. I think it was my last remaining illusion.

As an intellectual (of sorts), I had figured that the best way to improve rapidly during the Year and make it to the second stage of Q School, my goal, would be to use my brain. That would be my competitive advantage over guys who had done nothing all their lives but play golf. As a writer, I had been professionally trained to think and analyze, I was older than most of the guys on the mini-tours and presumably wiser.

But the mind is not the source of solutions in golf, the mind is the problem. If I'd learned one thing during the Year, that was it—over and over and over. And once this supposed advantage of mine had been taken away, I had to compete against guys like Baird and Stobbs on their terms, and on their terms—experience, skill, repetition—they were simply much better players than I was. It wasn't because they knew something I didn't, some secret, some grand unified field theory of golf that makes everything flow in sync. They were better simply because they had been competing since they were babies. Golf was their career. They had figured out over time what works for them and stuck with it.

But what did I expect? If it was easy to come out of nowhere and make it through the first stage of Q School, a lot of guys before me would have done so and the golf magazines would have told their Cinderella stories. Robert Landers, the "farmer" from Azle, Texas, who seemingly came from nowhere to earn a card on the Senior Tour a few years ago, triggered a media frenzy. But Landers had been a golf pro of one sort or another most of his life; farming was a sideline. Beneath his aw-shucks twang, Landers was as much of a golf obsessive as Fritz Gambetta.

As I drove across Alligator Alley, I had plenty of time to mull these thoughts and found to my surprise that I felt liberated rather than defeated by them. It was as if some ubershrink had lifted a giant neurosis from my shoulders. For months now I had been bearing the burden of trying to accomplish something clearly beyond my ability—not just making it through Q School, but more generally trying to compete head-to-head, on an equal basis, with the legitimate pros around me. Now I didn't have to.

For some reason I started thinking about Tom Lehman. The turning point in his career, he had told me, came in a tiny, pea-green hotel room in Japan. He had been playing like hell on the Asian tour and he and his wife, Melissa, were down to their last few thousand dollars. That night, for the first time, he opened up to Melissa. He told her how he felt like a failure and that he feared she wouldn't love him anymore if he continued to shoot high scores. Melissa almost laughed in his face. She couldn't believe that Tom thought her love for him depended on his golfing ability, and Tom couldn't believe that it didn't. That evening transformed his career. From that point forward, he knew he didn't have to play well to be loved, which freed him emotionally to become the star he did.

Well, I wasn't expecting my golf career to turn around. I was expecting my golf career to *end,* in about six days. But the time did seem ripe—how could it be riper?—for a major change in attitude. Comparing myself to the pros around me was an exercise in masochism, so I wouldn't do it. Trying to shoot four consecutive subpar rounds at Q School would be futile, so I wouldn't try. What I would do was accept who I was as a golfer—a decent player, on good days, albeit one who struggles with pressure—and do the best I could, considering. If things worked out well, maybe I could play a few long stretches of golf at Q School, perhaps even a whole round, at near the best of my ability. If things didn't go well, no matter. Unlike virtually everyone else in the field, I was not counting on a Tour career.

I pulled into Naples just as the sun, amid pink-and-blue Floridian fanfare, slipped into the Gulf. It was beautiful. I was nervous, but also excited. Maybe, just maybe, Q School would be fun. And that, I decided, would be my final, final End Game Strategy: to make Q School as much fun as possible.

A FRIEND'S PARENTS HAD AGREED TO LET ME
use their unoccupied condo in Naples for the
week. It was what you might imagine a snowbird couple from Rhode Island would own:
plush white carpeting, two bedrooms, a
dinette kitchen, and a bug-proof porch overlooking a big concrete pond. This pond was
called Hidden Lake, the name of the develop-
ment, although there really wasn't anything
hidden about it.

I spent the first hour after my arrival organizing my clothes and other belongings in the
master bedroom's closet and two chests of
drawers. I wanted everything to be just right
for the week. When finished, however, I was
dissatisfied with some of the placements I had

chosen—particularly my use of the closet—and spent another thirty minutes reorganizing. Then I hopped into Mr. Lucky, shopped at a twenty-four-hour market for groceries, and neatly stowed all my purchases in the kitchen cabinets and pantry. By the time I finished it was 2 A.M., but at least I was organized.

Early the next morning, a Sunday, I arrived at the swank, private Bonita Bay Golf Club for my first official round of practice. It was twenty minutes by car from the condo. At the perimeter gate a uniformed security officer gave Mr. Lucky's peeling paint a dubious glance, held up his hand, and inquired to the effect of where the hell did I think I was going.

"I'm here for Q School."

With alarm it occurred to me that I had no receipt for the three-thousand-dollar cashier's check I had airmailed to the PGA Tour two months before, only an unsigned "Dear Contestant" letter informing me of my assignment to the Bonita Bay first stage site. But I needn't have worried.

"Yes, sir," the guard said, practically saluting. "Take a right and then the first left to reach the clubhouse. And, sir?"

"Yes."

"Good luck!" He gave me a cardboard parking permit, good for one week, to put in the windshield.

In the pro shop I was treated with similar deference. The well-groomed young man behind the counter (a scratch handicapper, I felt sure, judging by his bred-in-the-bone golferly manner) obligingly directed me to the cart barn ("Take any one you want!") and to the range ("All the balls you'll need are on the tee!") as if he assumed I might be Somebody (a slumping Tour pro, perhaps) whose face he temporarily couldn't place.

"And is there a restroom?" I asked.

"Oh, yes, sir, we've got lots of them!" He explained the various options: pro shop, grill room, cart barn. If I'd asked, he probably would have done his best to pee for me.

The abundance of respect made me uneasy, but I tried to act as if all this were normal and motored on over to the course. My hope had been to play a few quick holes alone, get a sense of the course, and practice hitting the ball "over there" before Bonita Bay crowded up with the 186 other pros in the field. This was why I had arrived so early despite lack of sleep. But already the first tee was jammed with more than a dozen guys, also apparently hoping to be the first ones out, in an intimidating tableau. Brightly lit by the low morning sun, they clustered in groups of three or four, some on the raised tee box and some immediately below it, all deeply tanned, all wearing vividly colored golf shirts and dark heavy spikes. A few were rehearsing their swings—achingly beautiful, every one—while others idly bounced golf balls off the faces of their drivers as they chatted.

"My God," I thought. "Those guys look like Tour pros!"

So instead of warming up on the course, as I had hoped, I retreated cravenly to the range. Only a few other contestants were there, but even they made me feel inadequate. I stationed myself to the far left, so the other players' backs would be to me, and hit a few tentative wedge shots. So far, so good. No blunders. Then I hit one repulsively fat—the clubhead struck the turf four inches behind the ball—and looked up in panic like a cheating schoolboy to see if anyone was noticing. What did it take to get kicked out of Q School, anyway? If I hit three or four more fat shots in a row, would some observant functionary come over and ask to see my handicap card?

These were not positive thoughts. This was not the way a pro on the first day of Q School should be thinking. I reminded myself of my End Game Strategy: to play four rounds for myself at my own comfortable level, for the joy of golf, so as to bring together all I had learned during the Year in a glorious, fun-filled valedictory. I was not here to compete with the lifetime professionals. Even so, it was hard not to be swept up in the general atmosphere of tension, or for that matter simply to expunge from memory the many months of my own obsessions about Q School, the projections and imaginings and hopes that I might actually make it to the second stage. I felt lonely. Captain Kurt would be here to caddie, bless his soul, but not until the second round. He had a tournament commitment in

Orlando that would not end until Tuesday morning, the day of my first round.

Around eleven-thirty I noticed that the first tee box had cleared so I headed out for my solo practice round. By the third hole I began to find my rhythm. My putting in particular was sharp; lining up each putt, I could see the line as clearly as if laid out in chalk. On the fourth hole I rolled in a forty-five-foot left-to-right breaker, dropped another ball thirty feet from the hole on a different angle, and almost made that one, too—the ball lipped out.

"I saw that!" came a voice from behind me.

I turned to see another lone competitor standing near his cart in the fairway, waiting to hit. I acknowledged his remark with a wave of my putter.

"It's me, Danny Hyde," he called.

I hadn't recognized him from that distance. Danny had played a few events on the North Atlantic Tour and the previous week in Fort Lauderdale we had played a practice round together. He was one of the more likable and interesting characters I'd met all year. After a couple of years playing golf in college on a scholarship, he had dropped out to join the Navy, hated it, and then supported himself for three years in Boston by parking cars and winning bets on the golf course. Once, he said, he won five thousand dollars in a week. But now Danny was financing his pro career with the proceeds of an invention he had patented: masking tape ruled like a yardstick. "It's got a thousand and one uses!"

We played together and Danny's friendly optimism was a boost. "I'm gonna *win* this thing," he told me a few holes later. He was jazzed. "Let's *both* make something happen this week, how about it, pal?"

On the back nine we were joined by two pros neither of us knew. One was a scrawny, bespectacled, humorless fellow in his early twenties. If I thought I was apprehensive about the coming week, this guy was positively stricken. I tried not to look at him or even stand very close. I was afraid of picking up his vibes. The other guy, from Yonkers, New York, was more at ease. "Whatever," he shrugged after hitting a drive into the woods, and laughed dismissively. This seemed like just the right attitude for Q School: upbeat fatalism.

Between Danny Hyde and the guy from Yonkers, I was inspired and soon began playing comfortable, solid golf. On one hole I smashed a drive about as well as I'm able—it rolled maybe 290 yards, even on the cushy Bermuda fairway. Back home among the medium-handicappers I usually played with, a drive like this would have elicited ooohs, aaahs, and hosannas, maybe even some mock bowing. But here it was merely the second best among four drives tightly grouped in the fairway. This thrilled me more than if mine had been twenty yards the longest. It made me feel legitimate, a pro among pros. Hyde knew my backstory, but as far as the other two pros were concerned after watching me play for five or six holes, I was just another entrant. And why shouldn't they think that? I could play golf, some, when I allowed myself to.

By the end of the round I was feeling right perky. Maybe I wouldn't achieve my original goal for the year, to make it to the second stage, but I was suddenly excited about Q School. I was raring to see what I could make happen.

THE NEXT DAY, the last before Q School, began sleepily in bed with Dr. Bee. Through the miracle of recording tape, Dr. Bee and I had been bonding. Her somewhat raspy voice was becoming part of my psyche. Sleepily, before even coffee, I donned the Walkman headphones and luxuriated for forty-five minutes in her descriptions of my beautiful, relaxed, harmonious swing. This was followed, after breakfast, by a session on the bug-proof porch with Chuck Hogan. Under his tape-recorded tutelage I peeled an imaginary orange and played the water-tight ninth hole at Bonita Bay over and over. Then I stretched on the carpet and boiled down my End Game Strategy to a new, simple injunction: feel each shot before hitting.

At the course, a gaggle of pumped-up pros once again thronged the first tee, and once again I balked at joining them. I tried to tell myself that I wasn't intimidated, that these guys had no power over me, that I was there for entirely different reasons than they were. But my conviction was fragile. I could easily imagine winding up in a foursome with a couple of head-gamers or with one of the several former Tour players in the field who might let a few names drop and inadvertently incinerate my self-confidence. I needed this final day to fortify my courage, not test it. And by good fortune, I got that chance.

Fleeing the first tee, I drove to the tenth, where I would tee off the next morning. The tenth tee was a long ways off, several blocks down a suburban boulevard, and not easy to find. When I arrived, a grounds crew was mowing the fairway and the crew chief told me the back nine was not open.

"It'll be closed for another hour," he said brusquely.

I must have looked pretty forlorn. After a moment or two of heavy silence he took pity. "Okay, you can play," he said. "But don't tell anyone I said you could and don't interfere with my workers."

What followed was paradise. For the next three hours I had one of Michael Murphy's glorious golf gardens to myself. Except for having to halt once or twice to let mowers pass, I was in Eden alone. The Bonita Bay Creekside course, designed by Arthur Hills, winds among a few houses, but the back nine mostly trails through marsh-land and forest. The flora has a vaguely prehistoric quality—skinny trees rising from swamps, fan-leafed palmettos, bold tropical flow-ers—and the bird life is extraordinary. I saw great blue herons, snowy egrets, hawks, and woodpeckers.

One of the best things about this round was I could take my time. On the tenth hole, even after the mowers ahead had left, I stood absentmindedly on the tee listening to the birds chatter and swish-ing my club back and forth, relishing the peace. I didn't want the moment to end. The round which stretched invitingly ahead would be my last noncompetitive round of the Year, and it occurred to me that never again would I be likely to have as good a golf game—the touch, the skills, the whole package—as I did right then. The anticipation of playing such a round was like a sweet trance I did not want to break.

When I finally did step to the tee and smack my drive, it was a good one: a fine high draw that plunked down prettily right where I was aiming. The hole was a par five and from where the ball lay, 230 yards from the hole, I could have taken a three-wood and tried for the green. But I didn't want to. I wanted to lay up with a seven-iron because I wanted to watch my fresh white ball hang in the air against the tall green trees, lit from below by the morning sun. Hitting a lay-up seven-iron to a wide fairway is one of golf's most pleasurable shots, and I wanted to enjoy it.

The shot went just as I planned, and from where the ball came to rest I pitched over a pond onto the green and two-putted for par. There was nothing exceptional about this par—it was strictly by the book—but I savored it.

And for rest of the round, that is how it went. I traipsed along, unhurriedly, hitting many fine shots. Sometimes I stood behind my ball for as much as a minute or two waiting for the perfect crystal vision of the shot I wanted to hit to come over me. Sooner or later it always did, like a trout rising to the surface, and then I stepped forward with a simple mind and struck the ball, almost always with pleasing results.

It rained twice during the round, brief downpours, which only added to the dreamy wonder. During the showers I sat contentedly in my cart with my Gore-Tex jacket spread across my knees, humming tunes. One of the songs, I realized only after several minutes of humming it, was an old Baptist hymn. When I recognized this, I recalled the lyrics to the song: "Trust and obey / It's the o-o-nly way / To get closer to Je-sus / Is to trust and obey." The subconscious is a marvelous thing. I hadn't heard or thought about this hymn in years, but there I was happily trusting *something*—my swing, myself, Something Bigger Than Myself—as I hadn't since I was a kid.

I didn't keep score for the round, there was no reason to. Neither did I finish. With a few holes left, I hit two consecutive eight-iron approach shots to gimme distance of the holes. Both shots were nearly perfect, as precisely controlled as I was capable of hitting, and I figured, "Why go on?" If I wasn't ready for Q School now, the final few holes wouldn't help. So I climbed into my cart and motored back to the clubhouse.

THAT NIGHT BACK at the condo I laid out my clothes for the following day. My first thought was to go with my favorite khaki trousers and white polo shirt from Old Navy. This was an outfit in which I felt comfortable; it bespoke my regular guy aspirations for Q School.

But when I tried on these clothes to make sure and examined myself in front of a mirror, I thought they made me look too much like a milquetoast. They did not inspire confidence. So I substituted a jazzier shirt—royal blue, cut long in the sleeves in the current fashion—and this made me feel sharper, more aggressive. The problem was the shirt bore the logo of The Shattuck, that impossible course in New Hampshire where Kurt and I had met our Waterloo. Superstitiously, I rejected the shirt. I modeled another favorite—tan, roomy, no logo—but it clashed with the khaki trousers and my fashion confidence began to disintegrate. Maybe rumpled khaki was the wrong look in Q School trousers. So I tried on a pair of no-iron slacks—jet black, by Bobby Jones—and this made me think that perhaps I should go with a total power-golf look. The black slacks, paired with an assertive, red-and-black shirt from my sponsor, Maxfli, projected an image of unabashed professionalism. It was true that, regarding the outfit in the mirror, I felt like I was dressed for a costume ball, but I decided to go with the power ensemble anyway, on the theory that if I blended in with the power pros around me, I wouldn't need to think much about my attire one way or the other.

Having reached this epic decision, I laid out the elements of my chosen outfit on the living room couch in the order in which I would don them the next morning (underwear and socks closest to the bedroom, and so forth), talked to Polly on the phone (she wished me luck), and set two alarms for 5:30 A.M. I then tried to read a distracting novel, but this proved impossible. My heart was beating like a frightened bird's. How or when I finally fell asleep, I cannot remember, but I know it was after two.

The next morning I repeated my tape sessions with Dr. Bee and Chuck Hogan, stretched on the carpet, ate a nutritious breakfast, and walked out to Mr. Lucky. "What a beautiful day!" I exclaimed out loud, stretching my arms luxuriously overhead.

But the whole routine was a fake. I hadn't focused on a word Dr. Bee was saying.

Ba-bumb, ba-bump, ba-bump. I swear I could hear my heart beat on the drive to the course, even over the grinding throb of Mr. Lucky's engine. "Don't be silly," I told myself. "There's nothing at stake today. It's just a chance to show off, something to tell the boys back home about." Maybe this helped a little, but I doubt it. Time was whizzing through my cranium at warp speed, far too fast to hold on to any useful thought for more than a nanosecond. I wondered whether this was what soldiers felt during their final transport to the battle front. Every gas station I drove past seemed vivid and significant, as if it might be the last gas station I would ever see. Every red light was a blessing.

I chastised myself. "You're being silly."

Ba-bump, ba-bump, ba-bump.

When I reached the golf club I stayed in the car for fifteen unscheduled minutes. Fumbling for my Walkman, I sought a final benediction from Dr. Bee. "You have a beautiful, relaxed, harmonious swing," she assured me. I nodded affirmingly, the words going in one ear and out the other.

On the range I could hardly have felt less harmonious. I was so tight I could barely swing the club. Most of my shots were dead pulls. On the practice green, my putting stroke was twitchy. When I missed five three-foot putts in a row, I had the good sense to walk away.

"What's going on?" I asked myself, though of course I knew what was going on. I was freaking out, and it left me feeling betrayed and confused. I had expected to be nervous, but not nearly this much. I had thought that by scaling back my expectations and planning to play for "fun" and by feel, I would be mostly immune to the tensions the real-life pros around me would be feeling, but this was not the case. When I paid for a soft drink with a dollar bill, I noticed that my hand was visibly shaking.

"Maybe it's the socks," I thought.

My choice of socks had nagged me all morning. One of the problems with wearing black power-slacks to play golf in is the difficulty of finding thick, absorbent, athletic socks to match. The only black socks I had were thin, nylon-blend crews which made my shoes feel loose. Moreover, there was a chance of rain. Rain would be a *disaster* in thin socks. So I made an abrupt decision: on my way to the starting tee—for me, the tenth hole—I would drop by Mr. Lucky to change into the thick, gray, rag-wool socks I had planned to wear with my khaki pants. This would also allow me to pick up the PowerBars I had purchased for the round but left in the car. Then my mind would be clear of petty concerns and I could concentrate on golf.

When I got to Mr. Lucky I couldn't find the PowerBars anywhere. I scrabbled on hands and knees throughout the car, looking under the seats, in the glove compartment, everywhere, to no avail. I did find the socks, however, and changed into them. But as I banged across the parking lot in my cart for the tenth tee, I looked down and noticed excessive calf exposure. My slacks through repeated washings were a bit on the high-water side and the rag-wool socks had shrunk in the dryer. Thus, a generous section of my calf was visible. In addition to which, I was reminded, light-gray socks look dorky with jet-black pants, which had been my original reason for deciding against them.

Should I turn back? Or should I rush ahead to the tee?

I was on the horns of a dilemma. For a few panicky moments my mind simply refused to embrace the dilemma. I couldn't decide. If I showed up late for my tee time I faced a two-stroke penalty or possibly even disqualification. On the other hand, if I stayed with the rag socks, every time I addressed the ball I would be aware out of the corner of my eye that I looked like Jerry Lewis in *The Bellhop.* Ba-bump, ba-bump, ba-bump! My heart was in my throat. Finally I threw the cart into reverse, swerved erratically through traffic back to Mr. Lucky, grabbed the black socks out of the trunk, to give myself the option, and beat it to number ten.

As it happened, I needn't have hurried. Three groups were backed up at the tee. The PGA Tour official said the wait would be about twenty-five minutes. I took a deep breath. I took several deep breaths. I spent ten minutes taking deep breaths.

Some of the other waiting players were chatting amiably. A few were sitting in their carts, eyes closed, either napping or visualizing their rounds. After a while, however, I decided to use this unexpected opportunity to reorganize my golf bag. What with the possibility of showers, I wanted to make sure my towels, my rain suit, my extra gloves and extra socks (I changed back into my black crews), and so forth were near the top. This necessitated removing the entire contents of the bag—balls, tees, Band-Aids, grease-pens, sun lotions, PowerBars (so *there* they were!), visors, spare change, car keys, and so forth—and piling it all in the grass beside the cart and sorting through things and while I was at it throwing away some used candy wrappers and a few scuffed balls I didn't need and repacking the bag. I worked at this task with near-manic intensity, but to my surprise I still wasn't quite finished when the starter called our group to the tee.

Oh. My. God.

Twenty-five minutes had passed, I couldn't believe it. No, actually less than twenty minutes had passed—the starter's estimate had been off. But never mind. My mind boomeranged in every which direction at once. I was completely unprepared to play golf. On the tee the starter introduced me to the other two pros in my group, described a few special rules (in one ear and out the other), and invited us to hit away.

"First up," he said, consulting a list, "is Mr. Newport."

"I'll be right back," I said.

I had left my glove in the bag. I jumped down the three steps from the tee box, fished the glove out of a pocket, raced back up the steps, and teed up my ball. All the while I was repeating to myself, "This is it! This is it! This is it!"

Ba-bump, ba-bump, ba-bump! If my pulse rate was less than two hundred beats a minute, I would be surprised.

On the first tee of a PGA Tour–sanctioned tournament, there is only so long you can stand behind the ball waiting for a perfect visualization of the shot you intend to hit to crystallize. I waited that long, and then maybe twice again that long, before the starter intervened.

"Uh, Mr. Newport?"

"Yeah, okay, okay. Sorry."

Absolutely no image of a golf shot of any kind had crystallized in my mind. My main sensation was of tunnel vision, darkness crowding in from all sides. The merest glimmer of light flickered somewhere distantly down the fairway. I was no more ready to hit my first shot at Q School than I was ready to deliver an opening monologue at the Oscars, but I had no choice.

The time had come. The irredeemable moment was upon me. I took two deep breaths, stepped forward, closed my eyes, and lunged.

The clubhead made contact: excellent news! When my vision returned, I saw the ball easily clearing the nasty swamp immediately in front the tee and snap-hooking into another swamp that ran along the left side of the fairway. This was more good news! The swamp was marked as a lateral hazard, which meant I would not have to hit another ball from the tee box with everyone watching. I could drop a fresh ball near the hazard with just a one-stroke penalty. It was more than I deserved.

FOR THE FIRST hour of competition I played in a kind of hyperactive shock. Urgent, unignorable instructions flashed through my brain at the rate of two or three per second. Feel the shot. Concentrate on the target. Keep the right knee bent. Take a deep breath. Don't think about score. Stay behind the ball. None of them did any good. I had no rhythm, no focus, and no calm. Standing in the fairway consulting my course information book, I had difficulty computing the simplest distances—the numbers were a jumble. Twice I had to change clubs after addressing the ball when I realized my selection was grossly wrong—a pitching wedge is not the right tool from 175 yards. It's a wonder I didn't drive the cart into a swamp.

To say I was surprised at the degree to which I was freaking would not be accurate. I was too confused to be surprised, but I was dismayed. My carefully conceived End Game Strategy to "feel the shot" was a joke. The only thing I could feel was a knot in my stomach the size of a Ford Explorer. And, having put all my strategic eggs in one basket, I had no alternative plan to fall back on when hysteria hit. I simply floundered, yanking one dead pull shot after another and working the short game like the golf ball was a shot put.

When I finally began to recover the use of my senses around my eighth hole, I was already fourteen over par. According to the scorecard I had parred one hole (I can't imagine how) and bogeyed, double-bogeyed, or triple-bogeyed all the rest.

And then it occurred to me: what about the two innocents I'm playing with? What if my startling ineptitude prevents these two legitimate contenders, Chris Campbell and Sean McCarty, both of whom had forked out three thousand hard-earned bucks plus expenses to be here, from making it to the Tour? This possible consequence of my Q School lark had not occurred to me until this moment. Once it did I could think of little else.

For the rest of the round I had one objective: to play quickly and stay out of Campbell's and McCarty's way. In a way this helped soothe my nerves, by giving me a purpose beyond dissecting my own madness. Especially around the greens, I played fast. I spent almost no time planning my pitches or sizing up my putts. I simply kept hitting the ball until it went in the hole, like a cat playing with a mouse.

I straggled in with a 93—my second worst round of the Year. But McCarty and Campbell, thank God, did okay. McCarty shot a 69, which tied him for second place, and Campbell posted a one-under-par 71.

MY FIRST REACTION, after signing the scorecard, was to get away. I didn't want to see a soul: I was too humiliated, too ashamed. Zombie-like I trudged to the parking lot, loaded my clubs into the trunk, and sat down in the driver's seat of Mr. Lucky—and this was when I broke down. Oddly, it wasn't the thought about the 93 that sent me over the edge, or a sudden sense that my performance had made a mockery of the entire Year. These thoughts came later. At that moment I broke down out of sheer gratitude for Mr. Lucky. When I turned the key, that rusty old heap of junk started right up. Mr. Lucky was a trooper. Paying five hundred dollars for Mr. Lucky was one thing, at least, that I had done right this Year; the car had stood by me through thick and thin.

"YOU'RE KIDDING," said Captain Kurt.

"I wish I were."

"Ninety-three? How could that be?" he asked.

At least he appeared to be shocked. At least he didn't say, "Yeah, that's about what I figured you'd shoot."

"I'm a nutcase, that's how."

After the round I had spent an hour on the beach staring at the Gulf of Mexico and wondering whether France still sponsored its Foreign Legion. Then I had lunch at a Burger King and by pre-arrangement met Kurt back at the course, where he had just arrived from Orlando. When he found me I was lying on a grassy mound near the putting green, my cap covering my face, and I was not pre-disposed to move. But Kurt, for one, was not prepared to accept my performance so passively.

"Okay, tell me about it," he said.

I tried to explain how my choice of socks had thrown me into a tizzy before the round and how once the round started I couldn't think straight and how I had violently pulled almost every shot. Kurt seized on this last as something he could do something about. "Let's see the swing," he said.

Reluctantly I struggled to my feet, walked over to the range, and slapped a few desultory five-irons. For the most part they went where I was aiming—or so I thought.

"Do you have any idea where you're lined up?" Kurt said.

"I'm aiming at the yellow flag."

"No you're not."

He put a club on the ground flush to my heels and held another parallel to my shoulder line. Both were pointed about thirty degrees to the right of the yellow flag.

"That's awfully strange," I said.

"When did you start lining up like *that?*" he asked.

The truth is David Bakyta, the head pro at North Fork Country Club, had noticed something similar a few weeks before. During my flying visit to Orient, I had stopped by the club to practice a bit and Bakyta had looked at my swing on the range. I was nailing one perfect four-iron shot after another. "Take that on the road and you'll make some money," he complimented me. "You're too closed at the top, but that's okay, you seem to get it around."

"What do you mean, too closed?" I asked, instantly alarmed like a deer hearing twigs crack.

"Oh, nothing, nothing. Just something I saw, but, hey—you're hitting them great. Don't worry."

I knew perfectly well what "too closed" meant. It meant I was hooding the clubface, turning it too far to the left as I drew the club back, and once David mentioned it I couldn't help but be aware of this flawed action on every takeaway. I saw it in peripheral vision. During the two South Florida tournaments, this awareness had plagued me. Halfway into my backswing, no matter how focused on the target I had been to that point, fear of hitting a hood-faced pull overcame me and I instinctively compensated by pulling the hell out of the ball.

With time the problem went away—or at least I thought it had. But apparently I had merely adjusted my stance way to the right and that morning the problem had re-erupted with a vengeance.

Kurt set things right. He wouldn't let me leave the range until my alignment was dead-on and I'd hit ten reasonably accurate five-irons in a row.

That done, we staged our familiar pitch-and-putt contest at the practice green. On the North Atlantic Tour, we must have played this little game two dozen times, and now with the sky an incandescent orange and the tropical birds wheeling overhead, the little ritual felt like a calming vespers. Some feel for the short game returned.

Captain Kurt is not what you would call a touchy-feely guy. But his supportive, accepting, get-with-the-program attitude was just what I needed right then. I thanked him profusely for coming and bought him dinner and a beer or two at Applebees. By the time I went to bed that night, my brain was back on regular time.

I FELT MORE comfortable in round two. Walking helped. In round one I had had to drive my own cart, but now I could stroll while Kurt drove the cart—this was standard procedure for the caddies at Q School, since at Bonita Bay there were long walks between holes where carts were needed. During frequent long waits between shots (the pace of play at Q School is notoriously slow), Kurt chatted up Campbell and McCarty and after a while I joined in, too. Campbell, as it turned out, had a daughter named Annabelle exactly one month to the day older than my Anna Belle. He was one of the few other players at Q School in his forties, a prosperous teaching pro who had never quite rid himself of the Big Tour bug. Getting to know him helped diffuse the anxiety I had had about holding up him and McCarty.

"Take your time," he told me at one point on the green. "We're rooting for you." I don't know when a passing remark meant so much to me.

But try as I might, I couldn't really get my act together. The trauma of round one was too fresh. Every shot was tinged with fear and my rhythm was erratic. Around the greens I could not stifle the urge simply to get up, down, and out of the way as quickly as possible. My final score was 88: seven pars, eight bogeys, three "other."

After the first two rounds at Q School, the contestants are grouped by score, which meant I played with the other worst players in the field. Morale among us stragglers was hardly cheery—we had all basically blown three thousand dollars—but at least now I felt I could focus on my own game rather than the possibility of ruining things for someone else.

"Let's make something happen out there today, J. P.," Kurt said before the third round. "You never know."

"You never know?" I replied. "Like maybe I'll shoot two 59s and squeak into the second stage?"

This was a defeatist remark and Kurt regarded me with the disgust I deserved. "I want to see you play golf like I know you can. You're here, you've paid your money, there are two rounds left— let's do something good."

He was right, of course. I owed it to Kurt even if I didn't care for myself. But I did care for myself. Q School had never really been about getting to the second stage, it had been about testing myself at the end of the Year, to see how far I could get. And there was still a chance to validate the Year, in the final two rounds if not in the final four. And so I bore down. I tried hard. But it wasn't easy. If round one was the pits, the chills, the fever—a serious illness—I now found myself, in round three, back on my feet, shaky but game.

By the back nine I started to feel like myself again—the first sure sign of which was irritation at one of my new playing companions. This guy, call him Steve, revealed himself in various offhand remarks to be rather sniffy about my first round scores of 93 and 88. On one hand I can't blame him: I stunk. On the other hand, he had not exactly identified himself as a Tour contender with his rounds of 82 and 83. At the turn I was two strokes behind Steve and became obsessed with beating his sorry ass. Maybe this wasn't a good reason for wanting to do well, but my pride had been wounded and I didn't care. I scored seven pars in a row, two of them requiring gritty, determined up-and-downs, to pull within one stroke. But then the lucky bastard finished birdie-birdie and beat me by three, 78 to 81. For a brief moment there, however, I was actually having fun.

After the round, lunch, and some chipping, Kurt and I invented a new game on the range. One of us assumed our stance over the ball with, say, a five-iron, and the other called out "draw" or "fade." Without adjusting either stance or grip—that is to say, entirely through swing arc—the hitter had to comply. We were both surprised at our competence: firing at flags 180 yards away, we brought balls in from all directions.

"How is this possible?" Kurt asked. "I didn't know I could do that."

I hadn't either, and I certainly would never have had the guts to try it in a tournament. But I will say this: Kurt and I had some kind of fun that evening. We hit until after dark, like kids who didn't want to go home for supper.

WHEN I AWOKE on the morning of the final round, my first thought was, "Thank God the ordeal is almost over."

But instantly I rebuked myself. What did I mean, ordeal? I had one round left in a Year that was supposed to be a dream come true. Why couldn't I cherish the moment?

By the time I teed off on number ten shortly after 10 A.M., I felt whole and healthy and it showed in my game. Despite a couple of unnecessary mistakes, I made the turn in three-over-par. This wouldn't get me to the Tour but it was a measure of redemption.

I then parred the first four holes on the front nine, which meant that standing on the tee at number five, with five holes remaining, I had a solid chance to shoot a solid, mid-seventies round.

"Keep it up, big guy," Kurt said, slapping me on the back.

"Watch this," I replied. "I'm gonna blow the cover off the ball." And I did. I boomed a beauty. I felt fireproof. But I wasn't counting my chickens before they hatched. If I had learned one thing about golf from the Year, it was not to project ahead or behind. Take it one shot at a time.

And honestly, as I set up for a three-wood approach shot on the par-five fifth (my fourteenth hole), I wasn't thinking ahead. I was as much in the moment as I could be under the circumstances. But as we sow, so must we reap. And at the top of my backswing, for no reason at all, the fear returned. In an instant, I thought: I don't deserve to be here. I don't deserve to shoot a 74 or a 75 at Q School. And that flash was all it took. I flinched. The ball pulled into the jungle.

Oh, the dreary details. I scored a double-bogey on that hole, followed by a bogey on six and quadruple-bogey on seven. It's not worth talking about. Neither is my tee shot on the par-three eighth, which buried itself deep in the sand an inch below the lip of a bunker. A portion of the ball's surface no bigger than the tip of a pencil eraser was visible.

Rather than wait for a rules official—I didn't even want to know what my options were—I whaled away at this ball and succeeded in moving it from the top lip of the bunker into the bottom of the bunker. From there I blasted out over the green. The ball came to rest one foot from a pond.

If the Great God of Golf orchestrated my Q School finish, then I congratulate him. He's a wonderful comedian. With one foot stuck in the pond-edge ooze, I chipped the ball onto the surface of the green and watched it roll forty-five feet into the heart of the cup for a five.

On the tee box of the next and final hole of Q School, Kurt and I looked at each other and started laughing. We laughed loud. We scattered birds with our laughter. I can't say for sure why Kurt laughed (though Lord knows I had given him plenty of reason to), but I laughed because I finally got the joke, the joke being that golf will beat you in the end no matter what you do. It was all over now, and what good had a year's worth of escalating fear done me? Not one little bit.

Kurt handed me the driver. "Let 'er rip, big guy," he said. In the three previous rounds on this hole, which has water down the left side, I had always used a three-wood. But somehow Kurt knew I wanted a driver now.

I murdered the ball. I left myself a clean eight-iron to the pin and I lasered that shot, too, to within eight feet of the cup, no problem. The putt was not easy, a curving side-hiller, but I hit it without fear and watched it roll smartly into the high side of the cup. A birdie. My first of the tournament.

"Looks like you've finally got it going, J. P.," Kurt said.

As I always told Polly, if you can't accept that golf is absurd, you have no business playing the game. Or maybe it was she who said that to me, I can no longer remember.

Epilogue

✴

A fine golfer has only one fine thing:

his fine golf game.

—BYRON NELSON,
warning a young Tom Watson
of the perils of golf

E P I L O G U E

MANY YEARS AGO A WISE OLD BRAZILIAN
woman, the matriarch of a legendary family of
Brazilian jujitsu fighters, assured me that the
hardest issue for men to deal with is shame.
For women, she said, the hot button is
betrayal, but for men it is shame. At the time I
discounted her opinion as the grousing of
someone who lived in the company of proud
Latin males, but in the weeks after Q School I
began to wonder. Maybe growing up with the
notion of Original Sin hanging over my head
had not inoculated me from shame as much as
I thought.

"Golf's a bitch," Captain Kurt told me in
Naples as we shook hands upon parting. I
sensed he was trying to absolve me from

shame, but this only served to confirm that he thought I had something to be absolved from.

"Right," I said.

"You tried something hard."

"Right."

"You should be proud of your effort."

"I am."

"You stuck it out."

"I did."

But in truth I wasn't the least proud. As much as I could laugh at golf's absurdity, Q School had genuinely crushed my pride. At the start of the Year my hope had been that, through golf, I could transform myself into a *player,* a man in control of his emotional faculties, a winner—but instead I felt like a bigger loser than ever, or at least a bigger choker. If golf was "an X-ray o' the soul," as one of the characters in *Golf in the Kingdom* said, my picture was riddled with disturbing shadows.

From Naples to Orient, I had fourteen hundred miles to dwell on these matters. The first night I spent at the Hyatt Resort on Hilton Head Island, South Carolina, primarily because I had a coupon entitling me to one free room-night there. The coupon also provided for a free round of golf, but this I had no intention of redeeming. I never wanted to play golf again.

After checking out the next morning, however, the road happened to wind past the course and Mr. Lucky swerved unbidden into the clubhouse driveway. It was as if I were a criminal, irresistibly drawn back to his scene of the crime. I put on my spikes and reluctantly handed over the coupon. Without half trying, playing from the white tees with a couple of fellow resorters, I shot a 74: four birdies, one bogey, and one out-of-bounds triple-bogey.

"You ought to turn pro, young fella," one of the resorters joked.

"Right," I replied. "Ha, ha, ha."

You might think that shooting 74 would have boosted my spirits, but in fact it did the opposite. It certified that, yes, I could play golf at some decent level of proficiency when nothing was at stake, which meant that my problem was some colossal moral weakness. Faced with the Q School challenge that I had worked toward for an entire year, the best response I could muster had been to clench my sphincters as tightly as possible and never let go

For the rest of the drive home—three days of machine-gunned white lines on I-95—my thoughts did not grow any cheerier.

BACK HOME IN Orient, I made a show of resuming normal life. I organized my office, leafed through the notes I had accumulated during the Year, and tried to do extra housework to make up partially for the time I'd been gone.

But shame dogged me.

One bright autumn afternoon, a week or so after returning, I spent several hours raking leaves and tidying up the yard. The work was satisfying: peaceful, simple, well within my abilities, the kind of work they give to patients at mental hospitals. "Nice job," I told myself as I stowed the tools in our garage.

"Nice job?" a voice within me popped up. "Aren't you the same joker who shot 93 at Q School?"

The next week I received in my mailbox my regular subscription copy of *GolfWeek*. On the front page was a giant headline: PRE-TENDERS TAINT Q SCHOOL. The article beneath focused on the only ten competitors, from an initial field of 1,150, who failed to break 80 in any round. The words "deluded souls," "pipe dreamers," and "tragicomedy" were part of the lead paragraph. In the prominent chart accompanying the piece, my name (correctly spelled) was fourth from the top.

You'd be surprised how many golfers see *GolfWeek*.

A few days later I received a polite letter from the PGA Tour asking me not to apply to Q School again until I got a whole lot better.

My only safe haven from shame was Anna. Two-and-a-half years old now, she well understood shame as it relates to, say, the potty, but abstract, grown-up, existential shame such as I was suffering had no meaning to her. In Anna's eyes I was still simply Daddy, that lovable buffoon, and her delight was unconditional when we played silly animal games in the living room and spun round and round in the park.

With Polly the situation was more complex—though in the end more helpful.

I knew my dismal Q School scores didn't matter to Polly one iota—few people in the Western world could have been less impressed by Q School scores than Polly—but I felt humiliated before her nonetheless. The instinct was archaic, perhaps, but powerful. I had come of age in Texas, remember, where men were men and athletic failure was greeted sullenly by cheerleaders, their pompoms akimbo.

It was some months before I managed—in my own cowardly, indirect fashion—to confess my shame to Polly. One midwinter night we sat before the fire and fell into a discussion about the progress of the book. The hard part, I told her, was figuring out what to say about Q School. "Nobody wants to read about a loser," I said.

"But everyone wants a good laugh," she responded.

It had not occurred to me that Q School might be funny. Even then it didn't occur to me.

"Q School wasn't a joke," I replied testily. "It was a failure. It repudiated the whole Year. I couldn't have blown it worse. I shot 56 over par. That's how I summarize the whole Year now, with that one number, plus-56."

Polly looked at me with a combination of sympathy and amusement. The shame thing, quite obviously, had not occurred to her. She couldn't imagine anyone getting so worked up about golf that their sense of self-worth was in jeopardy.

"You silly man," she finally said. But she said it in a way, accompanied by a touch on my arm, that meant she understood. She didn't think I was ridiculous. She was on my side.

We talked about it some more, and soon it became clear that Polly's assumption was that the Year went well—perfectly, in fact. She said I had accomplished everything I set out to do: I had worked on my game and improved, I had competed on the mini-tours as I said I would and met lots of interesting people, I had come to understand some things about the nature of golf that I hadn't before, and I had followed through on my plans to compete at Q School, despite realizing toward the end of the Year that my goal of making it to the second stage was unrealistic. "So what's the problem?" she asked. "What did you expect? To make it to the TV tour?"

"Of course not," I scoffed. "Obviously not."

"Of course not?"

"Of course not!" But then I began to think: maybe I had. Almost weekly during the Year I had pronounced to anyone who would listen that I wasn't trying to make it as a pro, I was simply exploring what happens when an average, low-handicap Joe like myself works hard at golf for twelve months and tries to compete against the pros. How much could he improve? What were the obstacles to success? Thinking back over those pronouncements, however, I could now see that I protested too much. I kept telling myself I didn't care how well I did to hide the fact that I cared enormously. Without admitting it to myself, I *did* want to make it as a pro. Somewhere in that never-never land between what I was saying and what I was thinking, I nourished the fantasy that at Q School, if not before, I would make a breakthrough. I was Bill Murray in *Caddyshack*: "The Cinderella story, out of nowhere, a former greenskeeper about to become the Masters champion. . . . It's in the hole! It's in the hole!"

This lie, I think, is what did me in. At Q School the adolescent dreamer within me had surfaced and demanded his day, despite all my wise counsel to the contrary. As a songwriter friend of mine, Rinde Eckert, once wrote, "The pieces all came together. I fell apart."

But you've got to hand it to golf: unlike most things in our showy, image-driven culture, the game won't let you get away with this kind of bullshit. Not one little bit. And that authenticity, I think, is one reason people love and respect golf so much, even as they gnash their teeth.

· · ·

IN MAY THE following spring I took my clubs out of the garage for the first time since Q School and went to the course. I can't say I was excited by the prospect. The pain was still fresh. But some friends from the city invited me to play and I agreed. I hoped that a few, friendly rounds might flush the distress from my system.

Without any question my game was different than it had been before the Year. The biggest change my pals noticed was in my shot trajectory. Before the Year I hit my approach shots to the moon and back. Now they bore lower, which made them far less subject to the vagaries of wind and weather, and they held the greens with my increased backspin. For this improvement I credit Michael Hebron's leaning stick and the other changes he made in my swing.

Another major difference—the one I found most satisfying—was that now I knew how to fix my swing when it got out of kilter. Before the Year my efforts to cure an overzealous fade or a spate of pulled drives had been futile. Any solution was strictly accidental and usually unsustainable. Now that I understood what made a swing work and where its power comes from, I could diagnose problems fairly quickly and fashion a cure, although this didn't prevent me from falling into other bad ruts the next time out.

In that first round I shot an 83, which turned out to be the worst of my fifteen rounds that season. Individual hole scores of seven, eight, and nine virtually disappeared from my scorecard. Nine months of tournament play had taught me to play defensively and I seldom posted worse than double-bogey, even when I got into a patch of trouble. My negative handicap, based on the worst half of my scores rather than the best half, shrank from eleven before the Year to approximately eight.

On the other hand, this same spirit of caution kept me from having any ecstatic rounds. My best score all season was a workmanlike 73 (from the whites) and two-thirds of my scores were in the 77 to 80 range. My regular (positive) handicap actually rose from less than three before the Year to around five. Granted, I wasn't playing as much as I had before the Year, but still, this was disappointing. And I perceived—or maybe I projected—that my golf pals were disappointed, too. Their swing-from-the-heels buddy had gone off to spend a year with the pros and returned swinging from his tippytoes, choosing safety over risk every time in pursuit of, at worst, an old-fogey bogey.

The truth was I didn't like playing like this any more than they did, but I felt *encumbered* by the Year. It was as if the memory of the trauma I had experienced was hot-wired into my cerebellum. My overwhelming concern was simply not to embarrass myself, to hit a whopping slice or bladed wedge or to score a 93. Beyond that, I didn't much care how I played.

FOR THE NEXT eighteen months I didn't play much golf. We moved from Orient to a Hudson River town closer to New York, where getting onto public courses was more difficult and time consuming. Also, I had a lot of work to do, both on the book and other projects to keep my family's financial ship afloat. But I wasn't highly motivated to play golf, either. The game had not exactly been ruined for me—I usually had a decent time when I played and I still got a tingle out of catching a shot pure—but being around golf brought up a lot of *stuff*. I still hadn't made my peace with the Year.

I did, however, *think* a lot about golf, in particular about the two questions people asked me most frequently when I told them about my experience: What exactly *is* the difference, the Fine Green Line, between the pros who make it and those who don't? And what did I learn personally from the Year?

As for the first, there's no simple answer. At the start of the Year my assumption was that most of the difference was mental. In the uppermost echelons of golf, I reasoned, everyone knew how to hit the ball and the ones who made it to the Tour were simply those who had some kind of extra mental toughness. As the Year progressed, however, I retreated somewhat from this opinion. In every sport, those with truly extraordinary natural gifts rise to the top. In golf, pure God-given talent may be relatively less important than in sports like track and field or basketball, but it still matters. I noticed in my travels that at each step up the professional golf ladder—from the mini-tours to the Nike Tour to the PGA Tour—the players seemed more like *athletes*. They had bigger arms and stronger shoulders and moved with perceptively more animal grace. This wasn't a coincidence.

But of course physical talent isn't enough. History is rich with stories of gifted pros who never made it (like Bobby Clampett) and others with mediocre talent who did (like Corey Pavin). Hard work, perseverance, and practical intelligence count big time. This may seem obvious but it probably explains why 90 percent of the mini-tour troops don't get any further than they do. Most of the fresh pros out there simply aren't willing to do what it takes; they're too busy having fun or figuring out what it means to be a grown-up or bitching about how unfair golf is. In this regard golf isn't that different from any other line of work: success comes to those who are highly motivated and stay relentlessly focused on their goals.

Given two guys with equal natural talent and an equally diligent work ethic, however, and you're at the crux of the Fine Green Line. The one most likely to make it is the one who happens to have the best mix of personality traits for golf. You can't be too hyper, for instance, and make it to the Hall of Fame. Somewhere along the way you also have to have learned to separate your golf persona from the rest of your life. Dr. GolfPsych, Deborah Graham, has probably come as close as anyone to creating a useful roster of these psychological traits—her scales of cool, abstract, dominant, self-sufficient, and so forth—but I'm not sure how possible it is for a player to change these characteristics, except maybe at the margin. It's better to be born with them.

Luck plays a role, too, especially as it relates to confidence. Confidence is the number-one thing. The guy whose bad breaks come at the wrong time may lose his confidence and never recover. The guy whose good breaks come at the right time—that's the guy, in my opinion, who will be waving back at the others from yonder side of the Fine Green Line.

Plus, he's got to be a good putter. Some guys flat out seem to have a genius for putting. Maybe putting is that aspect of golf where Pure Confidence and Pure Will matter the most, or maybe it's magic, some people are just born with a sixth sense for seeing the line and feeling the distance. I don't pretend to know how they do it, but some players can simply make the ball disappear into the hole. And that's what it's all about.

As FOR THE other question, the one about how the Year changed me personally, the answer I settled on was that I finally learned to love golf for the right reasons. But this didn't happen during the Year itself, it happened only this past summer, when I played in my first golf tournament since Q School.

Long ago, when I first hatched the idea for the Year, I couldn't have told you what it was about golf that appealed to me so much. Compared to some people I had a knack for the game, that must have been part of it—people are always predisposed to like the things they're good at. Golf was a game, it was relaxing, it was sociable outdoors fun. Also, I was under the spell of *Golf in the Kingdom*, which hinted at unexplored spiritual and psychological dimensions to the game. My life at the time was in flux—I was emerging from a divorce, my career was at that late-thirties inflection point which so often spawns midlife crises—and golf vaguely seemed to promise some answers.

But whatever it was that lured me to golf, by the end of the Year that something was buried under layers of frustration. In twelve short months I cleverly managed to transform one of the things I loved most in the world into something that only caused me anxiety. This was very silly.

Looking back, I think the main cause for this transformation was the challenge I set for myself: I was doomed to failure from the start. It's clear now that my hope of advancing in one year from three-handicap amateur to second-stage PGA Tour qualifier was unrealistic, no matter how I went about it. Toward the end of the Year I realized this, but that didn't keep me from feeling deeply ashamed about my performance at Q School. As for my search for "answers," it never got off the ground. That search was subsumed by my more urgent-seeming search for a better swing.

But barking up the wrong tree, I should have realized, was more or less the point of the Year. As Polly pointed out, I did a bang-up job experiencing firsthand the barriers to progress in golf. I learned how complicated the golf swing truly is and how difficult it is to convert skills that can only be learned self-consciously into skills that can be deployed un-self-consciously. I experienced how tournament pressure preys upon the weak-minded and figured out that only time and experience can overpower it. Along the way I learned a lot of other things about golf, too, and saw my skills improve considerably. But in the thick of battle, it was hard to maintain this objective perspective. My failures got to me.

In the end, it took playing in another tournament to make me appreciate the things that had gone right. The event in question was a qualifier for the Met Golf Association amateur championship (I officially regained my amateur status from the USGA after a one-year "awaiting" period), which I entered primarily because, on a golf travel assignment two weeks prior, I had played nine rounds of golf in ten days and got my game into pretty good shape.

In preparing for the tournament, I told myself, "Okay, you've had a lot of time to think about it. What solid, practical advice from the Year would really help?" I came up with two answers. First, do your best over each shot to swing free and without fear. Second, think of each shot as a new ball game, don't give in to despair no matter what happens, play one shot at a time.

The observant reader will no doubt recognize this as practically the same advice I had given myself on the eve of Q School. This coincidence, if you want to call it that, made me feel better. I had been on the right track after all, it seemed. I had just run out of time. It also made me realize how impossible playing anxiety-free at Q School would have been. Back then—in my own fevered mind, at least—every shot was burdened with unnatural consequence; I had built up the moment to be of almost supernatural significance.

Now, on the other hand, truly nothing was at stake. It was a tournament out of all context. I knew none of the other competitors. I was not building toward any goal. I did not have a registered handicap to prove or disprove and, in fact, until the golf trip I had only played three times in the previous twelve months. Even if I qualified for the finals, which I doubted I would, I knew I wouldn't be able to play because I would be out of town. And so I was *free*, literally, to follow my own advice. The only criterion I had for the tournament was to play without fear. I didn't care what score I posted, so long as I swung freely on every shot and didn't let what happened get to me. And both my heart and soul were into this challenge, because the thing I most regretted about the Year—the thing that stuck in my craw every time I looked back—was the pointless fear I had experienced. This tournament was a chance to purge the fear.

And in this I succeeded beyond my most optimistic hopes. I had as much fun playing in that tournament as I had had playing golf since long before the Year—perhaps even since my magical round of 69.

For one thing, I proved to myself that, sure enough, I *did* have a golf game. Both the guys I was playing with were in their twenties— one had played in college—and could hit the ball a mile. But neither had a game in the sense I am talking about. They whaled away at every shot without strategy. Around the greens they used the same, blunt-instrument pitching stroke in every situation. And when their games started going south, as games inevitably do, both of them collapsed. They were versions of me before the Year, the me that had played against John Baldwin, the former Met amateur champion, in this same qualifier eons ago and fallen apart in exactly the same way.

I, on the other hand, got stronger as the round went on, despite the 101-degree heat and high humidity. I got off to a bad start, but played the last thirteen holes in one-over-par despite a triple-bogey. My final score was 80, which on that course on that day beat three-fourths of the field.

But the fun I had had nothing to do with score. I had fun because I played like I used to play. I swung from the heels. I trusted myself.

Without abandoning strategy, I played at the very edge of my ability. A few times I hit very bad shots, but I was exhilarated nonetheless by the sensation of having taken a risk. Each time I stepped to the ball I swung freely. I *defied* fear. And this, I realized afterward, was what had been missing from my golf. For far too long I had been too scared to let loose.

When you come right down to it, enjoying golf is a matter of how you frame the challenge. During the Year, I pursued golf in about as anxiety-producing a manner as you can; by the end, the only way I knew to judge myself was in comparison to the pros around me, a low-percentage proposition if there ever was one. But I'm still a big believer in playing for score, so long as the motivation is right. As a catalyst for organizing one's effort, score can't be beat. It's an honest and authentic arbiter. Score is what you put *at risk* with each shot, and risk—it may be trumped up risk in an absolute sense, but the rapid heartbeat it triggers is very real—is what makes golf thrilling.

And so, in that tournament, I reclaimed golf for myself by letting go of my fear and embracing risk—a minor victory in the grand scheme of things, but for me a significant one. I realize now that playing without fear—or *with* courage, as I prefer to think of it—is what I always loved about golf, though I didn't recognize it as such. It wasn't answers I wanted from the game, it was relief from the search for answers. Golf was one of the few places where I could escape the everyday burdens of anxiety and live life directly, if only in the brief graceful moments of a swing, at the edge of experience.

How much, if any, of this nonsense applies to the rest of my life, I don't know. Most of the important risks we citizens take in the modern world—in our careers, in our relationships—are attenuated. They play out over time. We seldom get the chance, as we do in golf, to roll everything into a ball and let it fly. But as a metaphor, golf at least is something rich to think about.

One of the personal ironies in the peace I have come to with golf is that my attitude toward the game—acceptance of my woeful limitations but a what-the-hell determination to swing for the bleachers anyway—is not all that different from the Original Sin Calvinism I grew up with. We're born as sinners, deeply flawed and profoundly weak, with no hope of salvation except through Grace, which God grants us based on the quality of our effort. In golf, the grace we occasionally receive are the rounds of 69, the five-hole stretches where we can do no wrong, the forty-five-foot putts that curl into the hole.

I find myself thinking often about Dan Bradley, the middle-age guy who won the Miami amateur championship at Key Biscayne. When he delivered his short acceptance speech his voice was cracking with emotion. "I don't care at what level you play, a victory like this means a lot," he said, and paused to gather himself. "I feel very humbled." Bradley knew what a gift he'd been given, to play as he had played in the event, to have had a glimpse, however brief, into the realm of perfection. When Tour pros on TV go all misty-eyed accepting their trophies, I no longer roll my eyes. They know this humility, too, and I'm sure their emotions well from gratitude and not from pride.

I suppose, given the title of the book, that I ought to conclude by tying all this to the Fine Green Line. Luckily, that isn't hard to do. The main thing I learned about the Fine Green Line is that you can't ever cross it. No matter how hard you try, no matter how much you improve, the Line will always hover just ahead, tantalizingly out of reach. That's the nature of the beast. But if you can ever learn to accept this about golf—in your heart and not just in your head—you'll have the hardest part licked. The rest is pretty much just fun and games.

A c k n o w l e d g m e n t s

SPECIAL THANKS GO to William Shinker, the founding publisher of Broadway Books. As a committed golfer, he understood instantly where I wanted to go with this book and gave me the wherewithal to do it. My editor at Broadway, Suzanne Oaks, was wonderfully insightful, encouraging, pleasant to work with and—above all—patient. Thanks, too, to her amazingly competent assistants, Ann Campbell and Lisa Olney. And to Kristine Dahl, my agent, for putting the package together so expertly.

During the Year itself, almost everyone I met was eager to help. Golfers are that way. I especially want to thank Michael Hebron, who was right all along, though I wish I could have proven him wrong. Great golf teachers like Hebron, devoting themselves empathetically one student at a time, seldom get the glory they deserve. For providing me and many other aspiring golfers with a friendly, supportive place to compete, I must thank Tom Eubanks and Sarah Stevenson of the South Florida Tour and, on the North Atlantic Tour, Buddy Young and Chris Young. Buddy claimed a fond place in many golfers' hearts and I am sad to report that after a lengthy illness he died in 1999.

Captain Kurt Kwader deserves particular mention for being such a pal. Thanks, too, to his family for their hospitality. (Kurt, by the way, has steadily pushed his tournament scoring average down to the even par range and, though still an amateur, last year won an event on the North Atlantic Tour.)

John Atwood, initially my editor at *Men's Journal* and now just a great friend, was enthusiastic about this project from the start. Others whose support has helped immeasurably include Chris Vetter and the friendly staff at Island's End, Bill Adams, John Kiernan, Nancy Lemann, and, especially early on, Phil Weiss and Cynthia Kling.

Mom and Dad: you set the example and gave me the tools. Thanks for a lifetime of support.

As for Polly and Anna, what can I say? Each in their way kept me from going off the deep end (I think). Polly made the book possible. She understood my need to understand golf and then, like Dilsey in *The Sound and the Fury*, she endured.

19381371R00179

Made in the USA
Lexington, KY
16 December 2012